CW01301956

PRAISE FOR *RETURN TO GROWTH* VOLUME ONE

"A rare, detailed diagnosis and set of recommendations to get the country back on course ... [Moynihan] incisively cuts through the UK's tax system, regulation, government spending and civil service, outlining specific savings, reforms and tweaks that could unleash growth and reduce impediments to it ... This is a highly valuable contribution to a debate that can often be short on detail."
Tej Parikh, 'The best new books on economics', *Financial Times*

"As (Lord) Jon Moynihan points out in his fine new book *Return to Growth*, public sector productivity has stagnated for a quarter of a century, a truly gobsmacking statistic when you consider the innovations that have happened during that time."
Matt Ridley, *Daily Mail*

"[Moynihan makes] many brilliant arguments [distinguishing] between things that reflect the modern ideological opposition to growth and things that are really policy measures that impact negatively on growth. The larger the government, the less growth we're going to have, and the higher the tax rate, the less growth we're going to have. That will make sense to a lot of people ... The book shows the extraordinary benefits that growth has accomplished for humankind and also for the planet that we live on."
Brendan O'Neill, *The Brendan O'Neill Show*

"The book is a collection of good judgements ... Moynihan offers something robust and thinkable ... He supports [his] suggestions with not only extremely close consideration of the facts, but also close examination of the economic theories that support his claim. His book is long, but can be read in a few hours if one reads it with the right attitude. And even a politician or civil servant should be able to make sense of the summaries of the argument which Moynihan conveniently places at the beginning and the end of the book. [It is an] important book ... A copy of this book should be on the desk of every politician, every civil servant, and every journalist."
Professor James Alexander, *Daily Sceptic*

"A must read for any would-be Chancellor. It is a compelling blueprint for how to end decades of economic malaise."
ANDREW PIERCE

"A trenchant, eye-opening and controversial tour de force from one of our foremost economic brains. Anyone who wants growth and wonders why it has become so elusive in western social democracies needs to pick up *Return to Growth* and take urgent note. Jon Moynihan shows, in crystal-clear and accessible prose, that you can either have ever greater government expenditure or you can have decent levels of growth. Contrary to cakeism, you can't have both. Rising public-sector expenditure brings greater debt, inflation and ultimately, if it is not controlled, national bankruptcy. A smaller state which does not crowd out the private sector is better able to preside over higher economic growth, which raises standards of living for the country as a whole. If the analysis of how we got into our current economic predicament is sobering, Moynihan's meticulously elucidated prescription offers a more hopeful way forward for those brave enough to take it. *Return to Growth* is an essential and compelling read for policymakers and general readers alike."
JUSTIN MAROZZI

"Jon Moynihan is right – it's time for a fresh look at how our economy should work. Growth and aspiration will only return when private-sector entrepreneurialism is allowed to thrive in a low-tax, free-market setting. More hard work and less regulation is the way forward."
LORD BAMFORD

"If Rachel Reeves is serious about her growth agenda, she should buy herself a copy of Jon Moynihan's book. Lucid, passionately argued, contemptuous of the groupthink that landed our country in debilitating stagnation; here is a manifesto to get Britain motoring."
ALLISON PEARSON

"Since the election, Conservatives have been desperately looking for a solution to Britain's economic malaise that isn't just a retread of the failed policies of the last twenty-five years. They need look no further. This book is the answer. Future governments will ignore it at their peril."
TOBY YOUNG

"Jon Moynihan combines serious business acumen with a firm grasp of the political big picture. *Return to Growth* is an important and timely book – a route map to a more dynamic, secure and prosperous Britain, by someone who knows what works."
LIAM HALLIGAN

"In terms that the economic layman can understand, probably because he's not a professional economist himself, Jon Moynihan lays out the economic, political, but also moral basis for how Britain can get growing again. These ideas are so practical, achievable, logical and overdue that his thesis is frankly unanswerable. It represents nothing less than a manifesto for national revival and has profound implications for economies beyond the UK too."
ANDREW ROBERTS

"This may well be the most important economics book of recent years. Moynihan's book is an urgent appeal to stop the decline and set western economies on the road to growth and prosperity."
MATT RIDLEY

"Moynihan challenges the bovine assumptions of 'social democracy' that will inexorably lead to fiscal collapse. No doomster, he asserts convincingly, 'We needn't keep doing things this way. We needn't keep digging our own graves.' Clear, readable, riveting and vividly illustrated."
LIONEL SHRIVER

"Moynihan reviews three enemies of growth: high expenditure, high taxation and high regulation. His inescapable – and well-supported – conclusion: raising taxes, bloating spending and bureaucratic meddling just make things worse. I love this book."
ART LAFFER

RETURN TO GROWTH
How to Fix the Economy
JON MOYNIHAN
VOLUME TWO

Biteback Publishing

First published in Great Britain in 2025 by
Biteback Publishing Ltd, London
Copyright © Jon Moynihan 2025

Jon Moynihan has asserted his right under the Copyright, Designs and Patents Act 1988 to be identified as the author of this work.

All rights reserved. No part of this publication may be reproduced, stored in a retrieval system or transmitted, in any form or by any means, without the publisher's prior permission in writing.

This book is sold subject to the condition that it shall not, by way of trade or otherwise, be lent, resold, hired out or otherwise circulated without the publisher's prior consent in any form of binding or cover other than that in which it is published and without a similar condition, including this condition, being imposed on the subsequent purchaser.

Every reasonable effort has been made to trace copyright holders of material reproduced in this book, but if any have been inadvertently overlooked the publisher would be glad to hear from them.

ISBN 978-1-78590-955-9

10 9 8 7 6 5 4 3 2 1

A CIP catalogue record for this book is available from the British Library.

Set in Adobe Caslon Pro

Printed and bound in Great Britain by
CPI Group (UK) Ltd, Croydon CR0 4YY

'We have been forced from the Gold Standard, so it seems to me, and others not unworthy of a public hearing, because of the insufficiency of money in the hands of consumers. Very well. I suggest to you that our contemporary anxieties are not entirely vested in the question of balance of payment, that is at least so far as current account may be concerned, and I put it to you that certain persons, who should perhaps have known better, have been responsible for unhappy, indeed catastrophic capital movements through a reckless and inadmissible lending policy.' … said Widmerpool. 'Now if we have a curve drawn on a piece of paper representing an average ratio of persistence, you will agree that authentic development must be demonstrated by a register alternately ascending and descending the level of our original curve of homogeneous development. Such an image, or, if you prefer it, such a geometrical figure, is dialectically implied precisely by the notion, in itself, of an average ratio of progress. No one would deny that. Now if a governmental policy of regulating domestic prices is to be arrived at in this or any other country, the moment assigned to the compilation of the index number which will establish the par of interest and prices must obviously be that at which internal economic conditions are in a condition of relative equilibrium. So far so good.'

… suddenly, the scene was brought abruptly to a close.

'Look at Le Bas,' said Templer.

'It's a stroke,' said Tolland.

ANTHONY POWELL, *THE ACCEPTANCE WORLD* (1955)

CONTENTS

Caveat to the Reader		xi
Recap	Three Key Drivers of Economic Growth	xiii
Prologue	Events Since Publication of Volume One	xxv
Introduction	Three Free-Market Approaches the UK Should Embrace Anew	1
Chapter 1	Let Free Markets Thrive	7
Chapter 2	Let Free Trade Flourish	51
Chapter 3	Let Sound Money Prevail	97
Conclusion	Returning the UK's Economy to Growth	187
Epilogue	And Here's How We Do It	195
Appendix A	Methodology for Chart 3.1	257
Appendix B	The Growth Model	259
Notes		267
Acknowledgements		279
Index		281

Readers who connect with this QR code can access web links to the referenced works in this book

CAVEAT TO THE READER

An important note about this book: as I caveated in Volume One, I am not an economist. Volume One was, and indeed this Volume Two is, about the UK's economy and the economic steps that governments can do, and sometimes do or don't do, to make it grow, and what practical steps we should take to make faster growth happen. Volume Two goes deeper into various topics that are very much the domain of an economist – for example, price theory, trade theory, monetary economics and policy. As with Volume One, I do my best to make it clear where I disagree with economists on these topics, while making my own prejudices clear.

On occasion, in both books, I slip into economists' language, talking as though I am an economist. I'm not. Any authority I have to say the things I say, I derive from my careful research into what economists have concluded and written about; from my decade or more working closely with the traders who actually deal with the financial commodities – currencies, exchange rates, tax rates, surpluses and deficits, regulations – that governments use to control and impact the economy; from the knowledge gained from my reasonably extensive reading; from my many decades of interacting (until recently) with economists at the MIT Sloan school, particularly the much lamented Rudiger Dornbusch, where I served for over twenty years on various advisory committees; and, above all, from having spent fifty years in business advising, starting and building firms that had to deal on a daily basis with the consequences of decisions made by governments over that time.

On some of the more recondite economic matters discussed in this volume, I have benefited more recently from listening to, and discussions with, economists, politicians and central bankers such as Tim Congdon, Patrick Minford, Roger Bootle, James Forder, Julian Jessop, Gerard Lyons, Don Lessard, Mervyn King, Terry Burns, Norman Blackwell, Norman Lamont and the late Nigel Lawson. Of course, I recognise that, as so often in economics, some of these economists might disagree entirely on any one particular point with other economists and even more so with any conclusions I draw. I have had to pick my own way among opposing views – and mention of these eminent economists in no way implies that any one of them supports any of the views I put forward here.

I hope all that is enough to make my conclusions in this book sensible and acceptable. I have throughout the writing of it benefited from research work and advice and reaction from the economics consultancy CEBR. All mistakes and misstatements are, of course, my own fault.

RECAP

THREE KEY DRIVERS OF ECONOMIC GROWTH

In Volume One of *Return to Growth*, I covered three 'devils' that inhibit a country's economic growth: too-large government expenditure, too-high taxes and excessive regulation. I showed how, before these devils came to be the norm in the UK, economic growth had taken off like a rocket for the past 200 years, in one of the greatest epochs of human history. Economic growth first made us the richest nation on earth and then, spreading to other countries, created numerous societies across the world whose citizens had their lives transformed.

I showed that without economic growth (and that has to mean economic growth per capita), our country cannot succeed. No growth per capita means, axiomatically, that no one in society can get a real-terms salary increase, ever, without someone else being paid less.[*] It means that aspiration is crushed and our society becomes dog eat dog. Capital that will be needed to start up new businesses won't be accumulated. Businesses that don't grow will wither and die because they don't have the resources to beat off competition, particularly from abroad. And a no-growth economy isn't static; it sooner or later shrinks because the unceasing demands of voters mean that politicians who want to be elected promise more

---

[*] Assuming equivalence with wages per capita.

money and more stuff at each general election. In the absence of growth, to pay for this largesse they have to put taxes up, higher and higher.

Chart A: Real GDP and Real GDP-Per-Capita Growth in Major Western European Economies, 1960–2019

Even pre-Covid, annual GDP-per-capita growth had shrunk to 1 per cent or less in major western European economies.

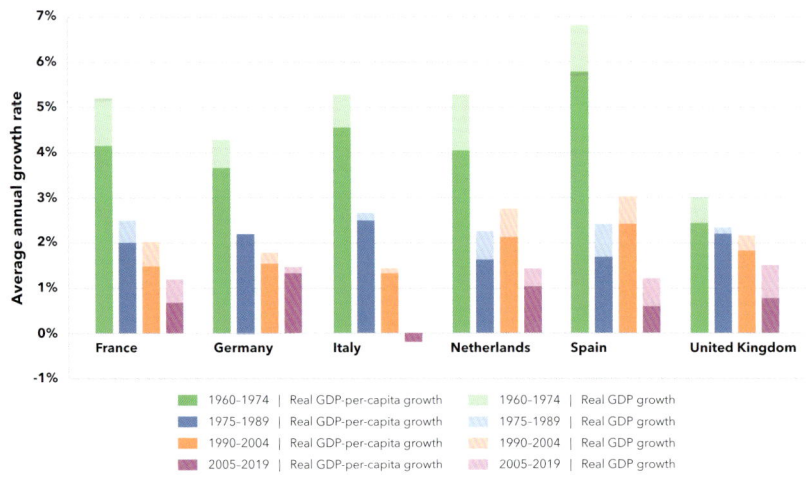

Source: International Monetary Fund, Maddison Project, moyniteam analysis
Also published in Volume One as Chart 1.7

As I show in Chart A, both growth and growth per capita have collapsed in the UK and in the major economies of the EU. Countries in other parts of the world have motored ahead, with much higher growth rates than ours. Why? Because social democracy, our and the EU's chosen political approach, is inimical to economic growth.

It's hardly groundbreaking to point out the importance of economic growth; indeed, the political weather has changed so much in recent years that at the time of Volume One's publication, each of the most recent three Prime Ministers, including Keir Starmer, discussed the lamentable lack of growth in the past few decades by saying that growth was their number one goal. Yet the policies each proposed to achieve that growth contradicted each other, and although politicians on the left and the right have ardently committed to creating growth, few of them seem to have a handle on how that can be done.

So how *is* economic growth generated, and what policies will promote it? In Volume One, I essentially argued that agreement on two key principles – neither of them very controversial – was necessary to create an environment where economic growth per capita could smartly accelerate.

The first proposition is that productive *jobs are created by people, not by government*. One of the more peculiar features of the modern era is the claim by government after government that they will 'create' jobs, often particularising this to their creating jobs in this or that sector. It's just not true to say that government is what creates productive jobs. The overwhelming experience of history is that the more government interferes with the economy and dictates what's going on there, the less will it grow. Economies that are run from the centre by those who say 'we know best' always have dismal economic outcomes. In the extreme, you end up with complete collapse as with Soviet Russia, Cuba or Venezuela.

There are plenty of reasons why this is so. In free-market economies, entrepreneurs and businesses invest their time, skills and capital where they think they can get the best return: they know that this will come from providing goods or services that will best meet the needs of the population. In socialist economies, however, central planning hands out resources, including capital, on personal whims ('we know best') and results in the misallocation of resources, and the production of goods and services that don't meet people's needs and wants (heat pumps, anyone?).* The more a government seeks to direct the economy, the more rent-seeking, crony capitalism and lobbying for subsidies occurs and the less opportunity there is for the entrepreneur to deliver effectively, all of which leads to economic stagnation. As Peter Mandelson immortally said about Labour's industrial policy in the 1970s: they thought they were picking winners, but the losers were picking them.

A particularly meretricious claim is that a government will create a host of 'green jobs'. It's nonsense, and I pointed out in Volume One that I was just one of many, from the *Financial Times* on, to say so. Do politicians really believe that they can be the driver of growth-producing job creation, particularly with doctrinaire central directives? If they do believe it, they must be very ignorant; if they don't, they must be wicked to say so.

The government can certainly create more *government* jobs, paid for through your taxes. Indeed, for most of this century, they have blithely done so – while productivity in the public sector has collapsed, and the quality of its services have declined. But government jobs do not grow the economy, except in the most make-work sense. Rather, they just expand the state and suck activity away from, while further taxing, the private sector – the place where true, growth-producing jobs are created.

These private-sector jobs are created by a combination of entrepreneurs, businesses and investors. The relatively free way in which,

---

* Handing out £400 or possibly £500 million, apparently on the whim of a senior government adviser, to OneWeb, a satellite company that was later sold to the French for peanuts, was one of the (admittedly, one of many) low points of the Boris Johnson administration. See Matthew Field, 'Taxpayers facing £200m loss on satellite venture OneWeb after Dominic Cummings engineered rescue', *Daily Telegraph*, 26 December 2023, https://www.telegraph.co.uk/business/2023/12/26/taxpayers-200m-loss-satellite-oneweb-dominic-cummings/; Oliver Gill, 'UK taxpayers put £400m into OneWeb. Now its tech "is a gift to France"', *The Times*, 4 February 2024, https://www.thetimes.com/article/656bd77c-c106-47c3-840b-674e9efc4f0e?shareToken=39c3f988388d0bf131945b0b0475491a; William Turvill, 'OneWeb satellite boss quits a year after French merger', *The Times*, 13 August 2024, https://www.thetimes.com/article/899e259f-74cb-4558-a2da-22defcdf17eb?shareToken=3dbc0b909af314785c80f389a26abbeb for the 200 years or so before now, private-sector actors, largely unconstrained by government, were able to work their magic, resulted in the most extraordinary level of economic growth in Britain's history: as I have shown, wealth, living standards, health outcomes, longevity and human achievement all increased dramatically, and in the process we pioneered an economic system that has given the entire world unparalleled prosperity.

Those same private-sector actors (entrepreneurs, small and large business investors) have always flourished when they could operate in environments such as the one we saw in Britain in those high-growth centuries: low tax, fewer bureaucratic constraints, altogether less regulatory interference from governments. Entrepreneurs are most likely to settle in countries that welcome them and allow them to get rich if they are successful, and their products, services and the jobs they provide add to human happiness and prosperity. In the same way, big businesses invest in countries that don't seek to suck the last penny out of them in taxes. Just ask AstraZeneca, who in 2022 were planning to invest £400 million in building a plant in the UK. Had they done so, that would have created significant economic growth and jobs. But they changed their plans when the then Chancellor, Rishi Sunak, increased corporation tax to 25 per cent: the factory is now being built in Ireland where, at 12.5 per cent, the corporate tax rate was exactly half. AstraZeneca, who had always taken great pride in their success in the UK, are just one of scores of companies that have fled the UK in the past two years – thanks, Conservatives. In sector after sector, companies have been leaving the UK. Depressingly, this has been particularly evident in some of the former crown jewel sectors of the UK – pharma, finance, oil and gas, and petrochemicals.

I recounted in Volume One how it was not just large companies that are leaving the UK, but we also had the third-largest number of millionaires in the *world* leaving the UK. This has been happening for a number of years and the number leaving has been increasing year after year, particularly in 2024. Non-doms were driven out. Entrepreneurs of all sorts looked elsewhere to make their fortunes. Most depressingly, the brain drain has started up again, with young high earners fleeing to the US, Australia, Dubai and elsewhere. High levels of taxes and regulation also result in many who could contribute to economic growth deciding no longer to do so: potential entrepreneurs and business builders are 'resigning from the economy', prematurely retiring or becoming 'digital nomads'.

The second key principle was that *while governments can't create productive jobs and growth, they certainly can create an environment that prevents the private sector from doing so*. What is that? It is something that has been studied over and over again, and the vast majority of conclusions from those studies say the same thing: a too large, unaffordable level of government expenditure,[*] too high a level of taxation to cover those expenditures[†] and finally, larger and ever-increasing amounts of regulation – the default option in recent years having been to pile one more regulation on top of another, with so many perceived problems 'dealt with' by passing a new law creating a regulator and introducing more regulations.

I showed how these three devils have increasingly dominated the social democracies and are in the main what is now keeping both our, and the EU's, level of economic growth so low.

---

[*] Several quantitative economists have claimed that the optimal size of public-sector expenditure is 26 per cent of the economy. Most politicians will assert this is too low a number to achieve in practice, but anyway, I would settle for government expenditures at, say, 33 per cent of the economy – a level that's not much lower than what we in the UK had just a quarter of a century ago.

[†] Growth is significantly decreased the more tax money you extract from the economy; I argued in Volume One for tax revenues that were lower than 30 per cent, with the UK government receiving inflows of another 3 or 4 per cent of GDP from other revenues, so a balanced budget could be maintained.

RECAP

It is irrefutable that a small state is a prerequisite for economic growth. I offered the following logic: if the public sector is sucking up 25 per cent of GDP, then three private-sector workers (the remaining 75 per cent) can divide up between them the burden of carrying one public-sector worker or beneficiary (the 25 per cent). At 50 per cent of the economy, however, each private-sector worker has to carry on their back, undivided, the 'entire burden' of an entire public-sector worker or beneficiary. How well is that likely to work out? I show in Chart B – one out of numerous studies that prove there is causation, not just correlation, between the two factors – that a large state results in low growth.

Chart B: Size of Government and Annual Growth of Real GDP in OECD Countries, 1960–2019

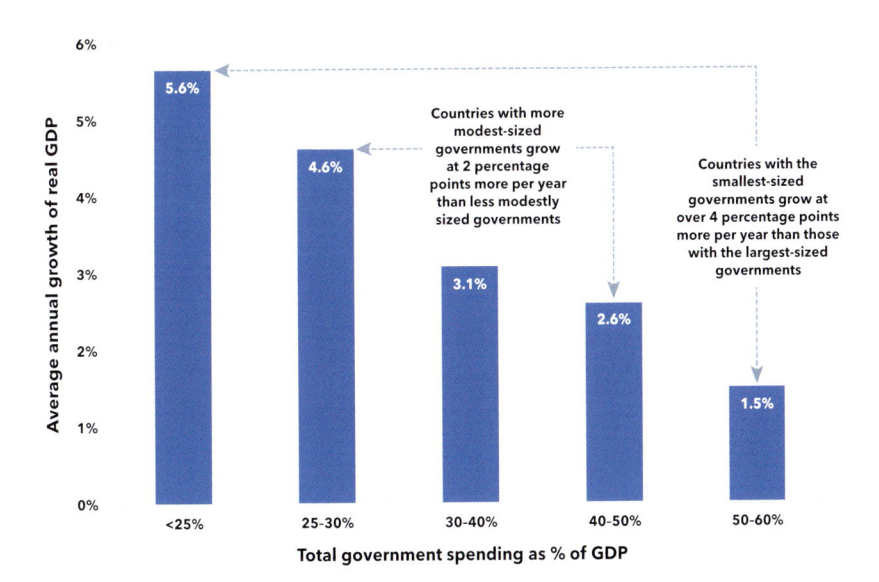

It is clear that small-sized government is a precondition for growth.

Total government spending as % of GDP	Average annual growth of real GDP
<25%	5.6%
25-30%	4.6%
30-40%	3.1%
40-50%	2.6%
50-60%	1.5%

Countries with more modest-sized governments grow at 2 percentage points more per year than less modestly sized governments

Countries with the smallest-sized governments grow at over 4 percentage points more per year than those with the largest-sized governments

Source: International Monetary Fund,[f] moyniteam calculations
An earlier version of this chart appeared in Volume One as Chart 2.5

And yet, in a short space of time, the size of the UK's public sector has increased from near 30 per cent of GDP in the last century to over 50 per cent during Covid – and even now, it is around 45 per cent, and looking likely to increase further under the new government.

Along with a large state comes the corollary: high taxes. I showed how academic studies have demonstrated that the higher the tax as a percentage of GDP, the lower the growth. Yet we keep raising taxes – even under Conservative governments. And when those governments meet resistance to their increasing income or corporation tax, they invent all sorts of unconventional taxes – often wrapping up the reasoning for them in faux-moral posturing, so that the taxpayer can feel bad about indulging in the activity while paying stiff taxes on it. But Art Laffer – still denigrated but always right – showed that these tax rises result in less compliance, less economic activity and less tax revenue than predicted.[*]

Large government and high taxes are bad enough, but what really kills growth is the third devil, excessive regulation. Bit by bit, governments fail to resist the temptation to interfere with wealth creators. Sector after sector gets more and more regulated and can innovate less and less. Capital requirements on banks steer them away from lending to small companies. Regulations on pension funds encourage them to invest in government bonds, not private-sector equities. The car industry is told what cars to make; the boiler

---

[*] As I write this, I hear news on the radio that the Liberal Democrat Party – usually the one to sneer most noisily and aggressively against the Laffer curve and the overall concept of dynamic responses to changes in tax rates – are campaigning for VAT to be removed from sun cream, so that more people will use it and thus less people will get skin cancer. That is a blatant and outright assertion of the power of the Laffer curve (see Volume One). See Claudia Savage, 'Lib Dems call for VAT cut on sun cream to tackle skin cancer', *The Independent*, 19 August 2024, https://www.independent.co.uk/news/uk/vat-daisy-cooper-lib-dems-government-nhs-b2598167.html

industry is told not to make boilers. Formerly privatised industries must be renationalised. The insanity of diversity, equity and inclusion (DEI), and environmental, social and governance (ESG) policies and the like (compulsory carbon literacy training, anyone?) forces companies to affirm and act with the primary purpose of achieving a fantastic social nirvana, rather than to deliver goods and services that people want. Good luck with that nirvana stuff, and in the meantime, forget about any economic growth.

So, two simple and fairly obvious principles, but, as I showed in the previous volume, most social democracies have taken the opposite view in the past fifty years, ignoring clear evidence on how to improve their citizens' wealth and living standards.[*]

I discussed three general models of how countries are run in this modern age. The first model, at the worst end, is the brutal bandit dictatorships such as Russia, Venezuela, North Korea, Iran, Nicaragua and Cuba, which mostly emerged as the logical endpoint of failed attempts to build socialism or communism, their leaders hanging on to power by abandoning any pretence at democracy, terrorising their own citizens and indulging in lethal military adventures abroad. The second model is social democracy. It takes a lot longer to fail, but results in economic stagnation and, in consequence, severe economic crisis – as is currently being predicted for France, for example.[2] The third model is the free-market economy, still pursued in many countries around the world. These economies show startling and continued levels of growth, bringing wealth, health, and usually longevity to their citizens. The US is still one (in the main), despite Obama's and Biden's efforts, and the wealth of

---

[*] Denmark's a unique exception – with a flexible labour market, a stronger working ethic, and lower regulation, even though it has high taxes and high spend.

its citizens grows at an astonishingly greater pace than that of the average EU citizen. The salaries and wealth in those free-market economy countries outstrip ours, further and further.

Post-war, western Europe at first used the free-market approach and so was successful at growing its economies, but bit by bit these countries moved from free-market structures to a social democracy framework, where saying you care but acting to damage is the norm. Their ever-increasing welfare bills led to the ravages of quantitative easing, and consequent bouts of inflation that we cannot be sure are fully behind us. Doctrinaire polemicists now spout more and more reckless social nonsense, such as claims that national wealth was built entirely on the fruits of rapacious colonialism and slavery, such as claims that modern monetary theory allows endless printing of new money, such as the promotion of diversity hires, such as the bizarre assertion that the UK's NHS, one of the worst health systems in the developed world, is a national treasure and the envy of the world.

I discussed in Volume One how leaving the EU had created the conditions for us to break away from the European social democracy model. But we haven't yet capitalised on that. Instead, since then, governments in the UK have, presumably with an eye to short-term political gain, doubled down on social democratic policies with predictably catastrophic results. Our economic model forecasts a dire long-term outcome from that (see Chart C).

In a review of the costs, taxes and regulations that we could get rid of, I showed in Volume One that it doesn't have to continue this way. In previous centuries, we led the world with a few basic principles, summed up in the term 'laissez-faire' – just let entrepreneurs, businesses and investors get on with building the economy, rather than stuffing them up with high taxes and drowning them in swamps of regulation. Other countries, such as Switzerland and

RECAP

Singapore, have shown us there is as yet no limit to the economic growth that a country can achieve if you rein in the state; in consequence, they deliver enormous wealth and benefits of all kinds to their citizens. There is, I argue, absolutely no reason why we can't do, and achieve, the same.

Chart C: Forecasted 'Status Quo' Development of the UK's Economy 2024–39

The outcome is predictable. If we continue with current policies, our annual growth in the long run will settle at below 1 per cent a year. GDP per capita will grow at an even slower pace, and government debt will inexorably balloon to some 150 per cent of GDP in fifteen years.

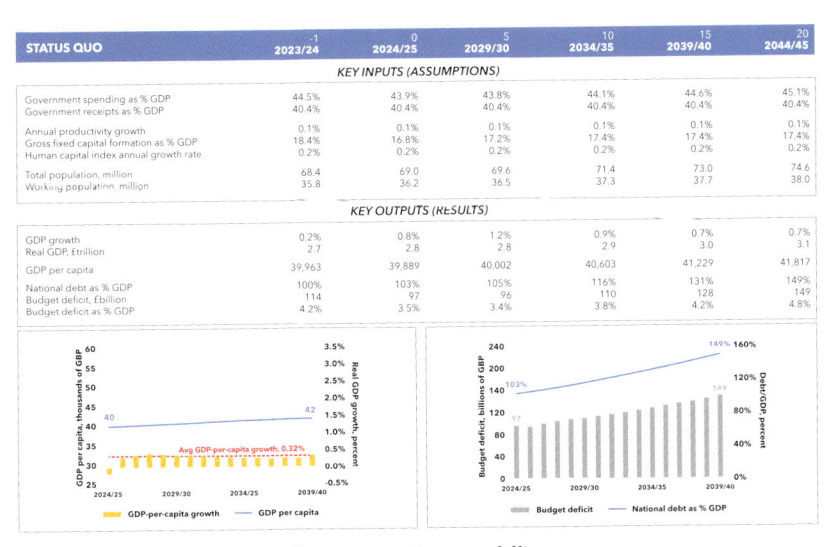

STATUS QUO	-1 2023/24	0 2024/25	5 2029/30	10 2034/35	15 2039/40	20 2044/45
KEY INPUTS (ASSUMPTIONS)						
Government spending as % GDP	44.5%	43.9%	43.8%	44.1%	44.6%	45.1%
Government receipts as % GDP	40.4%	40.4%	40.4%	40.4%	40.4%	40.4%
Annual productivity growth	0.1%	0.1%	0.1%	0.1%	0.1%	0.1%
Gross fixed capital formation as % GDP	18.4%	16.8%	17.2%	17.4%	17.4%	17.4%
Human capital index annual growth rate	0.2%	0.2%	0.2%	0.2%	0.2%	0.2%
Total population, million	68.4	69.0	69.6	71.4	73.0	74.6
Working population, million	35.8	36.2	36.5	37.3	37.7	38.0
KEY OUTPUTS (RESULTS)						
GDP growth	0.2%	0.8%	1.2%	0.9%	0.7%	0.7%
Real GDP, £trillion	2.7	2.8	2.8	2.9	3.0	3.1
GDP per capita	39,963	39,889	40,002	40,603	41,229	41,817
National debt as % GDP	100%	103%	105%	116%	131%	149%
Budget deficit, £billion	114	97	96	110	128	149
Budget deficit as % GDP	4.2%	3.5%	3.4%	3.8%	4.2%	4.8%

Source: moyniteam modelling

In addition to exorcising the three devils, there are of course many other things we have to do to get growth going. Key among them is improving our state education system, which the wonderful Katharine Birbalsingh's Michaela Community School has shown us how to do. It is also important that we break up the employee monopolies of the public sector and the semi-nationalised industries, banning strikes by public-sector workers. And third, we have to find a way, crucially, to get immigration down – so that economic growth per capita becomes possible. We *have* to do all these things, and more.

Finally, I showed that unless we return this country to growth, we can only expect decay, decline, and (eventually) financial default. One way or another, our economy has to be restructured. Better done sooner than later – although, I acknowledge, the chances of our having a government that will do that any time soon are slim to zero. My work across both volumes of *Return to Growth* can only hope to, at best, lay the foundations for future change. But I hope these volumes can be a good start for an eventual return to these principles, and thus a return to growth.

PROLOGUE

EVENTS SINCE PUBLICATION OF VOLUME ONE

The weeks between when Volume One was written and its launch were politically and economically active. (The further weeks more, that will take place between my writing these words and you, the reader, seeing them, will no doubt result in yet more change.) This short section is devoted to reviewing what changes have taken place so far since I wrote Volume One.

A new Labour government has come into power, with a large majority that will certainly see them through a five-year term. The new Chancellor, Rachel Reeves, had tweeted before Labour came to power, 'The lifeblood of economic growth is private sector investment which can create good jobs and spread productivity in every part of the country.' These words we can certainly agree with. They are better words than our previous Conservative government usually managed – although that is a low hurdle. She went on to say, 'I'm determined that the next Labour government is ready from day one to put our plan for growth into action.' Her words then, and since, have not, unfortunately, revealed the logic of what that growth plan involved.[1]

Let's look at progress on my three desiderata: smaller government, lower taxes, less regulation. First, what progress on reducing the size of the state? Remarkably, the new government came straight out of the box with one cut that I was gratified to see – one of my suggestions, removing winter fuel payments for those not in poverty. (Ignobly, I would have preferred that announcement had not been made so quickly, since as a result the book became available to the public only after Rachel Reeves had made her announcement, raising the possibility that I might have copied her and, in any event, making my suggestion far less interesting. But nonetheless, I approve of her action, of course.)

This was good news: a cut was being made in benefits. (Depressingly, the Conservative Party, maintaining its recently acquired modern reputation for fiscal incontinence, campaigned to restore them.) Labour's promising start was, however, obliterated by a flurry of expenditure commitments. More job destruction by raising the living wage by an above-inflation amount; a large increase to the state pension because of the commitment to stick with the pension triple lock; awarding public-sector workers well-above-inflation increases despite no increases in productivity.[2] The number of civil servants earning over £100,000 has now gone up by 40 per cent to a total of almost 3,000.[3] (Admittedly, most of that increase will have predated the new government.) Already overpaid rail workers received an 'above inflation' 15 per cent pay rise, but immediately after the £100 million award was announced, stated they will go on strike for three months in a dispute over working conditions.[4] Other public-sector workers, having noted that militancy works, also announced industrial action to get equivalently high pay raises.[5]

The public sector's impunity is further demonstrated by the news that a number of arm's-length bodies, such as the Bank of England, now offer private healthcare as a benefit to their staff at a cost to the taxpayer of tens of millions of pounds.[6] (So much for 'our' NHS!)

The cost of benefits continues to rise at a startling pace. The number of children under eighteen who are the subject of Disability Living Allowance claims has risen, since November 2019, from 534,000 to 730,000. Claims for neurodevelopmental conditions have gone up by a third to 337,000. Claims for ADHD are up to 72,000. The DWP is forecasting that almost 1 million under-sixteens will be in receipt of disability benefits by the end of the decade; the bill for health and disability payments to people of all ages is rising to some £100 billion a year.[7] Some 7 per cent of schoolchildren were receiving disability benefits in 2022.

This is not some simple case of complaining that money is being paid out to undeserving malingerers; it is far too hard to come up with some magic measuring wand that will say which young person is truly in need of disability benefit and which person just needs their behaviour adjusting through appropriate discipline at home and at school. There is no doubt that approaches to teaching; dubious diets; and the giant disruption that took place during Covid have accustomed many children to the idea that they are incapable of sitting still in class, behaving themselves or absorbing what the teacher is saying – so they need not do any of these things, and their parents receive payments to reward their non-compliance. The fact that there is a financial benefit at the end always distorts behaviour, and in this case guides the parent towards medicalising the condition, rather than finding a family-based solution. It would take an educational giant to parse out the problem and resolve all competing claims; in Volume One and here, I take the simpler view that the money is just not there for all this. Rachel Reeves has been quoted as saying that 'if we cannot afford it, we cannot do it'.[8] But they *are* doing it regardless. I agree that we cannot afford it. Unless we cut the coat of our compassion to the cloth of what we can afford, it is hard to see how we can get out of our economic problems. And for both children and adults, a 'tough love' (warm/strict) policy is the only way to get the numbers down.

At the time of writing, the autumn Budget has just arrived. Spending is up by almost 2 per cent, taxes ditto by £40 billion, with major increases in capital gains tax, inheritance tax, business windfall tax, and employer national insurance, all directly disincentivising business. Non-dom status is scrapped; more will leave.[9] So no, taxes will not be going down. And in the meantime, the Office for Budget Responsibility (OBR) is going even further in ruling the roost with its strange modelling formulations – ones which, despite the exciting lead set by the Lib Dems on their 'remove VAT on sun cream' campaign, implicitly reject that there is economic benefit from reducing taxes, or that there will be negative consequences from increasing them. The growth metric remains GDP, not GDP per capita.

Again, all of this is the result of using the wrong paradigm. More expenditure is said to be necessary or inevitable, a 'black hole' is declared to exist – all culminating in the narrative that there is no alternative but to raise taxes. The Overton window does not, it seems, currently allow a narrative that says: we can't afford all this, so here's how we are going to cut this expenditure, and when we do reduce our spend further, it will allow us to cut taxes and thus promote growth, so that eventually we *will* be able to afford more benefits for our people.

And regulation? Depressingly, in the run-up to the recent election, all major parties proposed swathes of new rules and regulations. The Liberal Democrats proposed 128 new major regulations. The Green Party proposed 104. The Labour manifesto included sixty-two proposals to increase the regulatory burden (along with thirteen proposed reductions). The Institute for Economic Affairs (IEA) estimates a £1,000 per year cost to each household from the ban on new petrol and diesel cars, a £1 billion cost from the renters reform bill, an £80 million cost for the football regulator, £2 billion for the smoking ban and £664 million for the junk food advertising ban.[10] Meanwhile, it's looking more and more like the new government won't allow much deviation from ongoing EU law across the UK (if only because of the ongoing malign influence of the Windsor Framework, which applies EU law to Northern Ireland; as a result, if we wish to preserve the union, we can't change things elsewhere across the UK). Blithely ignoring the clear public backlash against woke diversity initiatives, the civil service continues to double down on DEI. Diversity teams in various departments are being expanded, and pay rises are being offered to those who 'champion diversity'.[11]

What are the long-term expected outcomes from all this? It's going about as we might expect. Already, the UK's cash borrowing was £3 billion above the earlier OBR forecast in July 2024. Far from reducing electricity prices, the cost of 'renewables' is going up and up – costs which will come back to every household, but will also further drive manufacturing out of the country. The rich continue to decamp: Volume One described how every year, more and more millionaires had been leaving the UK. In 2022/23 that number was 4,200. Henley & Partners' annual report on wealth migration now tells us, startlingly, even before the Budget, that number has more than doubled, to 9,500 millionaires in 2023/24. This has to be shameful. The loss of capital, of entrepreneurial job-creators, of all sorts of tax revenue paid by those now departed is enormous; over the next few years we will find out what the negative impact was on tax revenues. The UK was for a century or more just about *the* top destination worldwide for millionaires. Now we are, astoundingly, the country with the second-highest rate of millionaires *fleeing* from it, with only China worse than the UK. How can that be considered a good thing? Are we really now agreed that the UK should have a policy that makes it highly unattractive for rich people to come and settle here? Because such a policy has now become the reality.

The ultimate outcome will, of course, be the collapse of our national finances. I predicted in Volume One that our national debt as a percentage of GDP would rise to some 150 per cent from its current 100 per cent within fifteen years if nothing is changed. In coming to that number, our modelling team sought very hard to avoid being overly pessimistic. And yet the OBR itself forecasts far worse; they said that by 2060 our debt-to-GDP number would actually be rising towards 300 per cent.[12] (It is worth noting that the gilt market ructions of 2022, allegedly caused by the Truss mini-budget, resulted from forecasts that were a tiny fraction of such numbers.)

So, overall, not a good start to our project of getting expenditure down, taxes down and regulation down. Instead, and particularly with an expected slow growth in GDP in the next few years, expenditure as a percentage of GDP is likely to rise; and tax *revenues* as a percentage of GDP will, most likely, and despite some swingeing increases in tax rates, not go up by nearly as much as expected. Nonetheless, the high tax rates will still keep GDP growth down. And regulation will, it seems, keep going up and up. Volume One's 'pessimistic' status-quo forecast for the coming years is therefore likely, if anything, to turn out as having been overly optimistic. The prospects for the economy and therefore for our citizens are poor, and the lives of frustration and anger for many, that will be the result of this, are painful to contemplate.

INTRODUCTION

THREE FREE-MARKET APPROACHES THE UK SHOULD EMBRACE ANEW

In Volume One, we discussed the three biggest drivers of faster economic growth: small government, low taxes, minimal regulation. But what about the surrounding environment in which an economy can best operate – the sea, as it were, on which a high-growth economy prefers to sail? Here, in Volume Two, we review the philosophical approaches that underpin the liberal free-market perspective. These approaches are timeless and well-established yet somehow, in recent decades, have fallen out of fashion. As we look at the growth-inhibiting philosophies and policies that are currently espoused by all the major political parties in the UK, it is clear that these traditional growth-promoting principles have to be rediscovered and re-explored with every new generation.

What, beyond the three social democracy 'devils' of large expenditure, high taxes and swamping regulation, are the mistaken approaches that governments take, which prevent a country developing a liberal free-market economy? There are, again, three further inhibitors: dirigism, mercantilism and Keynesianism.

Dirigism is most closely associated with France; its heyday there was under Charles de Gaulle, whose perfect economic ignorance allowed him to give full rein to the concept of national champions, directing investment into chosen sectors and parachuting senior civil servants into top executive positions in the private sector. While the French state was still small post-war, with low taxes and low regulation, capital could nevertheless be attracted into that economy, and large-scale investment (particularly from the US's Marshall Plan) led to significant economic growth. But the approach carried the seeds of its own defeat. When steel, transportation, energy, armaments and the like were in need of significant investment post-war, a dirigist set of decisions was unlikely to go very wrong in deciding where to invest and how to build capacity – particularly when the state could go arm in arm with a given industry in agreeing a regulatory framework that would support the rapid growth of the industry.

But once that capacity was built, and at the same time international competition began to challenge France in these industries, the disadvantages of the approach became stark. Sclerosis set in, with civil servants who were insufficiently trained in the given industry to understand its challenges and opportunities, and workforces who had been bought off with high compensation and stultifying work rules who were not prepared to be flexible in changing to meet emerging needs. By the end of the 1970s, the right-wing government was thrown out because of the major ructions that were taking place in the economy as a result of this sclerosis. It was left to a left-wing government, under François Mitterrand, to sort it out. He first tried to double down on this semi-socialist approach, but then, as things only got worse, wisely opened up the French economy to competition (across Europe, at least). The result, as Peter Hall of Harvard University has written, is that France has in the main stepped back from dirigism, and has embraced a more neo-liberal, competitive market-based approach.[1] (It might be said that the apogee of that change was Macron's decision, in 2021, to close the cradle of dirigism, the ENA, where future top bureaucrats had been getting their education.[2]) France today is still very far away from being a paradise of free-market policies, but it has learned its lesson regarding dirigism.

INTRODUCTION

And yet much of the dirigiste spirit survives across Europe, and that includes the UK. In the 1970s, the UK was happily dirigiste in many areas, such as banking. It took Margaret Thatcher to wrench the economy out of that approach. But then, bit by bit and particularly in the economic reign of Gordon Brown, and of successive Conservative governments that saw themselves as the 'heirs to Blair', the state reverted to interfering more and more in the economy. In the last decade or two, government after government wasn't able to help but be attracted to the idea that they were going to be able to pick winners, to tell companies how to run themselves, to interfere in different sectors. The dirigism impulse may not be as strong in the UK as elsewhere, but to interfere is so tempting, and the potential downsides are so little understood, that massive state interference in the economy has happened here, is happening here and will worsen here.* In the coming decade, as one sector after another is ruined, the staggering level of damage to the economy will become clearer. Will the situation then be turned around? It depends on how much will be left to salvage. In the meantime, the importance of free markets in liberating economic growth just has to be emphasised over and over again. As we discuss in Chapter 1, dirigism must be shunned, and free markets allowed to flourish instead.

Mercantilism, an approach to trade that dominated world commerce for hundreds of years, is a dog-eat-dog view of trade that reliably reduces worldwide economic growth, while impoverishing the population of those countries that adopt the approach. In simplest terms, it is the view that I should sell as much as possible of my output to you, while buying as little as possible of your output in

---

* See my earlier note on the fiasco of the £400 million investment in OneWeb in 2020.

return. I do this by being protectionist, and by seeking to monopolise certain sectors. In that way, I hope to accumulate wealth in my country. Instead, of course, my actions will encourage a retaliatory, even more mercantilist response from you. Evidently, mercantilism will work better for powerful countries with large armies that can threaten other countries; it doesn't work so well in a peaceful, mutually respectful world.

The Soviet Union imposed this system on its satrapies, and China is creating such a system, both with advanced economies and with its predatory behaviour towards many of the poorer countries around the world. Trump (at the time of writing not yet elected) threatens a supersized version of the mercantilist approach, evidencing his economic ignorance – although considerations of national security as regards chipmaking in Taiwan and many electronic goods manufactured in China and south-east Asia, for example, do complicate the question and give some credibility to his concerns. Biden, although more inclined towards free markets, didn't massively resile from the mercantilist policies of his predecessor (and his successor) Trump.

The problem with mercantilism is that by insisting on everything being manufactured at home, you raise the price of goods for your own people in many areas, and invite retaliation by other countries. Raising tariff barriers or quotas creates an additional cost to imports, again increasing the cost of goods for the population. (Tariffs are, of course, just another form of taxation.) As we discuss in Chapter 2, allowing free trade between free countries is essential to promote global wealth.

Keynesianism is the final of these three opponents of a successful economy. As Tim Congdon stated in an excellent recent CapX paper, the foundation of Britain's original economic upsurge was that our country 'conducted its public finances and international commerce according to a mere three principles: maintaining the

INTRODUCTION

gold standard, balancing the budget, and leaving British citizens free to buy whatever they wished – with no tariff or other impediments – from the rest of the world'.[3] For the first of these three, as Congdon points out later in his paper, the complexity of the world economy now makes maintaining the gold standard no longer feasible – a different approach to preserving price stability and managing the sterling exchange rate is necessary. That new approach is monetarism, combined with the general principles of balanced budgets and sound money – to which, as Congdon points out, there are no alternatives. These principles are discussed in Chapter 3.

Unfortunately, the tendency for governments to interfere means that they are constantly tempted to go against these simple principles. The idea that 'we know best' is so strong, bolstered by a reverence for the often vulgarly interpreted ideas of Keynes, plus modern-day policies that are still driven by a lingering belief that more government stimulus (as opposed to less destructive regulation on banks) is almost always the indicated response to any economic problem, that governments and central banks, as I describe in Chapter 3, find it hard to resist pouring money into the economy, whenever, however.[4]

As Congdon describes, the high priest of Keynesianism was Paul Samuelson, whose textbook went through nineteen editions, indoctrinating generations of economists. In its earlier editions, it confidently predicted the triumph of the Soviet system's planned communist economy. Obviously, that position became increasingly difficult to maintain, so the later editions removed it, but that did not prevent the gospel of stimulus from ruling the roost throughout the post-war period, almost up to the present day, extending so far as to give widespread recent credibility to a nonsense belief in the power of printing money without consequences (modern monetary theory or MMT). As Chapter 3 shows, allowing too much growth in the money supply has led to massively damaging bouts of inflation in the UK, impoverishing large parts of our society.

These three enemies of a well-functioning economy have to be battled against and eliminated. For a free-market economy to work and deliver satisfying and wealth-producing growth for its people, there must be a classical liberal economic policy, based around the core principles of small government, low taxes and minimal regulation.[5] This is achieved when, as opposed to the three devils described in Volume One, we embrace the three angels of the modern neoclassical, free-market economic approach:

- Chapter 1: Let free markets thrive
- Chapter 2: Let free trade flourish
- Chapter 3: Let sound money prevail

CHAPTER I

LET FREE MARKETS THRIVE

PRELUDE: WHAT IS MEANT BY A FREE-MARKET ECONOMY AND WHY IS IT SUCH A BIG DEAL?

A free market is one where transactions and exchanges between individuals and organisations take place without, or with only minimal, interference from governments, regulators, monopolists or other distorting entities. Its foundations are voluntary exchange, self-regulating price mechanisms, rule of law and sanctity of contract. Prices are determined by supply and demand, whereby the market (the locus where interaction between buyers and sellers takes place) discovers what price a purchaser is prepared to pay for a particular good or service and whether there are providers who are willing to part with the good or service for that price. Through a freely discovered price, only those goods or services are produced that buyers actually want to purchase and that other sellers are prepared to provide; both parties expect to gain from the transaction. Central planners are not allowed to impose their own concept of what prices should be.

The concept of a free market has been around for ever. In ancient Greece, a man with torn trousers could come to a tailor, who would say 'Euripides?' The man would reply in the affirmative and ask 'Eumenides?' All that would be necessary after that conversation would be for a price to be agreed, the transaction shaken on and the bargain ultimately fulfilled. Now, at first sight, the preceding words may appear only as my fruitlessly introducing a couple of feeble puns into my beige text, trying but failing to spice the book up. Not at all: the story is offered up as a near-perfect example of a pure free-market transaction between two autonomous citizens.[*]

But, of course, such a transaction would only work to the satisfaction of all if a variety of important circumstances prevailed in that ancient Greek town:

- First, there needs to be more than one tailor in town so that the trouser repairer could not gouge the trouser owner on price; *competition* was needed.
- Second, a true *free exchange* of money for services had to take place, leaving both sides reasonably satisfied with the transaction.
- Third, the tailor had to be a *free agent* to set his own price for the work, with an eye on what the competition charged and what the tailor's reputation, or otherwise, for quality allowed him to charge for his work. There could not be a government-set price for trouser mending.
- Fourth, there needs to be generally available *market information* regarding what different tailors around town charged and how good each tailor was at trouser mending. This would be the only way for discerning citizens to get their trousers mended well, and cheaply – in other words, at whatever combination of price and quality appealed to that particular citizen. (The preceding points add up to the needed conditions for a *price mechanism* that creates the setting for a free market.)

---

[*] The near perfection of the example is marred only by the well-known fact that the ancient Greeks never wore trousers; they considered them the garb of the barbarian.

- Fifth, sixth and seventh, there needs to be both *rule of law* and *sanctity of contract*, with appropriate *enforcement of the law* so that once any such agreement had been made between two parties, each could be confident that the other would stick to their side of the bargain – so that if there were to be a dispute, a court could rule justly on the ownership of the (well or badly) mended trousers, and on the payment that was due (or not) to the tailor.
- Finally, eighth, the tailors around town should not be allowed to get together to combine into a monopoly or fix prices at some unconscionable level; both *market collusion* and *monopolies* had to be prevented.

So, to generalise from this example, the key requirements for a free-market economy to operate are:

- sanctity of contract and rule of law
- presence (physical or virtual) of free and competitive marketplaces, with a price mechanism
- lack of interference from government or other outside forces, apart from enforcing sanctity of contract and preventing price fixing

With free markets operating efficiently, confidence in trade and transactions increases, and goods and services are produced and exchanged both in increasing volume and with increasing efficiency. Incredibly complicated markets spontaneously spring up, potentiated by a myriad of free exchanges. As Matt Ridley put it, '10,000,000 people eat lunch in London on most days, choosing what they have at the last minute and never going hungry, yet there is no London lunch commissioner, and it would be a disaster if there were.'[1] Compare the efficiency of this lunch provision with the chaos of provision of medical services by GPs in the UK, in our socialistic, centrally directed, no-competition NHS.[2]

Adam Smith, the eighteenth-century Scottish economist, is celebrated by many as the founder of the free-market school of thought. His concept of the 'invisible hand' (what technically might be called 'the market mechanism') explains how virtuous intent is not required for a merchant to do good and nor is central control needed for a market to work. Smith's description of how dividing the manufacture of a pin into eighteen specialised tasks could lead to the production of 4,800 pins per worker per day – as opposed to the near-impossibility of a single worker, working in isolation, producing even one pin in a day. This showed how entrepreneurs, benefiting from free interaction between different parts of the market, could drive prices down so as to create affordable mass markets for finished products. The well-known story 'I, Pencil' expands this concept to show how the spontaneous creation of many mini-markets leads to the ability to mass-produce ever-more-complex products at lower and lower prices.[3] Centrally directed economies are incapable of such ingenuity – as can be seen by the picaresque arch capitalist Armand Hammer becoming Lenin and Stalin's bosom buddy as he was awarded the pencil monopoly in Soviet Russia, due to their inability to replicate the quality of his pencil factories' output.[4]

Many economists over the centuries have developed these free-market principles, and thus our understanding of the free-market philosophy. Foremost among these are the so-called Austrian economists, particularly Friedrich von Hayek and Ludwig von Mises, and the Chicago economist Milton Friedman.

Hayek went beyond lauding just the *power* of free exchange. He showed that it was not just the best, but was in fact the *only* efficient way of creating economic growth that would provide enhanced happiness for humanity. He attacked those that I discussed in the chapter on regulation in Volume One: the ones who say 'we know best'. He did this by showing that it was impossible for governments, politicians or commissars at the centre to have sufficient understanding of people's individual desires, needs and buying power; or of providers' capabilities, concepts, and costs. He showed that it was impossible for anyone at the centre to be able to make rational decisions about products, prices and manufacturing volumes, or about what could successfully be created to be sold and what was likely to be bought.

Hayekians point out that the more you allow the centre to decide what the people should and should not have, the more you shut off entrepreneurial creativity. Does anyone seriously believe that a bureaucrat could have invented the iPhone or Amazon? No, but those authoritarians who have managed to seize power at the centre are now forcing heat pumps onto the populace. And it gets worse: if you tell the population that they must have heat pumps, it becomes highly unlikely that any new superior solution to heating homes will later find success, because you have cut entrepreneurs off from being able to try out their ideas in the marketplace. You've put in place regulations, laws, subsidies and so on that have made it nigh-on impossible for innovative inventors and entrepreneurs to get their new-concept heating products to be built – let alone for them to catch the interest of consumers, who aren't allowed to buy them.

The price mechanism is the way that information about the nature, quality, features and value of every item on offer in the economy – information that is too overwhelmingly large for a central government to capture, let alone absorb and rationally act upon – is transmitted, in the form of price signals, into the marketplace. At the same time, prices perform an equally important function by translating that information into transactions that drive an economy forward.

Hayek, in what has been called 'one of the most praised and cited articles of the twentieth century', 'The Use of Knowledge in Society', emphasised what a 'marvel' the price mechanism is, and how, if human behaviour had not adapted itself around the price concept, modern civilisation and wealth would not have been possible.[5] In two famous passages, he wrote:

> I have deliberately used the word 'marvel' to shock the reader out of the complacency with which we often take the working of this mechanism for granted … if it were the result of deliberate human design … this mechanism would have been acclaimed as one of the greatest triumphs of the human mind.

He goes on to explain how the unconscious, undirected way in which people's decisions to buy or not, at a given price, collectively results in the optimal utilisation of resources across society: 'The price system is just one of those formations which man has learned to use … after he had stumbled upon it without understanding it.'

It is Hayek's view that if mankind had not, more or less accidentally, embraced the price system, then some other entirely different way in which our civilisation organised itself might have emerged. Without the price system, he believed, our civilisation itself, and its evolution to its present-day success, couldn't have developed.

Building on Hayek, Milton Friedman has been called the 'prophet of the free market'.[6] So great was his influence that a commissioner of the US Federal Trade Commission, Christine Wilson, gave a speech in 2019 titled 'Milton Friedman is still right: marking the

35th anniversary of *Free Markets for Free Men*'.[7] Her speech lauded, and gave examples of the direct benefits of, Friedman's influence in eliminating regulation and promoting privatisation of state enterprises, which introduced the important elements of competition and a proper price mechanism, into the US marketplace. Friedman's original paper, which Wilson referred to, is a heartfelt polemic against government interference, regulation and price setting.[8] Friedman's extensive output, both in writing and on video (most of which can be found on YouTube), makes an unanswerable case for free markets.

. . .

How can a government muck up the effective working of a free market? Let us count the ways – in particular, looking at interference with the preconditions mentioned at the beginning of this chapter:

- limiting or eliminating *competition*
- interfering with *free exchange*
- regulating *prices*
- making *laws* or regulations that interfere with the free market
- setting *product standards* that sharply limit what can be offered to the public[*]
- failing to enforce, or interfering with, *sanctity of contract* and the *rule of law*
- allowing *market collusion*, *monopolies* or *oligopolies* to flourish

With regard to how well the UK economy does when judged by

---
[*] Health and safety standards may be beneficial, but many product standards have nothing to do with health and safety: they are instead just a form of protectionism for the incumbent producer.

this list, it is clear that to date, we have failed to use our Brexit freedoms to create a growth-promoting economy; the UK now comes up as only thirtieth in the Heritage Foundation's 2024 'Index of Economic Freedom'.[9] This index rates rule of law, government size, regulatory efficiency and open markets. Singapore, Switzerland and Ireland are first, second and third on that list. (If our close neighbour Ireland can do it, why not us?) New Zealand is sixth. Australia is thirteenth. Germany is eighteenth and the US is twenty-fifth. To repeat: the UK, once the standard-bearer of liberal market economics around the world, is now thirtieth.

Amazingly, price theory – one of the most fundamental building blocks of understanding how a modern market economy works – is hardly ever discussed these days. It is clearly not understood by most politicians, and now, the *Wall Street Journal* reports, it is disappearing from the curricula of most colleges in the US, including the most prestigious.[10] I would say from my own (admittedly only general) knowledge on this point that most UK universities are also getting rid of it.

A key requirement for a free market to operate effectively is untrammelled competition. Monopolies and oligopolies, whether private or public, are a conspiracy on the population, allowing goods and services to be sold that are inferior and/or overpriced, but that cannot (because of the monopoly or oligopoly) be replaced by better, cheaper goods or services: competition is suppressed. And the moment our government interferes in the free market by creating limits on what sort of product, with what features, can be sold (let us stipulate that this is unrelated to any genuine safety considerations), or encourages any other kind of monopolistic behaviour in any market, the public is cheated and economic growth is lessened because, as a result, less of the good or service is purchased.

There will always be less demand for a shoddier or more expensive item than there would be for an equally priced but superior one or a lower-priced one.

As alluded to earlier, one way that incumbents preserve their monopolistic or oligopolistic positions in the marketplace is through the apparently innocent and ostensibly desirable approach of 'product standards'. This is something that is particularly rife in the EU and holds back economic progress there; but, all around the world, few countries that allow product or service regulation are free of the downside created by these 'standards'. If a product becomes tightly defined, in a way that closely parallels what the incumbent currently offers to the market (which is what so often happens in the EU; and we in the UK have yet to shake off many such EU-originated regulations), then that shuts down the possibility of market innovation outside of those legally enforced standards. When that is so, any challenger company finds it near-impossible to enter that market with an innovative new product, even if it is one that consumers would prefer, because the challenger product has features that are outside those tightly defined product standards.

Trade unions often support product standards because their workers tend to have jobs with the incumbent and those jobs will be threatened by any new and superior competitor products. Very often, the 'product standards' are plausibly presented as a health and safety issue or as some kind of moral panic ('hormone-fed beef' or 'chlorine-washed chicken', anyone?) even when the costs to the consumer of the standard far exceed any supposed benefits. EU product standards often are aimed at competition from outside the heartland; the big American digital companies are often targeted with big fines for somewhat nebulously defined offences,[11] as were JCB and Dyson.[12] Indicating that there might be double standards in those fines aimed at US companies, it took the US, not the EU, to discover Volkswagen's perfidy in fiddling with its NO_2 emissions to meet the diesel product standards that, in fact, VW had both defined and subverted.[13]

It is well known that EU manufacturers follow a well-trodden and usually successful path, to persuade Brussels bureaucrats to specify product standards that reflect those manufacturers' existing product offerings – and which preclude introduction of better, more attractive products, whether homegrown or from abroad. (The laws of the EU are initiated and drafted by Brussels bureaucrats, not by the elected EU parliament.)

Equally unfortunately, media, politicians and other commentators are often unthinkingly quick to support such claims. Let us examine the moral panic claim that American chickens have lower product standards. This is discussed more extensively in the following chapter, but suffice it to note here that US-reared chickens do not, despite some scare-mongering headlines, have more health issues associated with them than UK-reared chickens.[14] The chlorine-washed chicken trope is merely a knee-jerk reaction that relies on anti-American phobia, augmented by the fuss over Brexit and the fact that many Remainers in the UK wish to remain within the trade orbit of the EU, regardless of the extra cost to consumers. The trope provides a good example of how rapidly protectionist the public conversation can become, propping up incumbents and suppressing free markets. Commentators can quickly be stirred up into decrying alleged violations of 'workers' rights' or 'health and safety standards', even when the proposed change or elimination of a particular product standard has nothing to do with either. Politicians flinch when faced with such campaigns, and quickly pull back from suggested trade improvements that will help the ordinary consumers – in the quoted case, blocking the provision of equally tasty, yet significantly cheaper, chicken.

More generally, monopolistic or quasi-monopolistic behaviour can be seen almost as the rule, rather than the exception, in many modern economies. The UK economy is riddled with such behaviour – rather than being properly free market, it contains many sectors that are monopolistic (either entirely or in part) or otherwise quasi-government.

An additional example is that of government activities. These are by definition monopolistic, as they allow little or no competition. Government workers – teachers, health workers, civil servants, MPs and the like – are able to extract significant concessions from their employer, especially when, as is the case with civil servants, they set their own remuneration (as discussed in Volume One), and collusively share rich perks, such as defined-benefit pension plans, with these politicians.

There are also outsourced government activities. In recent years, the outsourcing of activities to private-sector companies has been *claimed* as overcoming some of these problems, but while the outsourcing of that work to private companies does draw something of a veil over the size and cost of government, it doesn't reduce much, or even any, of the costs to the government of having that activity in the first place, nor does it make these activities much less monopolistic.

Quangos and other arm's-length bodies (ALBs) have already been discussed in Volume One. A recent report states that these bodies handle a staggering £265 billion of public money; the report just scrapes the surface of this problem by detailing where £5.5 billion a year spent by these bodies on politically motivated campaigns could quickly be saved.[15] These are not free-market activities!

Then there are quasi-public-sector privatised sectors. If we look at Network Rail, the London Underground, all the water and electricity supply companies and the like, these are, in the main, former entities that were nationalised in 1945 and thereafter by the Labour Party, and then were re-privatised in the 1980s and thereafter by the Conservatives. It's generally accepted that the privatisations have mostly led to better (albeit in many cases not great) services being provided by these organisations. However, there were mistakes made in the privatisations – in particular, the failure to create a competitive environment; and also allowing contracts that permitted excessive risk-taking. The privatised companies subsequently leveraged themselves up dramatically, paying out large dividends with the proceeds of the leverage. This then left the infrastructure of the privatised company decaying and unfit for modern service.[16]

Worse, many of these semi-public companies are unionised. Given their near semi-monopolistic status, because there is no or little competition to take business away from them, those unionised workforces can hold the country or the part of the economy they serve to ransom. In consequence, and despite those companies' stranglehold on convenience, the public, whenever there is an opportunity, steadily streams away from those services – as is illustrated by the enormous growth of long-distance coach services, providing cheaper and more convenient, albeit less efficient, service than the unionised railways.

These quasi-monopolies provide – as theory leads us to expect would happen – a much worse and a much more expensive service to the public. Consider, just as examples, the appalling leaks of water from water companies and the sewage they spill; the incredibly frustrating widespread 'not-spots' in mobile phone coverage; the enraging and apparently endless strikes by railwaymen and Tube drivers as they extort higher and higher wages while resisting the implementation of obvious and badly needed efficiency improvements; and the strikes by junior doctors who are apparently indifferent to unprecedented lengthy waiting lists in the NHS. These illustrate the major demerits that are attached to organising large parts of the economy in ways that are not in line with free-market principles.

The NHS itself represents the socialist nationalisation of formerly local medical services and formerly private doctors. Because the NHS has a near-monopoly on health services, much of its workforce can exert pressure through strikes to increase their pay. Astonishingly, this includes doctors. These are already among the highest-paid professionals in the land. Most of them in previous generations would have considered going on strike to be a grievous breaking of their Hippocratic oath. By contrast, in the US medicine is privatised. Hospitals and other healthcare providers compete to provide the best and cheapest outcome for their patients. Because of competition, doctors in any given hospital are unlikely to go on strike. US doctors get paid more than their UK counterparts. Competition means no waiting lists or the like: in the US, an appointment can be made within very few days of any health problem arising. (The same is, of course, true for that smaller but rapidly growing part of the UK's health service that is in the private sector; before Covid 10 per cent of the population were privately insured. Now, it's over 20 per cent and growing.)

Some so-called private-sector parts of the economy are de facto public, due to significant government control. These sectors of the economy are controlled by government to such an extent that they cannot be seen as operating in a free market. The most obvious of these is, as shown by Tim Congdon, the banking sector. No bank is now allowed to fail (because no citizen can be allowed to suffer from making the retrospectively foolish decision to give their custom to a bank that then goes bust); banks must do what the government (or the Bank of England or the Financial Conduct Authority (FCA)) requires of them at any time, particularly in deciding when and where they can lend and how much capital they must keep to do so. Tim Congdon has shown how draconian new state rules on lending slashed the number of loans to industrial and commercial companies, from some 23 per cent of total lending in 2008 to 19 per cent in 2019; and to unincorporated businesses (owned by sole proprietors, entrepreneurs and the like) from some 2.7 per cent to 1.3 per cent in 2021, shifting lending to the household sector from around 57 per cent in 2008, to 66 per cent in 2019.[17] He showed that foreign banks were quitting London, and the new capital rules had resulted in a 'severe deflationary shock'.

The automotive sector is another example; it is instructed what proportion, dropping to 20 per cent by 2030, of the cars it makes are allowed to be petrol or diesel driven (a breathtaking example of 'we know best').[18] The electricity generation sector now suffers massive distortion from mandates, penalties and subsidies, so much so that almost no one has a clue what the true cost of any particular type of electricity generation is. And then the residential heating sector: fines if a builder fails to install lots of heat pumps (even though few people can be found who want to buy them). And on the progressive trashing of free markets goes – after fourteen years of a so-called 'Conservative' government, and with things certain to get worse now that Labour is in power.

Beyond product standards, quangos and quasi-monopolies, a further major crimp on growth is the burgeoning 'government knows best' spread of regulation, as discussed in Volume One. Three economists – Ben Southwood, Samuel Hughes and Sam Bowman – have recently published research that identifies ridiculously embellished planning regulation, specifically in housing, transport, infrastructure and energy generation and transmission (in particular, nuclear), as the biggest obstacles to economic growth in this country.[19] They show a planning regime that, across many dimensions, is orders of magnitude more time consuming and expensive compared to those in comparable developed economies.*

What we have here is a creeping imposition of socialist principles, where the government sees itself as best positioned to know what future products will serve the people best, and imposes processes and requirements on new development and investment that make it nigh-on impossible for economic progress to be made. Having decided that, it interferes vigorously both to promote favoured approaches and to bar alternative – potentially better, potentially cheaper – products, cutting off many that might have been invented in the future. The result, as always, is the elimination of product innovation. Who could possibly be certain at this stage that there could not be any far better future replacement for both heat pumps *and* gas boilers? But what entrepreneur will now bother to innovate in this sector, if there is to be no market for their innovative ideas? Thus, we have a major reduction in economic activity because much of it is now banned or impossibly expensive to make happen – a cul-de-sac in the potential future of each affected sector, and a consequent deterioration in future human happiness.

A little later in this chapter, I go through a detailed case example

---

* An example of how quickly economic growth can return, and with it benefit to the people, can be seen in what has happened to housing in Argentina now that Javier Milei has scrapped rent control. (Ryan Dubé and Silvina Frydlewsky, 'Argentina scrapped its rent controls. Now the market is thriving', *Wall Street Journal*, 24 September 2024, https://www.wsj.com/world/americas/argentina-milei-rent-control-free-market-5345c3d5?st=vw5api&reflink=article_email_share.) The supply of housing being offered to renters has increased by an outstanding 170 per cent, while the costs of renting have declined by 40 per cent. Milei is systematically dismantling not just rent controls but also other price controls across the economy.

of just one such sector (nuclear energy) to illustrate the sweeping damage to both economic growth and public benefit that is produced by such constraints on market freedom.

Downstream from these government-influenced sectors, government interference has a castrating impact on multiple sectors beyond the ones they originally chose to mess with. Banks, cowed by past outcomes and present government oversight, have been taken over by social justice-oriented HR departments whose power comes from various 'DEI-style' regulations, frequently self-imposed. With little shareholder oversight or complaint, the social justice HR warriors went on an orgy of account-withholding and debanking, often for the most superficial of reasons, aided by extravagant new restrictive concepts such as the government-imposed concept of 'politically exposed persons' (PEP). The definition of a PEP is extremely wide, but any such is, amazingly, allowed to be treated as a threat to a banking institution.* (Remember, this was permitted under a Conservative government: further evidence that it is left-wing civil servants who run the government, not politicians.) The net result of all this wokery and over-regulation is that even the most innocuous individuals or new businesses often face draining difficulties opening a new account or retaining their existing one.

Far more damaging is the attack by doctrinaire campaigners on cheap energy sources and in particular on hydrocarbons. This has massively increased the cost of electricity in the UK, so that in 2023, UK households were hit with some of the highest electricity prices in the world – two and a half times higher per kilowatt hour than

---

* From my imperfect knowledge, my understanding is that the PEP legislation was originally thought of as a way to identify dodgy Russians who might have ties to Putin. Somehow, PEPs seem to have been defined in legislation as anyone involved in politics. Each such person now has to be assessed. The assessor could (it appears) say what they liked about each PEP and, if they wished, make a case for debanking the PEP. Step forward please the one who decided to debank Nigel Farage.

the US, for example, and nearly double that of Japan, Switzerland or Poland (and over five times the cost in China).[20] This, in turn, has been sending most energy-intensive businesses offshore, which in turn eliminates key feeder industries; the last ammonia plant in the UK had to close down recently.[*] [21] In the next chapter we will see how this has been rapidly shrinking the manufacture of goods in this country. All this is an inevitable result of the misguided war on hydrocarbons in the UK.

Rent-seeking sectors bolster their revenue and profits by spending much of their energy developing good relations with the government. They include:

- *Companies dependent on government favour*, such as those seeking North Sea oil licences, or any large company seeking legislation or regulation that is favourable to their own particular business model and which would fend off existing and potential future competitors.
- *Companies dependent on government contracts*, such as weapons manufacturers or nuclear plant developers, where success primarily depends on pleasing and placating a few civil servants.
- *Companies receiving government grants and subsidies*. The size of the pot is large. Capital grants to private-sector companies total £3.5 billion. Subsidies to private-sector companies total £19.1 billion.[22] To get a grant, you have to please both civil servants and, typically, a panel made up of not usually first-class former academics. The tendency or even ability of these 'wise men' to take a free-market and innovative approach is not fabled.
- *Sock-puppet charities*: these are, as discussed in Volume One,

---

[*] Ammonia is a crucial feedstock for many sectors, including for one of the UK's crown jewel sectors, pharmaceutical manufacturing.

charities and pressure groups, often politically motivated, yet getting their money from the government. They use some of that money to lobby the government so as to get more money from the government, all in the name of some alleged good whose achievement apparently couldn't possibly come about without vigorous public lobbying from the sock-puppet organisation.

The list of captive, formerly free-market sectors, and the size of each, is steadily expanding. As a direct consequence, the portion of the economy now occupied by free-market sectors is steadily shrinking.

In Volume One, I talked extensively about government spending being far too high to ensure a decent rate of economic growth. Quasi-government sectors, discussed above, are expanding. What about the non-government economy, where we see production of actual goods and services that are not linked to or supported by government? This, the only part of the overall economy that enjoys the free-market conditions that allow a good rate of economic growth, basically has to do all the heavy lifting. Is that 'real', non-government supported sector big enough to fulfil the imperative for the economy to grow?

In answer to that question, I create a taxonomy, based on the discussion in the prior pages, of just four sectors: government, outsourced government, quasi-government, and mostly free market. We show the size of each of these in Chart 3.1.[*] In terms of gross value added, the first of these is just 19 per cent of the economy. The second is just 3 per cent. The third is some 28 per cent – and growing! This means that the part of the economy that can properly

---

[*] See Appendix B for the methodology used to construct this chart.

run itself in relatively free-market conditions is less than half of the economy's gross value added. This, the part of the economy that has to shoulder primary responsibility for the job of economic growth, must grow twice as much as it would otherwise need to, in order to make up for the likely lack of future expected growth in the other (government-related) half of the economy.

Chart 3.1: UK: Free Market versus Captive Sectors
By Gross Value Added, 2023

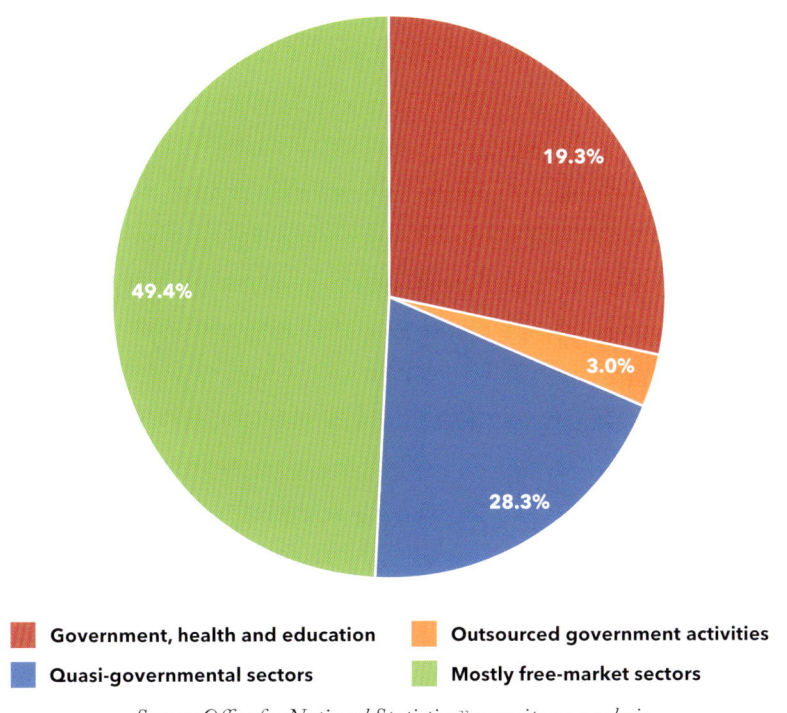

Properly free-market sectors take up less than half of the economy.

- Government, health and education: 19.3%
- Outsourced government activities: 3.0%
- Quasi-governmental sectors: 28.3%
- Mostly free-market sectors: 49.4%

Source: Office for National Statistics,[23] moyniteam analysis

What we see in Chart 3.1 overall is an economy where there is creeping growth in monopoly and oligopoly, especially in government-adjacent sectors. And even in the free-market sector, the economy, beset by burgeoning regulation, gets less and less 'free'. The government and the media become quick to interfere when it's politically expedient – for example, to accuse companies of 'price gouging' and then impose price constraints or to interfere with sanctity of contract, as in the home rentals market. To, in general, threaten the free market all over the economy. In such an environment, we can quickly understand – if we pay any attention at all to hard-earned experience, whether looking at the success of free-market economies or the failure of the many socialist experiments the world has seen over the last 100 or more years – that economic growth in the UK will increasingly become more and more difficult or unlikely.

The Economist has taken alarm, running an article headlined 'Are free markets history?'[24] They say that across the world 'the presumption of open markets and limited government has been [systematically] left in the dust'. The UK is, depressingly, a great exemplar of that trend.

A government must, if it wishes to ensure free markets are to be the primary mode of running the country's economy:

1. allow demand to express itself
2. allow a competitive market in supply
3. ensure that property rights are unambiguously respected through corruption-free rule of law
4. resist blandishments and pleas, from big business and 'social justice' campaigners alike, to regulate and constrain the economy
5. remove itself from the marketplace wherever it possibly can and let the market of supply and demand sort things out

Once it has done all that, the government should seek to promote every opportunity to give free rein to the law of supply and demand, relying on market equilibrium to assure the best price, best quality and largest variety of products and services. Currently, as we have seen, the UK fails to do this in a depressingly large proportion of the key sectors that its citizens seek goods and services from. We can see unnecessary and damaging interference in, for example:

- automobile manufacturing
- banking
- education
- employment
- health, energy and power supply
- home heating
- rental and home ownership

The consequence of the widespread failure to give full rein to competition and customer preference in key markets is that many goods and services that people need are constrained in supply, high in price and low in quality. This, as we discussed in Volume One, springs from what Hayek called the 'fatal conceit': the false idea that governments can intervene from the centre, impose constraints on a market and ensure that things can thus get only better. They don't; this approach almost always makes things get worse. What makes things better is deregulation, less interference, getting out of the way to let markets work, and allowing efficient markets to identify and satisfy the needs of commerce and citizens.

The following pages review this point in depth for just one of these markets: energy.

THE ENERGY SECTOR IN THE UK: A VIOLATION OF FREE-MARKET PRINCIPLES

The energy sector is a classic modern example of where enthusiastic politicians, responding to moral panic-style campaigns – often boosted by activists in campaigning organisations – start interfering aggressively with a particular sector. In the case of energy, an extraordinarily accelerated process has, in a very short number of years, laid waste to almost any free-market activities. In 2019, in the waning days of Theresa May's government, while the focus of the public and the commentariat was almost exclusively on Brexit, a legal commitment to get to net zero by 2050 was rushed through Parliament, imposing stringent requirements on the automobile and the residential heating industries by 2035.[25] No cost-benefit analysis was done on this mandate; no evaluation of its feasibility, or what the true impact on the economy (including secondary repercussions) would be. These were policies pushed as much by leftist civil servants as by politicians.

And then, amazingly, less than a year later, Boris Johnson's government fecklessly accelerated May's already ludicrous 2035 deadline to 2030.[26] Again, this was merely a wonderful feelgood feast of virtue signalling, with the worst parts of both the impact and the cost only coming far off into the future – so that those politicians who were imposing these requirements could be comfortable that they would not be anywhere near the public eye at the time the chickens would come home to roost from their policies. Blame for the consequences would be shouldered by others. (The impossibility of the 2030 deadline was so obvious in some areas that Rishi Sunak pushed some of the legislation back to 2035 – but most of that is now being reversed again by Labour.)

Chart 3.2: Change in Contracts for Difference Strike Prices from AR5 to AR6 versus Recent Intermittent Market Reference Price (£/MWh)

In recent allocation rounds, offers to supply wind power have been at higher and higher prices. If the cost of wind power was declining, as has been claimed, the opposite would be the case. Clearly, the cost of wind power is, although concealed by subsidies, far more expensive than is asserted. The greater the renewables sector becomes as a proportion of our supply mix, the greater our cost of electricity will be.

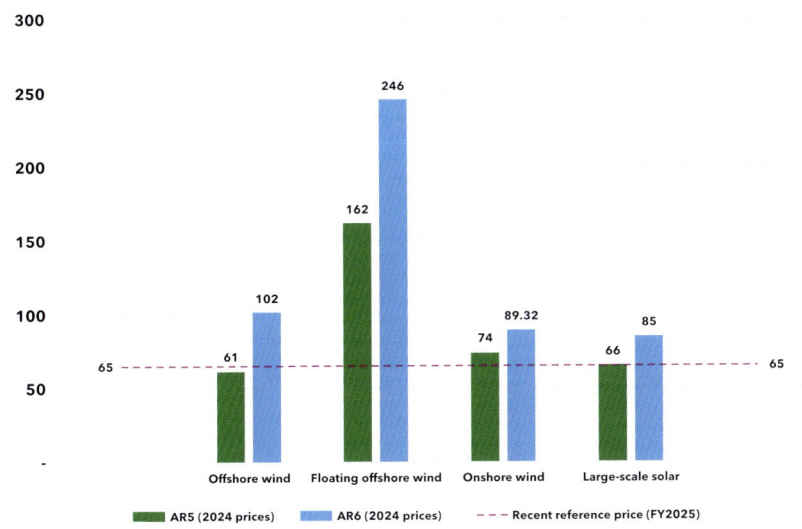

Technology	AR5 (2024 prices)	AR6 (2024 prices)	Recent reference price (FY2025)
Offshore wind	61	102	65
Floating offshore wind	162	246	65
Onshore wind	74	89.32	65
Large-scale solar	66	85	65

Change in renewable offer prices from AR5 to AR6 compared to market prices (£/MWh). AR5 and AR6 are the previous and the most recent rounds of bidding by wind farm owners or developers to deliver power supply to the grid.

Source: David Turver in the Daily Sceptic [27]

So far, all we have here is a number of impossible-to-achieve mandates for 2030 and 2035. But the anti-growth net-zero crowd had been waiting and working for this moment for many years, ready with policies, and binding laws and treaties. Soon, a sequence of regulations and requirements was rolled out. If not soon reversed, they will in the fullness of time have a large part of industrial Britain, and indeed much of our overall economy, lying in ruins. The religious-style process goes as follows:

- *Identify the 'sinners'.* Hydrocarbons fit the bill very well. Just as the devil must be exorcised, so hydrocarbons must be eliminated. Ignore the science, ignore the cost. (If you want to lower CO_2 emissions, the country that has lowered its carbon emissions the most in the world is the US.[28] It has done so by fracking for gas, a relatively low carbon emitter. As a result, the US is now energy self-sufficient and has been able to replace coal-fired energy generation plants, cheaply, with gas-fired ones. (Gas has a much lower carbon footprint than coal or indeed other hydrocarbons.) But here in the UK, gas is an emanation of the hydrocarbon devil – so no, we won't frack.)
- *Identify the 'saints'.* Renewables fit the bill very well for this: primarily wind and solar. Here, 'we know best' comes into its own. The great advantage of the religious approach is that you can call on your higher purpose to impose whatever you like on the populace, ignoring market forces. Potential problems are ignored, although if we continue with the renewables approach, intermittency will lead to brownouts and blackouts over the country.[29] There is also the issue of converting diffuse energy to concentrated energy, which with renewables creates enormous additional distribution costs; and the problem of efficiency conversion, where renewables are several orders of magnitude less efficient in creating energy than hydrocarbons or nuclear.[30] These problems are ignored, but all have massive future negative repercussions on our ability to generate or benefit from affordable power.
- *Tax the consumer and spend the proceeds on subsidising the 'saints'.* By a massive series of subsidies, credits, and impositions of cost on both consumers and industry, the government has created

a totally false market in electricity. The cost is such that other forms of electricity generation – such as nuclear, which offers a more free-market approach – are starved of funds, at the same time as they are hobbled with economic regulatory costs.

- *Give vast bungs to saintly ancillary markets,* such as mega battery factories. These then unfortunately – but to a degree, inevitably – go bust.[31]
- *Lie about the cost and the level of success.* In particular, claim that the cost of wind is going down (falsely asserting that economies of scale, or whatever, are kicking in) when, in fact, as Chart 3.2 shows, the settled cost of wind from off-shore farms is going up and up as the costs are discovered to be ever greater.

The off-shore wind business is already being subsidised at the enormous rate of £4.3 billion annually.[32] That amount will only increase – and this is before the hidden and rarely mentioned large costs for standby energy that intermittent sources such as wind need.[33] It also ignores the reality, as shown in Chart 3.2, that subsidy costs continue to increase – rather than, as is being barefacedly but untruthfully asserted, declining.[34]

Despite the obvious fact that it's going terribly wrong, we double down on the strategy. We ignore the endangerment to national energy security. We do that despite the fact that energy imports are touching modern highs, and our gas reserves are at a modern low, way below that of other countries, and despite the enormous damage done to the economy by the spike in gas prices in 2021.[35] That price spike did not occur in the US, where fracked gas was in plentiful supply – this is because in the US, they fracked. Note that because of their abundant gas supply, US energy companies now make enormous profits by shipping fracked gas from Texas to the UK.*

---

* These profits could have been made by British companies had we fracked in the UK – which would therefore have meant they paid much larger taxes here, and employed British workers. The pricing of taxes for fracked gas in the UK could (as was done by the Dutch with their own gas bubble) have been made to vary with the global cost of gas, thus protecting the UK against the damaging impact of price spikes).

Importing fracked gas means in practice that the UK is, hypocritically, enjoying the benefits of fracking while claiming to be virtuous because there is no fracking actually in the UK.* The consumer loses.

A few years ago, it was already astonishing that policymakers and governments in the UK had insouciantly ignored the obvious danger that our anti-hydrocarbon approach offered to our energy security. It led directly to increasing reliance on Russian hydrocarbons, in the UK as well as across the EU. Now that Russia has shown what kind of actor it is – having barbarically invaded initially Crimea, and then deeper into Ukraine, not to mention its having murdered individuals in the UK and worldwide, seemingly at will over the past few decades – our continuing with that insouciance can manifestly be seen as incomprehensible stupidity.

As Chart 3.3 shows, our prospects for economic growth are ruined by the massive increase in energy costs in the UK arising from these foolish decisions. Note in that chart how coal is, over time and now, much cheaper than gas and much cheaper than electricity, which has to carry the cost of subsidising renewables (as Chart 3.4 shows, our electricity prices are among the highest in the world). Countries from China to Germany still use coal. In fact, Germany is currently building a large new coal mine, dismantling a wind farm in the process.[36] Couldn't make it up. (But, should *we* do the same – a mortal sin.[37])

As a result of all of this, our economy suffers.

---

* The claimed awfulness of fracking – earthquakes, taps on fire, whatever – is, experience has now shown, nonsensical hysteria. (Michael Lynch, 'Fracking opponents ditch science, embrace hysteria', *Forbes*, 9 July 2015, https://www.forbes.com/sites/michaellynch/2015/07/09/fracking-opponents-ditch-science-embrace-hysteria/; Ronald Bailey, 'The top 5 lies about fracking', Reason, 5 July 2013, https://reason.com/2013/07/05/the-top-5-lies-about-fracking/.) Russian disinformation and involvement in this hysteria has been long-documented. See Keith C. Smith, 'Gasland: Russia and hysteria regarding hydraulic fracturing', American Diplomacy, February 2014, https://americandiplomacy.web.unc.edu/2014/02/gasland-russia-and-hysteria-regarding-hydraulic-fracturing/

Chart 3.3: Fuel Price Indices for UK Industry
In real terms, including Climate Change Levy, Q1 2010–Q1 2024

Unlike in many other parts of the world, fuel prices in the UK are now astonishingly high.

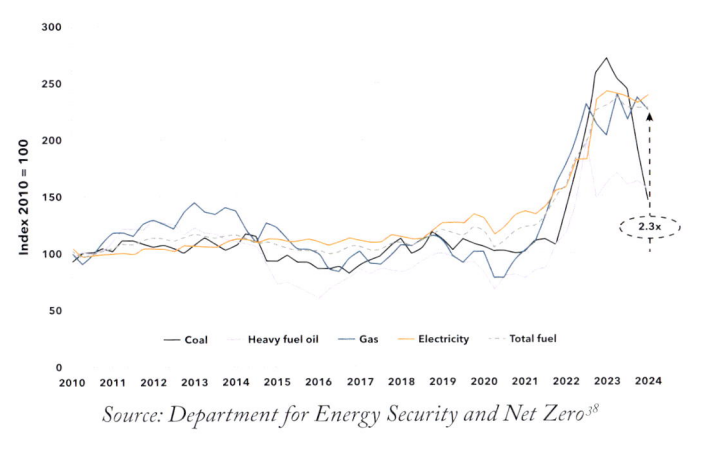

Source: Department for Energy Security and Net Zero[38]

Chart 3.4: Electricity Prices for Households
Select countries, in pounds sterling per kWh, as of December 2023

Because of subsidies for ever-more expensive renewables, UK households face, quite unnecessarily, some of the highest electricity prices in Europe.

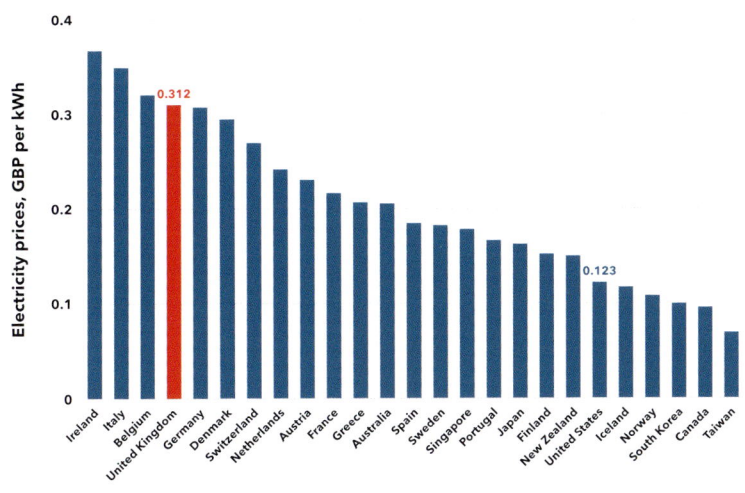

Source: Global Petrol Prices[39]

We have ignored the obvious ridiculousness of our driving manufacturing industries offshore to China, where the products, previously manufactured in the UK, are now made (using much dirtier energy) and then imported back to us with the additional carbon footprint of their travels. As China builds up these industries (because we have closed them down in the UK), they construct two coal-fired stations every week.[40] China have adopted the Saint Augustinian approach to carbon neutrality: they say they want to be made virtuous but not quite yet. Whether they actually will turn to virtue in some far-off future remains to be seen. Permit me to doubt it. The current situation, the only one we should base our actions on, is that their carbon generation increases in leaps and bounds. In view of China paying no attention to other international treaties,[41] it is arguably the height of self-delusion for us to believe that if it gets in the way of their economic development or jobs, China will pay any attention to its official net-zero obligations.

Regardless, the net result of impoverishing our nation and destroying our position in key industries, which then are offshored to China and elsewhere, is that, because the other countries have dirtier electricity than us, far more carbon is released into the atmosphere than if we had not adopted those foolish climate-related policies.

We have also further distorted the market by subsidising households whenever electricity costs get too high. The spike in gas prices in 2022 that led to very high electricity bills was unbelievably painful for consumers, creating real-life hardship. The Truss government felt it necessary to subsidise household bills through the Energy Price Guarantee, and the Sunak government retained these subsidies (at a still costly, not enormously different level), not ending them until March 2024.[42] Given the political pressures, it is hard to second-guess those decisions, but the pressures were as large as they were because of the original foolish energy policy. Had there not been such huge green subsidies to pay, and had there been a steady source of fracked gas in the UK, the impact could have been both mitigated, and largely cost-neutral.

The end result of this sorry litany has been the prevention of economic growth in the UK. Consumers have had to use what little discretionary income they have to pay their increased energy bills – and these bills are increasing even more, from having to pay for the renewables subsidy, from any future geopolitically created spike in the price of gas, from any uptick in wind pricing due to the increasing apparent higher cost of wind farms, or from the upcoming Carbon Border Adjustment Mechanism (CBAM), a particularly foolish EU protectionist measure. Industries are moving offshore, with losses of UK jobs, tax revenues and economic activity. New businesses, or even whole new industries, are denied the opportunity to set themselves up in the UK. Just the loss of ammonia as a feedstock massively reduces potential future business opportunities. All in all, a tragic tale whose full disastrous impact on the UK is only just beginning to be seen.

Worse: the reader should not assume that energy is some exceptional 'special case', one where an acceptance of alarmist claims on global warming can be held to justify this interference. As shown, the outcomes of government interference are actually destructive of the carbon-reduction objectives that the government is attempting to achieve. But in any case, similar interference is being implemented, usually using similar religious-style rhetoric, in multiple other sectors. The banking industry needs to be closely supervised because of the appalling excesses of global capitalism. The automobile industry must be tightly regulated because of, again, global warming.

Overall, government or regulatory interference is increasingly extending across the entire economy, now often using the justification of 'social equity', ESG or DEI.

The point of this particular discussion is not to relitigate the topic of global warming or any other such movement-inspired issue. Rather, it is to point out that when government gets into the business of 'we know best', the situation hurtles towards the disastrous. One day, whether soon or possibly a decade or two into the future, it will be decided that a horrendous mistake was made, that the interference was foolish, the proposed solutions were massively more expensive than claimed, the proposed solutions didn't work to reduce any impact on global temperatures or on lowering carbon in the air, the claimed 'green jobs' didn't eventuate, the impact on the UK economy was catastrophic. But by then, untold and quite likely irreversible harm will have been done. As Hayek painstakingly pointed out, government direction of an economy doesn't work, doesn't come up with the right solutions and is fatally conceited.

It will be tragic if this lesson has to be learned over and again by successive generations, even when we have, plain before us, the lessons of China under Chairman Mao, Russia under so many leaders, Cuba under Fidel Castro, Venezuela under Hugo Chávez and Nicolás Maduro, and numerous other socialist examples.[43]

So, let's take a detailed look at one specific energy sub-sector: nuclear energy.

THE NUCLEAR SECTOR IN THE UK: THROTTLED BY GOVERNMENT

Nuclear energy furnishes around 10 per cent of the world's electricity supply.[44] We have nearly three quarters of a century's experience with it. It is, in terms of deaths and injuries, the safest form of conventional energy supply.[45] Relative to renewables, its safety record is perched between those of wind and solar power – minuscule levels of danger.* [46]

Like all parts of the energy sector in the UK, and in particular because of its association in the popular mind with nuclear warfare, nuclear does not find itself in a free market. The government allocates subsidies, punishment taxes, and cruel and unusual regulation across all of the energy sector – but far more so on nuclear energy. Above all, when it comes to nuclear electricity generation stations, the government decides where, what and when to build. It might seem that this is normal, but it isn't. In the US and Canada, the power-supply companies – highly regulated but nevertheless part of the private sector – decide what types of generation station to build and where and when. While some states, such as New York and Connecticut, make it almost impossible for new nuclear plants to be built, others don't. Georgia Power has recently announced that its new Vogtle plant 3 has commenced its nuclear operations and it expects Vogtle 4 to commence generation within months. Vogtle will then be the largest nuclear power plant in the US.[47] In Canada, Ontario Power Group has commissioned a small modular reactor (SMR) that will be completed by the end of this decade.[48]

Given the emotional feelings many have about anything with the word 'nuclear' attached to it, none of these new nuclear power stations could have been built without close government cooperation – and often with government encouragement, and sometimes subsidy, reflecting the high costs of early adoption of new technologies. So, it is impossible to think of nuclear as being, at least for many decades into the future, a fully free-market sector. But the

---

* Three Mile Island, Fukushima etc. actually bolstered nuclear's safety record. Many of the newer forms of nuclear energy remove all likelihood of meltdowns or similar accidents.

experience of France shows how a combination of a large number of plants, long-term planning, standardisation, and efficient and valuable use of spent fuel can result in both a major competitive advantage for that nation's industry, and a satisfied citizenry that basks in the consequent low cost of electricity.

In the UK, our *current* approach to meeting future energy needs is, in the main, reliant on three things: renewables; a single (incredibly expensive) new nuclear power station; and electricity imports. (Think about those three components of our energy strategy, and it's easy to see that things are not going to work out well.)* Green subsidies are already so high (and, based on recent wind auctions, would seem to be steadily moving higher) that it is very difficult to contemplate any further decent-sized government subsidy to any other new power generation.†

Nuclear, however, presents multiple attractive options. Even after decades of repression by successive governments, there is still a nascent nuclear development industry in the UK, encouragement of which could mean that if a wide-ranging nuclear strategy were adopted, a new era for the industry could be created, with the potential for the UK to seize a leading global role and thus for there to be massive creation of real new jobs.‡

Nuclear encompasses a plethora of different approaches and

---

* Britain was the second-biggest importer of electricity in the first half of 2024 – a telling outcome of its feckless energy strategy. (Power Engineering International, 'Steep rise in GB power imports in first half of 2024', 7 August 2024, https://www.powerengineeringint.com/coal-fired/strategic-development-coal-fired/steep-rise-in-gb-power-imports-in-first-half-of-2024/.) Which country is going to suffer most when, inevitably, there are energy shortages in Europe in the years to come?

† Despite some ludicrous lobbying, the enormous costs, risks and general impracticability of tidal power have proved too great even for the taste of the UK's incontinently spending and heavily lobbied governments of this century.

‡ To be clear: there is no guarantee that any particular new nuclear technology will prove to be the magic bullet that takes over from hydrocarbons as a viable baseload energy source. But there is a reasonable possibility that, sooner or later, at least one and possibly several new nuclear technologies will prove workable and be rolled out on a wide scale. This is all the more reason why each should be getting explored thoroughly and speedily.

opportunities, most of which offer promise. Some – for example, fusion – could ultimately – no guarantee – resolve the world's energy issues in a long-term cheap and, of course, carbon-free way.*

Overall, if nuclear works out for the world, then the decarbonisation, and thus deindustrialisation, of our country through renewables subsidies will have been a complete waste of time and money – but by then, much of what will have been lost will be irrecoverable.

Charts 3.5, 3.6 and 3.7 show what a large landscape of technologies and what considerable promise the nuclear industry offers.

Chart 3.5: Allowing Free Markets to Work by De-Constraining Nuclear
Current Taxonomy of Nuclear Energy Approaches, with Illustrative Competitors

Around 10 per cent of the world's power generation is from nuclear energy. A plethora of mostly unexplored opportunities extends hope for long-term cheap and plentiful power.

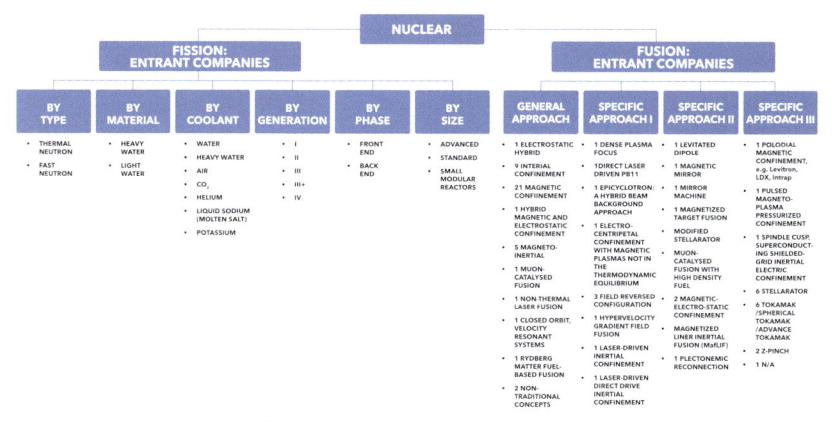

Source: Global Fusion Association[49]

---

* Fusion is a technology with many unsolved issues, some of which are not guaranteed ever to be resolved. So, it is a bet, but at this stage one well worth taking – and it is private sector money that is, in the main, currently financing fusion's development.

Chart 3.6: Illustrative List of Commercial Competitors in Two Representative Nuclear Technologies

Although it currently does receive some government subsidy, the nuclear industry exhibits many of the needed attributes of free-market competition, attracting considerable competition and private-sector investment.

LIQUID SODIUM FISSION (MOLTEN SALT)	FUSION
• Terrapower	• TAE technologies
• Moltex	• Helion
• Terrestrial	• Commonwealth (CFS)
• Thorcon	• General fusion
• Elysium	• Tokamak energy
• Seaborg	• General atomics
• Holtec	• Kyoto fusioneering
• Kairos	• Renaissance
• Many others	• Many others

Other non-commercial approaches include ITER in France ($22 billion of multinational funding) and three fusion reactors in China, South Korea, the EU etc.

Note: Many major economies (China, India, Indonesia, Canada, Texas etc.) are exploring building molten salt reactors. Declaration of interest: this author has an investment in one molten salt company.

The important thing to note here is that most recent nuclear technological development was created in much the same way that any new technology today operates. Science first arrives, mostly out of universities, then entrepreneurs take these scientific breakthroughs and develop them into marketable technology, then capital is applied to the technology to innovate, experiment and test against the market. Somewhere, in that large list of companies and technologies that we saw in Charts 3.5 and 3.6, there is likely to be one, or indeed several, attractive technologies that will prove far superior to renewables. In the ferment of the free market that we see in those charts, the cross-fertilisation of ideas and knowledge could, in a supportive environment, lead to a rapid explosion of capability and progress.

Chart 3.7: Responses from Fusion Companies

While they are probably overly optimistic or propagandistic, most industry players are predicting that fusion will be up and working well before the 2050 net-zero witching hour. If that were to happen, the ongoing destruction of UK industry on the altar of net zero would have been entirely unnecessary.

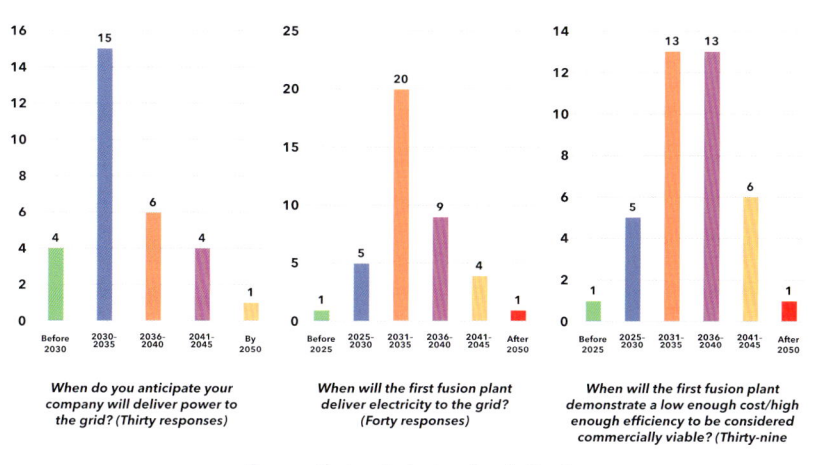

Source: Fusion Industry Association[50]

To take just one technology as an example, several competitors around the world are in a race to make nuclear fusion work through use of a tokamak machine (tokamak is just one of a number of different technological approaches to fusion). It is quite feasible that one or more of the tokamaks will succeed; it is also highly likely that each company will use intellectual property from the others in what they finally develop. While this also happens in industries that are ancillary to the renewables sector (for example, battery technology), the pervasive interference of a dirigiste government has led to less technological development in batteries in the UK (because one or another technology is favoured with a giant subsidy, and the others give up). As a result, what development there is, some of it exciting, tends to be in China or Japan, not so much in the UK. The 'choosing of winners' in the UK is crowding out potentially exciting innovation in technologies that are competitive with renewables. The nuclear sector shows better what happens when human ingenuity is allowed free rein, and capital is allowed the liberty to run after the most promising ideas.

An aside on safety: the fear that many have is that an uncontrollable 'runaway' nuclear reaction could lead to leakage of radiation or even a nuclear explosion. In new fission technologies, such as molten salt, such a meltdown is not a possibility.[51] With fusion, the secret's in the name – any problem would lead to a harmless, nanosecond-long implosion inward, not an explosion outward.[52] Nor does fusion produce nuclear waste, and molten salt technologies hold the potential to use up existing nuclear waste for their fission materials. (It's strange – albeit drearily predictable – therefore that the government's nuclear subsidy programme is concentrated entirely on using traditional fission SMRs, since with newer nuclear technologies, nuclear safety concerns that apply to traditional reactors are no longer needed.)

How could a more free-market approach work for nuclear in the UK? For example:

- A level playing field could be created for subsidies, so that renewables don't get such an unfair advantage.
- For new developing technologies, a 'thousand flowers' could (should)

be allowed to bloom, with demonstrator projects being built across the UK and incentives given to local communities to host them.
- Regulation could be reviewed and modelled, to allow power companies more freedom to bring nuclear options on board.
- Consultation could take place with all sorts of nuclear organisations to find out how best to adapt regulation to encourage growth in the industry.

To repeat, there is no guarantee that any particular nuclear technology, whether fission or fusion, will provide the answer to the need for cheap, reliable, baseline energy. Indeed, respected and knowledgeable commentators throw a great deal of doubt on fusion, while safe fission still seems to get short shrift.[53] But the range of potential technologies and the far superior potential energy conversion levels of nuclear relative to renewables (and especially not having the problem of intermittency, as with renewables), make nuclear the essential technology to focus on if we indeed are going to abandon hydrocarbons.[*]

The key is to understand the overwhelmingly negative impact of regulation in the UK on our nuclear industry. A depressing article in *The Spectator* titled 'Why Britain is building the most expensive nuclear plant' shows how we have been stopped in our tracks from getting more nuclear technology into the UK.[54] A build cost that, *mostly because of regulation*, is almost five times as much as in other parts of the world. Hugely expensive workarounds to save a few fish.

---

[*] A possible sighting of blue sky among these clouds is the news that fourteen of the world's biggest banks have issued a joint statement agreeing to help finance the goal of tripling the world's nuclear energy capacity by 2050. (Lee Harris and Malcom Moore, 'World's biggest banks pledge support for nuclear power', *Financial Times*, 23 September 2024, https://www.ft.com/content/96aa8d1a-bbf1-4b35-8680-d1fef36ef067?shareType=nongift.) This not only indicates that they no longer expect to be demonised for supporting nuclear; it also implies that they think the sector is commercially attractive and financeable.

Billions of pounds of regulatory-imposed cost per expected life saved. And so on. The obvious way to save our energy sector is to entirely reapproach and rewrite the safety and other regulations, thus lowering cost, so that we can get ourselves cheap nuclear power. Alternatively, a failure to establish a leading position in nuclear will, as things stand, leave the UK holding only the busted flush of renewables.

• • •

Can we quantify the beneficial impact of free markets on growth separately from our previous quantification of the variables of small government, low taxes and minimal regulation? The importance of free markets is widely acknowledged.[55] Yet the debate on free markets versus a social democracy/welfare state approach continues; it is often somewhat tangled, with the two sides talking past each other.

Much of the impact of having an economy that is based, or not, on free-market principles was already discussed in Volume One. Using as a measure the relative growth of different countries compared against their differing scores on the Index of Economic Freedom, we showed the major positive impact of a free-market approach on economic growth, and thus on prosperity for all.

From the free-market side, there are plenty of academic studies showing how free-market principles – often taken to mean 'capitalism', but in fact comprising much more than just the efficient allocation of capital – lead to greater economic growth. We have reviewed some of these studies in Volume One, but a general summary of the issue, commented on by the Hoover Institute, is offered by economist Edward Lazear.[56] In his Human Prosperity Project essay 'Socialism, Capitalism, and Income', Lazear analysed decades of income trends across 162 countries. He studied how incomes for low and high earners change, as countries shift from government-controlled economies to more market-oriented economies. He concluded:

> The historical record provides evidence on how countries have fared under the two extreme systems, as well as under intermediate cases, where countries adopt primarily private ownership and economic freedom but couple that with a large government sector and transfers. The general evidence suggests that both across countries, and over time within a country, providing more economic freedom improves the incomes of all groups, including the lowest group.

Advocates of socialism tend to swerve such discussions, focusing instead on 'fairness', 'equality', 'social justice' and other appealing-sounding notions that have as yet to show any payoff at all, let alone enough to justify their stultifying effect on growth. Search the internet, and you quickly find a myriad of such approaches. The poster child of this view is the entirely unreliable Thomas Piketty. Of his work, the World Socialist Website stated:

> The facts produced by Piketty from an analysis of objective data argue that there is no possibility of combating social inequality other than the overthrow of the capitalist social order, which produces inequality, by means of a socialist revolution carried out by the international working class.[57]

Does socialism lead to a fairer society? No, it doesn't.[58] There's very specific evidence that free-market economies create fairer societies than do redistributionist ones. This is not just the argument, true as it may be, that people get richer overall, as shown in Volume One. It is the argument that, in addition, free markets create a

RETURN TO GROWTH

more equitable split of wealth *within* society as well. The evidence for this focuses on something called the Gini coefficient.

The 'inequality' discussion is wrapped up in misleading language and concepts, but this Gini coefficient is a well-accepted and standard measure of inequality. A Gini measure of 100 would be found in an imaginary country where one individual had all the wealth, and all others had none. A Gini measure of 0 is one that would be found in an imaginary country where every single person was exactly equally wealthy. World Population Review have created a map of Gini coefficients in each country, which we emulate here.

Chart 3.8: Income Distribution by Country
Gini Coefficient

Gini coefficients show better economic equality in most of the capitalist democracies (with the exception of the US).

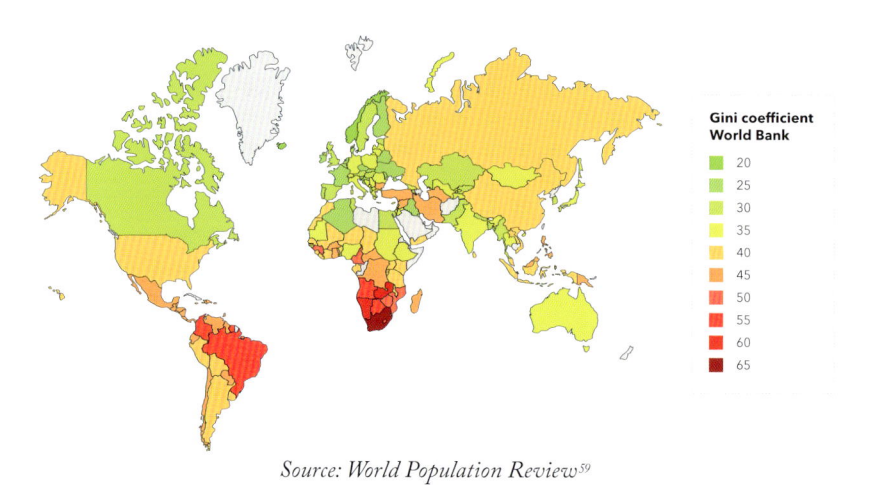

Source: World Population Review[59]

As can be seen from the chart, it is western free-market countries

46

that tend to have the best Gini coefficients, while socialist countries such as China have worse coefficients.[*]

We can go further even than that. If we look at the matter more closely, using just the Gini measure means we will miss some key considerations. In particular, consider two societies: 'society one', where everyone is rich, but some are much richer than others, and 'society two', where there is much equality, but all are poor. (Bear in mind that, as the map shows, the latter type of society isn't that frequent in the world, since in most cases the poorer the country, the more inequitable is the distribution of wealth.)

Which of these two societies is preferable?

To prefer society one is to believe in individual versus collectivist dignity, and the right for all to have opportunities for wealth and happiness. We create such a society when all are given equality of *opportunity*. There will always be inequalities of *outcome* in the world; they occur because of, say, inheritance, or parentage, or acquired skills, or beauty, or luck. They can't be wished away; they will never, in future human history, disappear. The more important and realistic hope is to bring equality of *opportunity* to all – and through this, as much wealth as possible to each. All of society benefits from such an approach – but, admittedly, some more lucky or gifted individuals will always, inevitably, benefit more than others.

To prefer society two (lots of equality but lots of poverty) is to seek to dampen the vigour and entrepreneurial spirit of the more inventive and go-getting members of the population. This will have the inevitable outcome of damping growth. It will also bring the

---

[*] With admittedly not quite so good a performance by the US – but, as we will see in a few pages, because of high GDP per capita in the US, this leaves the poorest quintile in the US just comparable to the poorest quintiles in other large, rich countries.

vice of envy to the surface, encouraging deprecation and the pulling down of those who have done well. (In Matt Ridley's magisterial book, *The Origins of Virtue*, he emphasises that one of the key requirements for a virtuous society to emerge is for all of us to supress the instinct to be envious.[60])

So, there's a strong argument that the first kind of society (some inequality, general wealth) is preferable.* As it happens, though, there is further evidence that free markets don't result in making the poorest in society poorer – in fact, the opposite (i.e. society two is only rarely found in the world). Have a look at Chart 3.9 and the spread of wealth across the different earning quintiles of various wealthy countries. Compare Singapore, possibly the most successful free-market economy in the world at the moment, with France.

Chart 3.9: Income by Quintile, Developed Economies, 2019

The poorest quintile in Singapore is as rich as or richer than the poorest quintile of all those countries shown, except for Denmark, and Singapore's other four quintiles are all *much* richer than the comparable quintiles of every one of these countries.

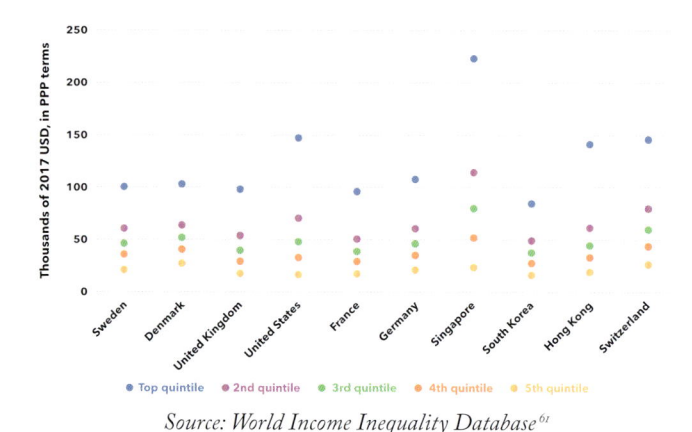

Source: World Income Inequality Database[61]

---

* And remember, even the poorest quintile in the UK is much richer than the middle quintiles of many middling-rich – not just poorer and developing – countries.

France, we are told, has a Gini coefficient of 30.7.[62] Singapore has a Gini of 45.9 – much less equal. The UK's is 32.6, just slightly less equalitarian than France and much more equalitarian than Singapore. From the point of view of wealth, which kind of economy would we rather have, the equalitarian France and UK or the less equal Singapore? Well, we can see from the chart that the *bottom* quintile Singaporean is far richer than the bottom quintile Frenchman or Brit. The *second-poorest* quintile in Singapore is richer than the *second-richest* quintile in France (and about as rich as the second-richest quintile in the UK). The richest quintile in Singapore is by far the richest group of citizens shown in this chart. That's why the most talented are emigrating to Singapore.

Thus, free markets offer one of the few examples of successful cakeism; through a free-market approach, you can have your wealth and spread it throughout society too. On this evidence, the argument that social democracy is necessary for spreading wealth to all of society fails completely.* China's Gini is 37.38, Russia's is 36, Venezuela's is now up to 45, Mexico's is 45 and Nicaragua's is also 45. When we get to full-blown authoritarian socialism or communism, we get, as a result, both poverty and inequality.

In other words, inequality does not, as Piketty claims, create poverty in advanced economies such as ours. *Equalitarianism is the thing that creates poverty.* All that is necessary in a high-Gini economy is to supress, as recommended by Matt Ridley, any envy of your richer neighbour, and just enjoy your own wealth – while having an excellent opportunity to create more of it. The way that we in

---

* The one exception to this is, as already discussed, the bottom quintile in the US – the one US quintile that fails to rise above almost all of the other depicted countries. However, social transfers are larger than in most of the other depicted countries. See Tim Worstall, 'America has the world's second-largest social welfare state', *Forbes*, 8 October 2015, https://www.forbes.com/sites/timworstall/2015/10/08/america-has-the-worlds-second-largest-social-welfare-state/

the UK punish success, with high taxes and our extensive welfare safety net, results in our being one of the more 'equal' societies in the world. But the outcome of that, as shown in Chart 3.9, is that few – particularly in the lower quintiles – get rich.

SUMMARY

If free markets are not allowed to flourish in any country, then its economic growth will suffer; the point is both logically compelling and demonstrable. Free markets do not promote inequality, and Gini coefficients shrink (i.e. people become more equal) as economies become more open. (In most cases, as economies develop, *all* quintiles move upwards in wealth.) In recent decades, the encroaching size of the state and the onward march of ever-greater regulation have been steadily shrinking that portion of the UK's economy that can be described as free market. The implications for economic growth, and indeed for the wealth of our lower quintiles, are negative.

What to do? The general prescriptions of Volume One – smaller government, lower taxes, less regulation – will promote more free markets, but the more specific prescriptions in this chapter – rule of law, property rights, and abolishing rent-seeking, subsidies and crony capitalism – are key to restoring proper entrepreneurial capitalism to its rightful, growth-promoting place in the economy. Any new government bent on promoting economic growth must pay attention to, and create improvement, in these areas.[*]

---

[*] One absolutely necessary concomitant of free markets is free speech: the more censorship there is, the less opportunity for price discovery, for prevention of cronyism and for not allowing distortion of markets. Free speech is becoming one of the key battlegrounds of the economic and political – indeed, moral – landscape of the twenty-first century.

CHAPTER 2

LET FREE TRADE FLOURISH

Openness to trade – making it easy for other countries to sell their goods and services to us and doing our best to persuade them to make it easy for us to sell our goods and services to them – is unequivocally important for boosting a country's economy.[1] As the OECD stated in 2010, 'The large body of empirical work on the topic strongly supports the theoretical presumption that trade liberalisation reduces poverty on average and in the long run.'[2] As this chapter proceeds, I review a part of that 'large body of empirical work' in more detail.[*]

The value of free trade is one of the most studied topics in economic theory, starting with Adam Smith's work in the eighteenth century, on through to the insights of David Ricardo and Frédéric Bastiat in the nineteenth. Now, in the present day, almost all economists who study international trade highlight the important contribution of free trade to economic growth. (Why many such economists simultaneously praise the free-trade-phobic EU is one of life's many little mysteries.) Recent in-depth reviews of the power of opening up an economy to free trade confirm that adopting such an approach can have a big positive impact on growth. Post-Brexit, with Britain now free to trade globally on its own terms, our GDP growth (were we to take proper advantage

---

[*] An earlier version of this chapter appeared in Max Rangeley and Daniel Hannan (eds) *Free Trade in the Twenty-First Century* (Springer, 2025).

of our opportunities) could accelerate significantly, just as Britain's GDP grew rapidly in the second half of the nineteenth century after the abolition of the Corn Laws – a step which, at the time, resulted in the UK becoming the world's largest and most successful economy.

Popular nationalists, EU-philes and anti-globalists – all of them work hard to obscure the clarity of proper free trade's importance. A further negative complication is that even those who support free trade talk, in mercantilist terms, about the advantages to be gained from increasing our *exports*, and ignore the even bigger benefit to our populace that would come from *importing* better and cheaper goods and services for our citizens' enjoyment and consumption.

One additional dimension: there is a general lack of appreciation of the difference between trade in goods, and trade in services; and how the UK is different to the EU in that respect. With the UK, about 80 per cent of our economy is in services – the highest percentage among the developed economies, and extremely dissimilar to the profile of the other EU countries.[3] The UK is the second-largest exporter of services in the world, behind only the US. In 2022/23, our services exports rose by about 14 per cent, and a further 4 per cent in 2023/24.[*][4] Services are – whether we like it or not – the present, and even more so the future, of UK exports. As far as increasing exports is concerned, it is therefore primarily a matter of finding markets for our *services*, and only secondarily (although still of course not unimportant) for our *goods*. That then takes us to a further key point: our services are less suited for exports to the EU than they are to the rest of the world, because the rest of the world contains many English-speaking countries that share far more with

---

[*] Real-terms chained volume measure.

us in their business and economic structures than the EU does. In particular, they base their legal system on our common law, as opposed to the EU's Napoleonic Code approach. (See Volume One for more detail on this point.)

The arguments in the UK for and against free trade have suffered recently in the ideological battle around Brexit. Many of those who would, in theory, be expected to advocate Britain opening its economy up to the world – a grouping which should, ostensibly, embrace most economists in the UK and other eminent economists in transnational bodies and in prominent American universities – instead argue muddleheadedly yet fiercely against Britain being allowed to conduct its own trade policy, claiming that the EU is a beacon of free trade to which we should entrust our trade negotiations, rather than acknowledging that the EU is a protectionist cartel. These EU-embracers go along with the cant that EU standards and directives from Brussels are primarily for consumer protection, and won't acknowledge what, in the main, they actually are: carefully constructed, protectionist non-tariff barriers designed to fend off outside competitors, at the direct expense of the EU's own consumers.

According to research by the Resolution Foundation, the UK's exports of services have grown 3.6 per cent more than a typical OECD country since the UK left the EU, replacing its membership with the EU–UK Trade and Cooperation Agreement in early 2021.[5] In the post-Brexit environment, the British services sector has, according to *The Economist*, 'enjoyed one of the best performances in the G7'.[6] Chart 3.10 shows that over a longer period, 2014–24, the UK has persistently performed at or above the average of the G7, and considerably better than the large economies of the US, France and Germany.

Chart 3.10: UK Services Exports
Compared to Other G7 Countries, 2014–24

Britain enjoys good performance among the G7 countries in exports of services.

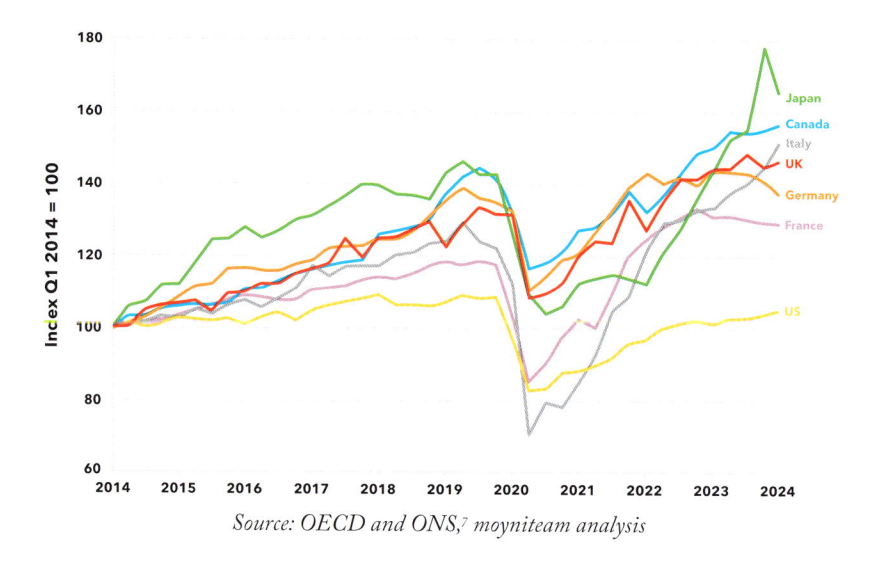

Source: OECD and ONS,[7] moyniteam analysis

Goods exports, although not nearly so important as services exports, have not done so well, performing considerably below the rest of the G7. See Chart 3.11.

Why have we had such a poor goods-exporting performance since Covid? The answer is a combination of a changing UK economy, a general attack on manufacturing (and indeed other) businesses over the past few years (high taxes and high regulation in particular) and the disastrous impact on our energy-intensive businesses of net-zero and high-energy-cost policies. This last has led to shutting down refineries, steel production, oil drilling, production and transmission, and ammonia production. All of these have significant knock-on effects on other manufacturers, so that manufacturing has shrunk in the UK, and manufacturing exports have shrunk commensurately.

As Chart 3.12 shows, the changing mix of goods versus services in the UK economy has been altering substantially over the past couple of decades, and continues to do so. In particular, the size of the manufactured goods economy in the UK has stayed flat since the turn of the millennium. Consequently, the UK is increasingly a services economy: goods have dropped in that period, from 27 per cent of GDP to now only 20 per cent.

Chart 3.11: UK Goods* Exports
Compared to Other G7 Countries, 2014–24

Goods exports have not recovered to pre-Covid levels, unlike in other G7 countries.

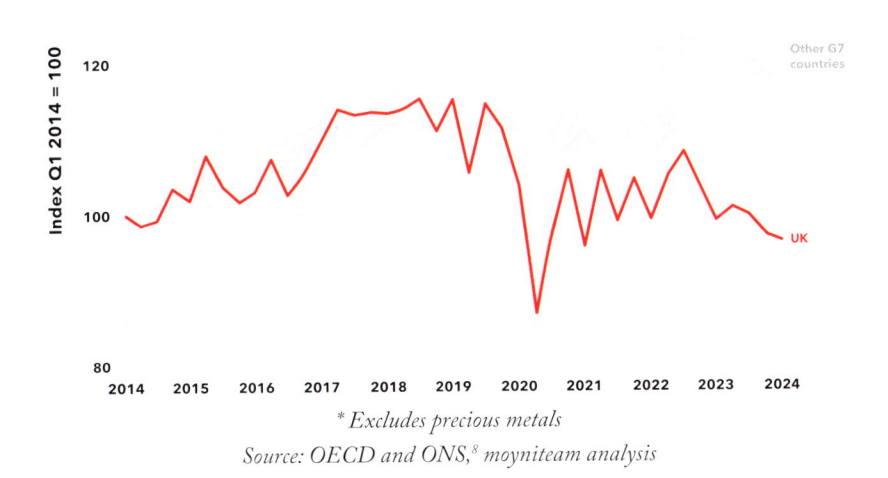

Excludes precious metals
Source: OECD and ONS,[8] moyniteam analysis

This would not necessarily be problematic if that evolution followed the rules of competitive and comparative advantage, where emigrating the workforce from lower value-added manufacturing sectors to the higher value-added services economy would create more and more export opportunity. However, any natural trend away from goods manufacture seems to have been exacerbated by the self-inflicted wounds, whether from tax policy or from regulation in general, of the disastrous impact of net-zero policies. As shown earlier in Chart 3.3, these led to some of the highest electricity costs in the developed world, causing energy-intensive manufacturers to close down or move away from the UK. This in turn has meant we haven't had nearly as many manufactured goods available to export – a large reason for the drop.

Chart 3.12: Evolution of the UK Economy, 1999–2023
Goods by Gross Value Added (GVA)

Over the past two decades, the goods/manufacturing part of the economy has not grown at all, so its share of the economy has dropped from over a quarter to one fifth.

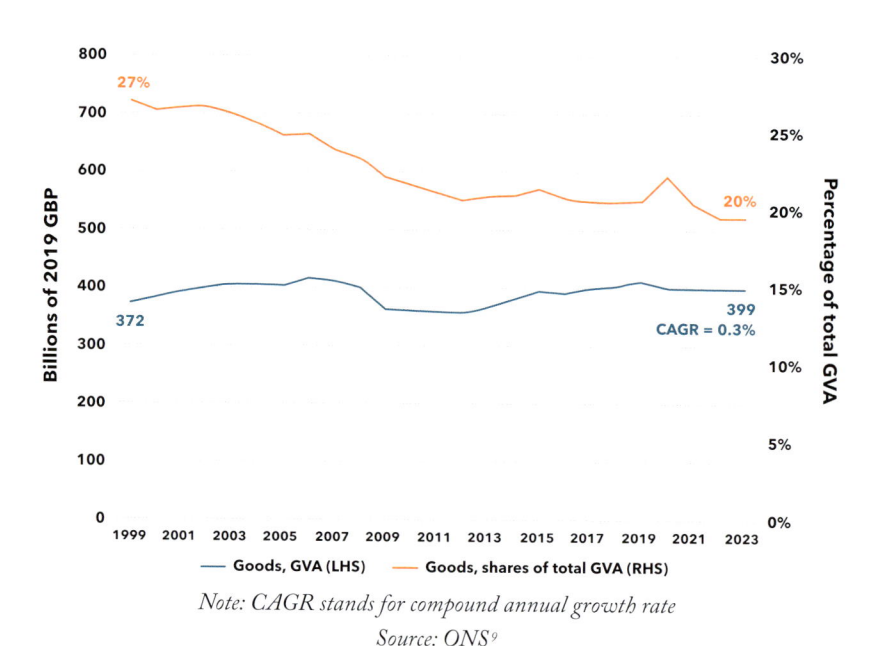

Note: CAGR stands for compound annual growth rate
Source: ONS[9]

As part of that dynamic, the war on hydrocarbon fossil fuels, from past and present governments, has contributed to a range of business closures in the UK, including the closing down of one of our few remaining petroleum refineries and the closing of the UK's last ammonia plant.[10] The war on North Sea oil has also led to a steady drop in production, and therefore export, of crude and refined oil products since 2020 – see Chart 3.13. (If we had permitted fracking, this would, of course, have led to either an increase in goods exports of hydrocarbons, or a drop in goods imports of hydrocarbons; or both.)

Chart 3.13: UK Oil Exports 2014–24

A significant part of our decline in goods exports has come from various governments' war on North Sea oil and on hydrocarbons generally.

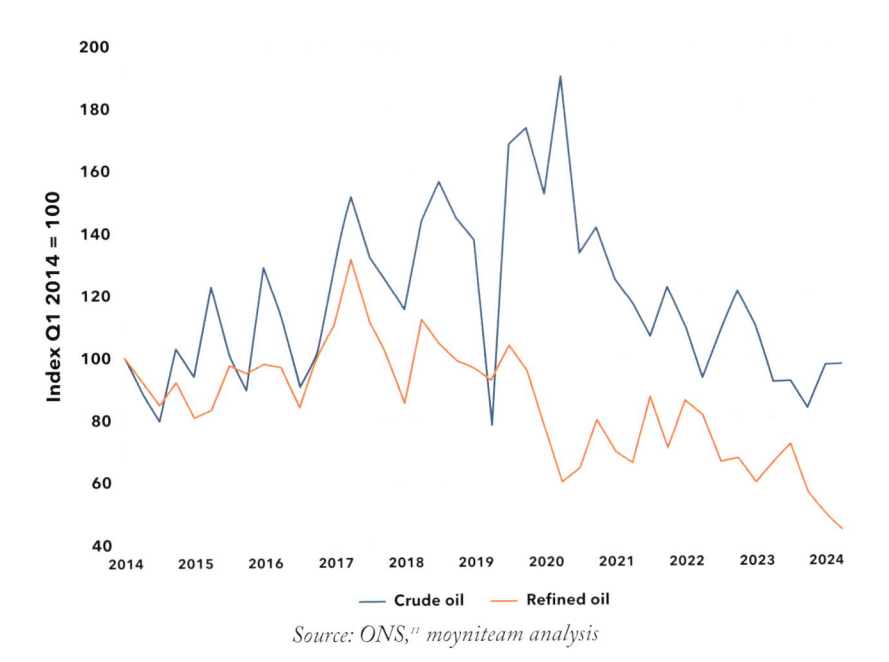

Source: ONS,[11] moyniteam analysis

Our decline in goods exports has been more pronounced with the EU than with the rest of the world. Later in this chapter, I discuss the Commonwealth in particular, emphasising our close links and trade opportunities. On services, as Chart 3.14 shows, the growth in exports since 2016 to the Commonwealth, the non-EU rest of the world and even the EU itself has been excellent. Our drop in goods exports has been to all parts of the world, so was not a function of our leaving the EU. But as, post-Brexit, we turned to face the world and signed new trade deals across the globe, rather than focusing so much on the EU, we have seen our goods exports performance do better worldwide, and particularly with the Commonwealth, than in the EU. This performance elsewhere mitigates the lessening of our trade (as a proportion of our overall mix) with the EU. That change in mix is partly a result of the EU, due to its anaemic growth, becoming smaller and smaller in the overall picture of world trade. It is also because of the other influences, in particular our better suitability to trade with the Commonwealth, that I reviewed earlier. It's clear that our export future is more with the rest of the world, than with the declining EU.

This difference in outcomes is an inevitable consequence of the UK leaving the protectionist barriers of the EU, being now free to engage with the entire world.

As mentioned earlier, a key reason for our changing mix of exports, moving away from the EU, is the sluggish growth of the EU itself. Even with its faster-growing eastern members, we can see from Chart 3.15 that the rest of the world is leaping ahead of the EU in its growth rate, and that the Commonwealth, which was 9 per cent smaller than the EU in 2016, is now 10 per cent larger than the EU. The reason for this is that the EU embraces the low-growth social democratic model of large government, high taxes and excessive regulation. In consequence, the EU grows slowly and is increasingly unattractive as a trade destination.

Chart 3.14: UK Exports of Goods and Services, 2014–24
Commonwealth, Rest of the World, EU

As the UK distances itself from the EU, its exports to the rest of the world, and particularly the Commonwealth, begin to prosper.

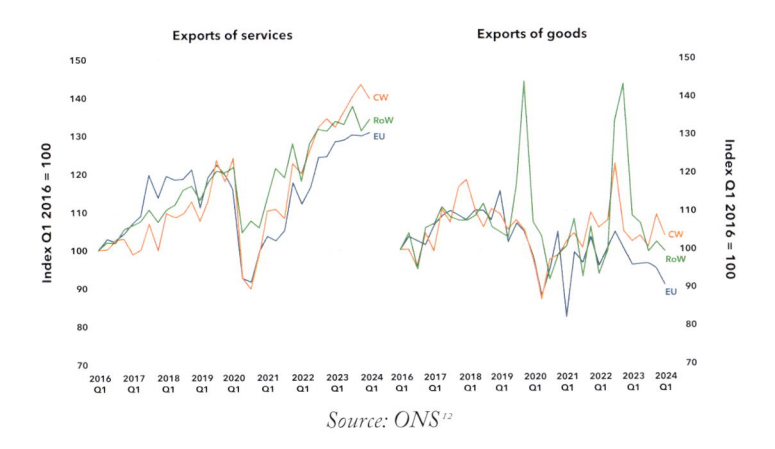

Source: ONS[12]

Chart 3.15: Growth of EU versus Rest of the World and Size of EU versus Commonwealth, 2016–24

Both the Commonwealth and the rest of the world are more attractive export markets than the EU.

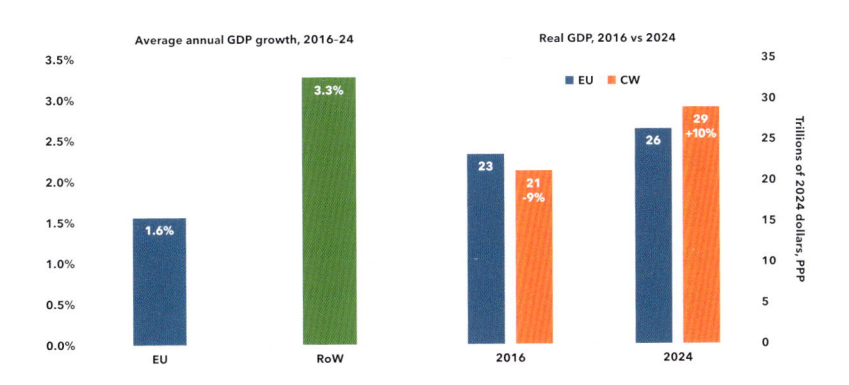

EU, Commonwealth (CW) and rest of world (RoW) figures do not include the UK
Togo joined the Commonwealth in 2022 but was added to the 2016 figures for ease of comparison
Source: International Monetary Fund[13]

What are the best policies for ensuring that our services-export success goes up a further notch and that, equally importantly, we encourage imports of low-priced goods and services into our country that our citizenry could be, but currently aren't, enjoying? The bets policy perspectives to focus on, listed below, are reviewed in the remainder of this chapter:

- Economic theory demonstrates why, and practical experience proves that, openness to trade accelerates economic growth.
- Britain's economy, as we now pursue our own trade policy, can benefit greatly from further opening itself up to the world.
- To benefit properly from opening up its economy, Britain must recognise protectionism for what it is and avoid it. Now that we have left the EU, we must avoid replicating its cartel-like protectionist behaviour.
- The UK should focus instead not just on developing our capabilities in high-value sectors, but also on exploiting any sector where we have competitive and comparative advantage.

We develop each of these points in the following sections.

OPENNESS TO TRADE ACCELERATES ECONOMIC GROWTH

In recent decades, academics around the world have increasingly focused on understanding the potential and actual benefits of free trade. This is an interesting throwback to the eighteenth and nineteenth centuries, when works by economists such as Adam Smith, David Ricardo and Frédéric Bastiat led to the eventual major breakthrough for free trade in the UK – the abolition of the Corn Laws, with consequent unparalleled growth in the British economy.

GDP grew so fast at that time that Britain cemented itself as, and for many decades remained, the largest and the most successful economy in the world.

As the nineteenth century went on, many large economies followed Britain's free-trade lead. However, by the twentieth century things started to regress. At the beginning of the Great Depression, the imposition of the Smoot–Hawley Tariff Act in the US, and the creation of other trade barriers worldwide, resulted in a catastrophic collapse in world trade, and consequent immiseration within the populations of many countries, including the US. All over the world, tariff and non-tariff barriers – protectionism in general – sprang up and persisted for many decades. The majority of economies did not start opening up again for half a century or more, especially in developing countries, and quite a few not before the 1990s.

The change back to open trade, as slowly as it came, was precipitated by an event that occurred much earlier than the 1990s. This was the formation of the General Agreement on Tariffs and Trade (GATT) in 1948, which led to a slow, cautious opening of economies over the following decades. GATT was probably one of the finest achievements of the modern economics profession, gradually rolling back the disaster of the pre-war protectionist era, but it took several decades to bear fruit. There were, at first, a few cases of opening up in the 1970s, then more in the 1980s and then, with the great opening up of China and India from the mid-1990s on, the commencement of enormous enrichment of populations around the world. Billions of the world's citizens, formerly living in poverty, started to receive better wages and living conditions thanks to the application of the capitalist model in those countries and the willingness of western countries to have open-trade policies and to buy those countries' goods and services – for example, admitting

China to the World Trade Organization (WTO) in 2001. GATT was made more operational through the establishment of the WTO in 1995, bolstered by the resistance of many countries against pressures created by holdout protectionist trade cartels around the world and despite ongoing populist protests against 'globalisation'.

In consequence, the world has, over the past couple of decades and until very recently, enjoyed a positive period for free trade, a situation that many around the world still work hard to improve even further.* The UK has exited the protectionist EU, which has also dropped its tariffs by a significant amount in recent decades (though the EU still to this day maintains many 'non-tariff barriers', often under the hypocritical guise of those pesky 'product standards' that are allegedly designed to protect consumers).

There is a persistent and frequent reappearance in politics of empirically and endlessly discredited socialist beliefs – among which are the reappearance of populist/protectionist policy proposals. The latter stem partly from geopolitical considerations and partly from perceptions that countries such as China don't 'play fair' with trade (and yes, they don't, particularly when it comes to industrial espionage, but that is not an argument for blanket, anti-free-trade policies when dealing with China). Biden, Trump, Harris – all leaned heavily protectionist.[14] When the US goes protectionist, others unfortunately follow. But that doesn't mean that protectionism is smart: the value of a free-trade approach abides. The UK, an independent sovereign country with its own trade policy, sitting at number two in the world on the measure of soft power, is now poised to take a leading role in, and benefit greatly from, this

---

* The split of the world into two geopolitical camps, with the western powers aligned against China, Russia, Iran, North Korea and others, poses a large challenge to further global trade liberalisation. But there is no reason why trade liberty should not continue to develop among the western powers and the non-aligned states.

still-enduring era of global free trade – and we need to resume and increase our traditional global trade leadership role in advocating it.[15] (We are better positioned to do this now because, having left the EU, we resume our own independent seat at the WTO table.) Constant protectionist counterattacks, attempting to reverse trade freedoms, proliferate around the world – as described in a recent *Economist* special report.[16] It is essential that free-trade advocates such as the UK fight protectionism wherever it occurs.

. . .

Adam Smith is universally acknowledged as having laid the foundations for classic free-market economic theory and, in particular, as having given an early push to the world to move from a 'mercantilist' economic system to a free-trade one. In his era, that predominant mercantilist approach asserted that the way for a country's economy to flourish was in essence to sell as many goods as possible to other countries, while inhibiting those countries, as much as possible, from selling anything back. Smith's 'liberal markets' approach was grounded on his more general analysis of how economies can grow through specialisation and by frustrating any monopolistic behaviour. For example, famine in a country can occur if other countries are prevented by tariffs (imposed primarily to benefit monopoly/oligopoly providers) from selling affordable grain into that country.

Ricardo refined Smith's ideas with what is often claimed as one of the most important (and counterintuitive) economic ideas ever: the theory of comparative advantage.[17] This says that country X should produce goods and services only when it can do so at a lower opportunity cost *relative to the other goods and services it could produce instead*. In other words – and this is the part that most people find surprising – it should, in certain circumstances, import products in sector A from country Y, even when it could itself make sector A products more cheaply than does country Y. This is the case if, even though country X has a competitive advantage in sector A, within X's economy is another sector, B, where X's advantage over Y is even greater than its advantage in A; and X can transfer resources (people, capital) from A into B. Observing this rule moves country X up the value chain to the position where it can focus on the sectors in which it can add optimal value, creating the most wealth and economic growth for its own economy. (Note the key condition for this to work: mobility of people and capital between sectors.)

When all nations in the world follow that rule, there are two consequences. First, every country can find *some* demand for its goods and services, even if it is outperformed in every sector across the board by other nations. Second, and yet more counterintuitive, even in those cases when a given country's own productivity does not improve, any increase in the productivity of *other* countries will make it wealthier – because those other countries. through their higher productivity, move to higher value sectors. This affords more economic opportunity even for the country that has had no productivity improvement.

Competitive advantage – the basic ability to produce a good or service better or cheaper than other countries – is, of course, *also* something that is key for a country to develop; it was the foundation of Adam Smith's original argument for free trade in 'On Treaties of Commerce'. Ricardo's concept of comparative advantage goes beyond that in saying even those countries that are superior to other countries in *all* economic sectors will still want to trade with other countries, in order to be able to move resources from one sector within the home country to another, higher value-added one;

and in order to move capital and people out of those sectors where comparative advantage is least, and into those where it is most. A country can do that only if it has good mobility of capital and labour. Any difficulties in hiring and firing, such as those imposed by taxes or regulation, will inhibit that. Artificial costs placed on housing, such as planning regulations (see Volume One), or stamp duty, prevent workers from moving to locations where the jobs in the most advantageous sectors are. Arguably, the now very high rates of stamp duty on the more expensive houses in the UK will have been particularly damaging in that respect, as they act directly in preventing mobility among those higher-paid employees whose value-added contribution in moving to new sectors could be the greatest.[*]

So, a final point about Ricardo's theory, whose comparative advantage concept is nowadays almost universally accepted among economists: when followed (and after appropriately structuring the economy through infrastructure investment, a sensible tax code and low regulation) it further magnifies the benefits all countries can get from free-trade agreements.

How is competitive – and, from it, comparative – advantage created within a country?[†] There are some basic foundations that can underpin its attempts to build and exploit advantage. The UK is replete with such foundations – for example, being a country that speaks the English language, our reasonably good education system, our excellent science base and our entrepreneurial national spirit.

Beyond these basic foundations, we can see high-value competitive

---

[*] For some time now, the imposition of stamp duty has resulted in people spending money on digging basements and converting lofts, rather than losing money through stamp duty by moving house.
[†] Strictly speaking, there is comparative advantage to be found in the most moribund economy, one that has little competitive advantage anywhere; in *all* economies, opportunity cost varies between sectors. But for a thriving economy, exploiting comparative advantage is key; this mobility (of both capital and labour) is an essential component of a dynamic, upward-moving economy.

advantage being built up in business ecosystems, where clusters of capability reinforce each other and create formidable advantages. One such (exemplary) UK ecosystem would be 'Motorsport Valley', the Oxfordshire and Midlands cluster of high-tech companies that feed the Formula 1 racing industry.[18] In this community, a combination of expertise, manufacturing capability and suppliers both large and small have led to such a formidable interlocking set of capabilities that a full seven of the world's ten Formula 1 competitors are located within an hour of Oxfordshire. Such dominance in this area has enormous downstream benefits to other related industries for example, Jaguar Land Rover in nearby Birmingham benefits enormously from this high-tech nearby presence.*

Another example is Silicon Fen, which developed around Cambridge and has created enormous economic success and growth for the UK. With over 1,000 high-tech companies established just in 1992–7, that ecosystem continued to grow and develop, now boasting over 5,000 tech companies in fields such as biotech, AI, chips and fintech.[19] A similar science cluster more recently sprang up around Oxford. The Bristol ecosystem, built around aviation and other high-tech, high-design manufacturing, is another example. Tech hotspots have sprung up in London (Silicon Roundabout), Birmingham, Manchester, Edinburgh and elsewhere, with the UK consequently emerging (at least until recently) as a global tech hub.[20]

All these activities help to create competitive advantage, which in the majority of these cases will translate into comparative advantage. The theory then says that workers must move out of existing, less competitive sectors and into those ones. Several problems with that: first, most of these new sectors require a high level of education.

---

* This will possibly not be the case in the future, in our new, wonderful, internal combustion engine-free automobile industry. Will Formula 1 teams, and this entire business cluster, also emigrate to China?

Second, workers must be prepared to move, but the Briton is often famously reluctant to do so.[*] Third, this view is in direct opposition to Boris Johnson and Michael Gove's 'levelling up' concept, which envisaged bringing jobs to people, not people to jobs.[†] A gifted leader in the north such as Ben Houchen might do wonders in creating a local environment where entrepreneurs flourish, with consequent economic successes such as we are seeing in Teesside. These would not require an upheaval of mobile labour, but such wins are rare, and in general, levelling up is the opposite of what is needed to migrate labour from low-value sectors to high-value ones. It is just another form of likely-to-fail industrial strategy.[‡]

Indeed, the problem one has to be careful about with any focus on competitive advantage is that it can quickly develop into a yen for industrial policy. Governments can certainly support creation of competitive advantage, by working to have well-educated citizens and encouraging a great science base through cheap energy and low taxes. Governments can also, unfortunately, waste a colossal amount of money pursuing the chimera of 'industrial policy'. This often consists of 'picking winners', doling out subsidies (whether to entire subsectors, as is the case with green energy companies, or to individual companies in the UK such as the disastrous OneWeb example referred to earlier) or anointing specific products, such as heat pumps or electric vehicles, that are then legislated to have a full or part monopoly in the marketplace. Abandoning any fantasy that we can pick winners will, as discussed in Volume One, help reduce government spending and interference by a significant amount.

And since competitive and comparative advantage come from

---

[*] Not to mention the high rate of stamp duty, which charges, for the more expensive houses, 12–15 per cent of their value when you buy them. Not a huge inducement to move house.
[†] Abandoned, but not vocally, by the new Labour government.
[‡] It is to be hoped that the Labour government persists with its stated intention of not pursuing it.

ecosystems, if the government attacks any sector that is an important part of the supply chain for that ecosystem, it cascades down the value chain and damages further opportunites for competitive, and thus also for comparative, advantage. The attack on hydrocarbons has created a major problem for the UK's valuable business ecosystems – as discussed, the closure of Britain's last ammonia plant, and of a major oil refinery in Scotland, will inevitably have calamitous knock-on effects on the UK's economy overall and exporting ability in particular, leading to loss of advantage in advanced sectors. This is not to argue for subsidies for those plants, but rather for removal of most of the newly introduced punitive taxes, of green charges, and of the regulations that played a large part in raising the cost of energy and thus the costs of running large plants, driving UK businesses in such sectors out of existence.

In any event, it is clear that competitive advantage and comparative advantage go hand-in-hand: development of the latter can be facilitated, and its advantages more fully realised, by the former.

Ricardo propounded the concept of comparative advantage in 1817. At that time, the UK – thanks originally to the commercialisation and industrialisation of Richard Arkwright's water frame – had a comparative advantage in textiles, as compared to agriculture where it did not. It took decades after Ricardo's death for his arguments to bear fruit, so powerful was the instinct towards protectionism and the consequent imposition of tariffs. But eventually, the repeal of the Corn Laws led to wealth creation and a major shift in Britain's economy, away from agriculture and towards textiles and on to other manufacturing.

Bastiat, one of the most fluid and amusing of economic writers, focused on the flaws of protectionism in particular. His misfortune was to be born and live in France, where protectionism flourished in his time – just as it does now. But his ideas received much greater appreciation in Britain, where they were highly influential on Richard Cobden, the father of Corn Law abolition.* [21]

As mentioned earlier, the topic of free trade has become, somewhat absurdly, embroiled in the Brexit discussion. Remainers, ostensibly pro-free trade but in their arguments protectionist,† still hanker and argue for a return to the EU's customs union and/or single market. One of their chief arguments, which they believe bolsters this position, is the so-called 'gravity theory' of trade, which states that the amount of trade you will find yourself doing with another country can be expressed mathematically as a function of (a) the size of that country's economy and (b) the inverse of its distance from your own country.‡ It's an apparently reasonable possibility, though doctrinaire and simplistic. In any case, it's one that – in the modern era and particularly for a country with 80 per cent of its economy in services – is quite clearly, and increasingly, wrong.

Starting after the Second World War but with a major accelerating trend since the 1990s, the face of global trade has changed dramatically. From 1945 to 1980, despite GATT, most countries around the world practised some form of protectionism. At the same time, the costs of trade could be high, particularly when it came to trade with distant countries. It's possible to argue that back then, as distinct from our own modern era, distance had more importance. Jeffrey Frankel and David Romer, using data for the period up to 1985, were among the more influential of early authors studying

---

* An excellent short review of this period, leading all the way through to the 1930s when it all started to go wrong, can be found in the first section of Radomir Tylecote's 'The New Trade Route'.
† Primarily, and weirdly, protectionist on behalf of the EU, not of the UK.
‡ It is inspired by the gravitational law in Newtonian physics where the gravitational force between two objects is proportional to their masses and inversely proportional to the squared distance between them. There is no compelling logical or scientific reason why Newtonian physics should translate directly to the laws of trade economics.

the issue.[22] They identified that countries with a larger amount of exports and imports as a percent of their GDP tended to have higher income per capita, but they could not find arguments for there being a correlative causal theory that said overseas trade led to wealth (much as you or I might find that idea intuitively obvious). They moved on to analysing pre-1985 trade success and ended up focusing on geography (specifically, proximity of one country to another) as a determinant of that. Their work seems, unfortunately, to have led to a misplaced obsession with the aforementioned gravity theory among modern economists.

All of Frankel and Romer's data was from the era pre-1985. Starting around 1985, and increasingly after 1995, a dramatic improvement in trade liberalisation had begun to take place across the world. There was also the arrival of a little something that people initially called the World Wide Web. Due to both these things, massive changes to global trade eventuated. Most trade liberalisation, most prominently in the two most important countries, China and India, started shortly after 1995. Frankel and Romer had emphasised that their conclusions on the gravitational power of propinquity were weak, but in any event, we can now confidently say that their findings on distance, ambiguous as they already are, have more or less zero relevance to the modern world (as is illustrated by the enormous trade success nowadays of so many countries who have found ways to sell their goods and services to countries on the other side of the globe).

The gravity-model theory continues, however, to be enormously influential on establishment trade economists – in no small part, one might suspect, because it conveniently supports these economists' obsession that the UK must return to the EU; an obsession that bemusingly still grips so many influential economists. Even the more recent analyses of the gravity model use pre-1995 data; they can say nothing about whether modern-day data support or rebut the theory.

In the pre-1995 period, the distance-abolishing internet had not arrived. Containerisation (with its enormous potential for transporting goods cheaply from far-off countries such as China) had not been invented. Digital trade had never even been thought of, let alone become the enormous economic force that it now is. Neither China nor India had liberalised. No Zoom, no AI, no Google Translate. The gravity model ignores all that. It is superannuated, and irrelevant to the modern world.[23]

A country seeking to improve its exports – particularly a services-dominated country like the UK – should, in the age of Zoom, WhatsApp, email and AI, pay little attention to whether the country it is seeking to sell to is nearby, or otherwise. (Chart 3.14 brings this point home forcefully.)

. . .

Trade policies, trade deals: they matter. To properly examine the impact and implications of the new liberal trade order, and the value of opening up one's country to trade with others, one really has to use post-1995, preferably post-2010, data. Douglas Irwin (2019) has written one of the most quoted and up-to-date survey papers on the subject.[24] He noted that review papers that used sample periods ending in the early 1990s tended to be ambivalent about whether a liberal trade policy was positive for the economic growth of a country. He then, however, reviewed papers that used later data; they came to very different conclusions. In his summary, he stated:

> The findings from recent research have been remarkably consistent ... there appears to be a measurable economic payoff from more level trade policies ... Economic growth is roughly 1–1.5 percentage points higher than a benchmark after trade reform ... this gain cumulated to about 10–20 per cent higher income after a decade.

So, if you liberalise your trade policy, your GDP is likely to be 10 to 20 per cent higher ten years from now than it would otherwise be. Think about what an enormous impact an improved growth level of that size would bring – growth that would be over and above the additional growth that we have identified would come, as discussed in Volume One, from small government, small tax and low regulation.

Irwin gives examples of countries that implemented trade reform, such as Indonesia. He states, 'Indonesia's per capita GDP soared. It was 40 per cent higher than the estimated counterfactual after five years and 76 per cent higher after ten years. These results are robust to placebo testing.'*

Pretty impressive.

One important and obvious caveat is that Irwin's study is mostly of developing countries, less advanced than the UK; but there is no reason to believe that his result is not applicable across the board. Robert J. Barro, whose work we referred to in Volume One, also found that countries that embraced free trade grew faster, but was pessimistic that developed countries could, despite their past growth, expect to grow more than 2 per cent per capita per annum.[25] Barro's

---

* This example addresses the causation versus correlation issue: it says that if you implement trade reform, you then see extra economic growth.

concern has, some twenty years on, been robustly demolished by the undeniable examples of recent economic progress in such countries as Switzerland, the US, Singapore, Taiwan and South Korea. (And of course, even just 2 per cent per-capita growth per annum would, at this time, be an achievement gratefully embraced by the larger EU countries, and indeed by us in the UK, in a world where anything greater than 1 per cent sustained growth per annum, let alone a similar level of growth per capita, currently seems nigh-on impossible for any of our western European economies to manage.)

Going beyond Irwin's and Barro's reviews, there have been a number of other surveys, such as Kim and Lin (2009),[26] or Singh (2010),[27] that also robustly demonstrate the positive impact on growth of trade liberalisation in the modern trade era.

For a summary of this important and excellent point about the power of openness to trade, economists Matt Palumbo and Corey Iacono provide a table (Chart 3.16) of multiple studies of the early 2000s.[*] They all found (apart from Rodriguez and Rodrik, who were neutral) a positive impact on growth stemming from trade openness.

Our own analysis shows the same result. Using the Fraser Institute's measure of trade freedom (based on the size of trade tax revenue, mean tariff rate and standard deviation of tariff rates) at the beginning of each five-year period from 1975 to 2019 for the twenty-three OECD countries considered in Volume One, we found a positive association between the level of trade freedom, and subsequent economic growth over those five-year periods (Chart 3.17). The lower the trade barriers, the higher the economic growth.

---

[*] Reproduced with permission.

Chart 3.16: Palumbo and Iacono's Summary of Reviews of Trade Openness

There have been hundreds of studies of the impact of trade openness. Palumbo and Iacono summarised seven different meta-reviews of these studies. All but one found a positive impact.

Study	Method	Conclusion
Burg and Krueger (2003)[28]	Literature review of more than 100 studies	Positive effect of trade openness on growth. Trade reduces poverty by increasing growth
Hallaert (2006)[29]	Literature review of approximately fifty studies	Positive effect of trade openness on growth
Cline (2004)[30]	Literature review of more than 100 studies	Positive effect of trade openness on growth. Trade reduces poverty by increasing growth
Baldwin (2003)[31]	Literature review of more than thirty studies	Positive effect of trade openness on growth
Winters (2004)[32]	Literature review of approximately fifty studies	Positive effect of trade openness on growth
Rodriguez and Rodrik (2000)[33]	Literature review of over 100 studies	No effect
Srinivasan and Bhagwati (2001)[34]	Literature review of more than fifty studies	Positive effect of trade openness on growth

Source: Palumbo and Iacono[35]

The impact of trade openness on economic growth, shown in this chart, is of the same order of magnitude as Irwin's overall finding. In the case of the UK, the chart shows how in 2000, by the Fraser Institute's measure, we had one of the most liberal tariff policies in the OECD. Our growth rate that year, well over 2 per cent, was at – indeed slightly above – the level predicted by our regression. By 2015, however, the UK's policies were much worse – we had dropped to the middle of the pack – and our growth rate had dropped commensurately, from some 3 per cent to around 2 per cent. (It is now even lower.)

Chart 3.17: Trade Freedom versus GDP Growth, 1975–2019

Trade liberalism is correlated with economic growth. The growth in a protectionist versus a liberal country is, the regression implies, up to 1.5 percentage points per annum less. This is generally accepted, yet the UK's trade freedoms have diminished in recent years.

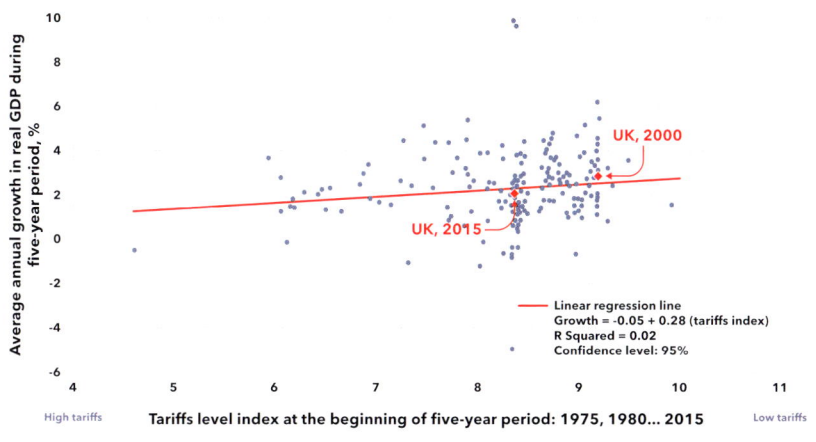

Source: Fraser Institute,[36] Groningen Growth and Development Centre,[37] moyniteam analysis

The indicated impact of Chart 3.17 implies that *if* the UK could improve enough from its current position to get back to where it was in 2000 (which would still make it not quite as liberal in free trade as, say, Singapore currently is) then our GDP growth rate would, if it followed what is implied by Chart 3.17, increase by around 0.3 percentage points or more annually. Growth at that rate compounds each year, to produce a GDP that would be over 3 per cent higher, in just ten years, than it would otherwise have been. That's over £80 billion in additional wealth in today's money: more potential tax revenue, more individual wealth and, of course, more potential benefits and state spending on things like growth-producing infrastructure. So, trade freedom is a hugely important driver of economic growth.

BRITAIN'S FUTURE ECONOMY CAN BENEFIT GREATLY FROM OPENING ITSELF UP TO THE WORLD

The world, in our post-Covid era, is certainly something of a puzzling place when it comes to trade. If the prior decades saw a golden opening up of trade around the world, there now seems to be a bi-polar global model emerging, creating barriers that we predict will reduce economic growth all round.* Russia and China, on one side, use a mostly mercantilist or similar (in Russia's case, actually imperialist, with its mercenary force the Wagner Group) approach to trade, seeking to wrap as many other countries as possible into their embrace. On the other side is the 'free world', with many different approaches but with a worrying, not insignificant number of its member countries in retreat from the Clinton-era North American Free Trade Agreement, WTO, generally open approach. The US now seems increasingly locked into Trump-inspired protectionist rhetoric (although the US economy is still not entirely protectionist). Both the Republicans and the Democrats mostly embrace America First-style language. Within the EU, even though it has gradually lowered tariffs over recent decades, a forest of non-tariff barriers continues to be maintained and augmented, frustrating other countries' attempts to sell into that economy.[38]

When the UK joined the European Common Market in 1973, we were required to lodge ourselves behind its tariff wall. This automatically destroyed large swathes of existing commerce that we had with Commonwealth countries. Trade with all these countries

---

* This is not to argue that this bipolar model can be avoided, given the emergence of countries that are increasingly difficult to trade with, and that threaten the security of western nations.

rapidly diminished as Britain ended up being essentially required to buy much of its goods from within the EU – in particular, agricultural products. The difference in the pattern of the UK's imports and exports, pre-joining and post-joining the Common Market, can be seen in Chart 3.18. In 1960, half of the UK's imports were from the Commonwealth and only three were from Common Market countries. By 1980, there was only one Anglosphere country in our top ten of countries we imported from – the US. The Commonwealth had not a single country in the top ten; seven of the ten were Common Market countries. The story is similar with exports – three Common Market countries and six Commonwealth/Anglosphere countries in 1960, but by 1980, eight (if we include Sweden*) Common Market countries and just the US and Nigeria from the Commonwealth/Anglosphere. As depicted in Chart 3.18, even just seven years after joining, a massive shift in trade patterns had occurred.

Why were exports affected by our joining the Common Market just as badly as were imports? The answer is because when we joined the EU, which made us put up barriers against the rest of the world, the rest of the world in turn put up retaliatory barriers against us. So, we couldn't have quite as cosy a trade relationship as we previously had with the US, for example. And, as can be seen from the chart, once the UK joined the Common Market, trade with Australia, New Zealand and Canada fell off a cliff. By 2019, thanks to the protectionist barriers of the EU, the Commonwealth had been increasingly shut out of trade with the UK. In that year, goods exports to the EU were 46 per cent of the total (22 per cent in 1970), while they were 9 per cent to the Commonwealth (19 per

---

* Sweden joined the EEC in 1985. The Common Market (or European Community) became the EU in 1993.

cent in 1970).[39] This was despite the fact that the collective economies of the Commonwealth were at that point about as large as the economies of the EU (the Commonwealth's economies are now, as we have seen, 10 per cent larger than the EU). The loss of so many of our trading ties to the Commonwealth during that period was, frankly, a tragedy.

Chart 3.18: UK Main Goods Trading Partners, 1960 versus 1980

The geographic pattern of the UK's trade shifted towards the Common Market after we joined the European Economic Community in 1973 and away from the Commonwealth.

	Imports, 1960	% imports		Imports, 1980	% imports		Exports, 1960	% exports		Exports, 1980	% exports
1	United States	16%	1	United States	12%	1	United States	10%	1	Germany	11%
2	Canada	11%	2	Germany	11%	2	Australia	7%	2	United States	10%
3	Australia	9%	3	France	8%	3	Canada	6%	3	Netherlands	8%
4	New Zealand	8%	4	Netherlands	7%	4	Germany	5%	4	France	8%
5	Germany	5%	5	Belgium-Luxembourg	5%	5	South Africa	4%	5	Ireland	6%
6	Netherlands	5%	6	Italy	5%	6	India	4%	6	Belgium-Luxembourg	6%
7	Sweden	5%	7	Saudi Arabia	4%	7	Sweden	4%	7	Italy	4%
8	Kuwait	4%	8	Switzerland	4%	8	Netherlands	3%	8	Sweden	3%
9	India	3%	9	Ireland	4%	9	New Zealand	3%	9	Switzerland	3%
10	Denmark	3%	10	Japan	3%	10	Ireland	3%	10	Nigeria	3%

Commonwealth countries and the United States
Countries in the European Economic Community before 1980 and Switzerland

Source: International Monetary Fund[40]

While EU tariff levels have dropped considerably in size since the Common Market's high barriers of the 1970s – so, in theory, non-EU countries should now be able to sell their goods more easily to the EU and to the UK, so long as we keep our own tariffs low – the EU has also created non-tariff barriers that are even more formidable than the original tariff barriers. The single-market approach uses the sneaky device of highly detailed specifications for products, and detailed local required qualifications for a swathe of markets, with mandatory requirements for companies exporting to the EU to have local offices, companies and officers. Thus, goods and services from outside the EU are successfully kept out of the single market, while those fixated on singing the praises of the EU's single market point out, in a misleading distraction, that the EU itself is a trade-free zone – which is, to some degree, true – but only at the expense of blocking out so much potential free trade with the rest of the world.

The EU's protectionist stance is maintained through these bogus 'standards', along with the faux moral panics mentioned earlier (e.g. chlorine-washed chicken and hormone-fed beef), and it is also continued through a protectionist tariff regime. That situation is particularly dire for some of the poorest developing countries, which are forced into remaining underdeveloped by a tariff regime that is low to zero for raw materials that the EU's manufacturers need (for example, 0 per cent for raw cotton).[41] The regime is middling for intermediate goods that are still useful for EU-made items (6 per cent for cotton goods) and high for finished cotton goods that are directly competing with EU manufacturers (12 per cent for clothes). It's a similar story with palm oil: crude oil is at 2 per cent, oil refined for industrial use is 4 per cent and that which is refined and packaged for human consumption is at 12 per cent. Poor countries are kept poor; they're not allowed to use their home-grown resources to ascend the value chain, but instead only to sell them at rock-bottom prices, in their raw, undeveloped form.

Those wishing the UK to still be tied to the EU seek to keep us in line with the bogus 'standards' approach. As a result, we still import 35 per cent of our chicken, very expensively, from the EU, and our trade negotiators have kiboshed a trade deal with Canada over the issue of 'hormone-fed' beef. (The real reason behind the ban has to be the desire to protect our own beef farmers from having to compete with potentially better beef at lower prices.)[42]

Britain is now, post-EU, in the process of establishing a new era of trade freedom. For the first time in fifty years, we can strike our own trade deals. Deals that benefit the UK, not deals negotiated by the EU with the UK as a captive member, negotitated when we often had no seat at the table at all during the negotiations, and got saddled with deals that contain detailed clauses structured around the specific protectionist concerns of one (or several) of the other twenty-seven other countries of the EU – concerns that had nothing to do with us. And then, cherry on the cake, the EU negotiator would assent to additionally damaging demands from the other party, in order to achieve that damaging-to-the-UK concession. Having left the EU, we are now able to negotiate separate deals – deals that won't need to accommodate twenty-seven countries' multi-fold needs or the protectionist needs of the EU's big businesses.

To repeat what we should be trying to achieve with our trade policy: the common, superficially arrived at understanding is that we are trying to maximise our exports while minimising what we import (the mercantilist approach). But as demonstrated by Smith, Ricardo, Bastiat, and Cobden, among many others, it is actually the opposite that is the case. What our most important overall objective should be, if we focus on the interests of our consumers, is trade freedom, particularly for *imports*. We should deliver for our people the best possible goods and services, regardless of source, at the cheapest prices, and this can only be achieved if we allow the world's producers to come to us, and compete with our domestic producers at world prices.

What that means, of course, is lowering tariffs and non-tariff barriers as much as possible. As an open economy, we can remove tariffs without a trade deal, thus immediately benefiting our consumers. The only point of not reducing barriers until we have a trade deal with a given country is to make things better for our exporters through reciprocal-benefit trade deals. So, this should be done – but not religiously – we should always recognise the harm we do to our own citizens by maintaining tariffs. A noteworthy breakthrough came in April 2024, when the UK finally suspended the tariffs on tropical fruits and nuts, among other things.[43] Dan Hannan persistently cites the example of Moroccan tomatoes.[44] (Why did we ever have these tariffs in the first place? The EU, of course!) But oddly, all those tariffs are at best only suspended – the Moroccan tomatoes still incur penal tariffs to favour non-tariffed, more expensive EU tomatoes. Any and all such tariffs should be abolished.

The prime advantage to the UK of removing tariffs and other barriers, whether unilaterally or through trade deals, will be in getting cheap goods and services from abroad, with access for British goods and services to markets abroad as a beneficial by-product of that. Ever wondered why items that sell for dollars in the US sell for the same amount in pounds in the UK, despite sterling being some 30 per cent higher than the dollar? Ever wondered why Argentinian beef, famous around the world and enjoyed cheaply and copiously by Argentinians, is not available, equally deliciously and cheaply, in the UK? Ever wondered why Australian wheat, so abundantly and inexpensively produced (and cheaper than UK wheat even after the cost of transporting it from Australia to the UK) is not sold more in the UK? Each is the result, in the main, of *our own* trade protectionism, a policy that worsens the cost of living for all citizens. With a free-trade policy, we could both lower the cost to, *and* raise the standard of living of, our citizens.

Who is to blame for the failure to demolish the protectionist barriers that constrain those goods? The answer is, in the main, the UK itself. Still in thrall to the EU view of the world, we impose import charges, product standards and sometimes quotas and inspections on these and so many other goods and services, in a counter-productive effort to provide protection for our domestic producers. What we actually achieve is to increase the cost of living for the UK consumer.

For almost fifty years, we were required to impose protectionist costs because we had no independent trade policy; we had to follow the EU's. Now that we are out of the EU, we have had to spend much of the time that has since elapsed replicating (necessarily, so as not to have to take a large step backwards) the suite of EU trade deals around the world. Only recently, and in particular with the Comprehensive and Progressive Agreement for Trans-Pacific Partnership (CPTPP) deal signed in mid-2023, have we started to go significantly beyond those deals.

For the past few years, entering the CPTPP was said, vociferously, to be unachievable. Now it has been accomplished, a reverse ferret is attempted, alleging that the impact will be insignificant. Equally negative predictions were made about how we would struggle to replicate EU trade deals – but we have done that, and in some cases, we have improved those deals.[45] The impact on growth of these deals (which can be further improved over time) will be significant.[*] Organisations such as the OBR have asserted, by torturing the data in the most improbable manner, that we will lose 4 per cent of GDP as a result of Brexit – yet, they assert, we will only improve GDP by 0.08 per cent from joining CPTPP (a trading area that is somewhat

---

[*] The achievements of a series of Trade Secretaries and Foreign Secretaries in concluding these many deals, at fast pace and with officials who inevitably had little experience in negotiating such deals, have had scant recognition. Liam Fox, Liz Truss, Anne-Marie Trevelyan and Kemi Badenoch all deserve credit for making that happen.

LET FREE TRADE FLOURISH

larger than the EU).*[46] James Forder, for the IEA, has effectively and comprehensively rebutted that non-credible negative claim about our CPTPP accession.[47] As regards that OBR claim, how on earth can it be true that we lose 4 per cent from leaving one trading block, and yet gain less than 0.1 per cent in getting access to a market of larger size?† In any event, the predicted immediate loss in GDP from Brexit didn't occur, and the new claims (counter-reverse ferret) that the GDP loss *will* still occur, but slowly, over time (the 'leaking balloon' theory), now have only the discredited (and, of course, merely theoretical, invalidated by modern-era data) gravity model for their justification.

As Patrick Minford pointed out in his book *After Brexit, What Next?*, the Treasury's forecast was for an even worse outcome than the OBR predicted: a 7.7 per cent reduction in GDP from Brexit (when our trade with the EU is only 12 per cent of GDP!).[48] As Minford has shown, if more reasonable assumptions were fed into the exact same model that the Treasury used, that 7.7 per cent shrinkage would reverse to a 4 per cent *gain* in GDP, and a reduction in consumer prices of 8 per cent.

It is certainly true that the EU did its very best to punish the UK for leaving the EU, temporarily imposing all sorts of constraints. These penalties punished its own citizens as much as they did the UK.) Such self-damaging attempts certainly constrained trade for a while, but as the EU's strop over our leaving subsides, the problems are disappearing fairly quickly:

- Disruption in the first few days of Brexit on the Dover/Calais crossing, leading to long lines of trucks backed up from Dover,

---

* Predicated on our not getting a deal with the EU (spoiler, we did) and other bizarre assumptions.
† It is this sort of outlandish, non-believable claim by the OBR that in the next chapter makes me advocate, even more enthusiastically than I otherwise would, for the abolition of the OBR.

did not last more than a few days. Despite shock-horror articles in the Remainer media at the time, this can now be seen as having been merely a toddler's tantrum by France.
- Aggressive behaviour by the fishing fleets of France – a two-week wonder.[49]
- Forcing UK citizens to queue up in non-EU lines, despite the technology being present to allow us e-passport entry – an almost certainly finite tantrum that we are told will eventually be rescinded sometime after the introduction of the (also somewhat irrational) much-delayed EU Entry/Exit System scheme, as each country realises it costs them more to use humans rather than machines, with no benefit to them, and a difficult-to-deny appearance of petulance in the meantime.[50]
- Forcing UK citizens travelling to the EU to not stay more than ninety days – these restrictions are gradually disappearing as, again, these countries realise that it is themselves who are punished by these restrictions, since the excluded Brits then spend their money back home rather than in that country.[51]
- Pet restrictions, whose justification necessitates the intriguing hypothesis that rabies is endemic in the UK – in distinction from the reality that it is in continental Europe where *la rage* is found. Again, we predict these restrictions will be removed within a few years.[52]
- Multiple petty restrictions and costs on exports from the UK, particularly low-ticket ones, to EU countries.[53] (This is being worked around, with digital apps created by such commercial shippers as DHL and by the government for companies exporting to the EU). Most exporters of low-ticket goods, having found and employed the workarounds, no longer complain about this.

- Cutting off trade between Northern Ireland and Great Britain.*54 The surrender of Northern Ireland is one of the most sordid events in the Brexit saga and is the one blow to trade that is, so far, *not* going away. Politicians, from May to Johnson to Sunak, are responsible for this entirely unnecessary and damaging situation. The Windsor Framework eventually can and must be reversed, but we need a government that is prepared to fight hard and ingeniously to get rid of it. Until then, this is one appalling, unnecessary and entirely self-inflicted negative outcome of the Brexit negotiations, whose damaging nature for now persists.

It is evident that one by one, apart from the final point, these restrictions are dropping away as different EU countries come to realise that each restriction, satisfying to vengeful EU bureaucrats and politicians as it may have been at the time, is harming the citizens of the EU as much as it harms the UK. Once these barriers are dropped or reduced, that in turn will result in a greater volume of trade between the EU and the UK – but at no detriment to the UK's growing exports to, and imports from, the rest of the world.

We now face the ongoing task of creating entirely UK-oriented free-trade deals, whether with the EU or the rest of the world. The Department for Business and Trade (DBT) is rapidly gaining a reputation for responsiveness and negotiating expertise, and this

---

* A totally unnecessary and damaging concession by the UK, apparently conceded originally by the Remain-disposed Theresa May, cemented in by the inattentive, impatient and ignorant Boris Johnson and now encompassed in the Windsor Framework deal struck by the hapless Rishi Sunak. All such deals have been dishonestly and unconvincingly presented to the UK's citizens as preserving unrestricted trade across the United Kingdom and essential for maintaining free trade with the EU. Their major repercussions (possibly intended by both sides) include the fact that whenever mainland UK diverges from EU law, so as to improve our economy, we have to leave Northern Ireland behind – so, to prevent that, and any accompanying negative publicity, we do little diverging. As a result, our economy suffers – but, good for Remainers, the possibility of a partial return to the EU, however unlikely, is thereby kept (at least theoretically) open.

will lead to great success, so long as their political masters continue to champion the free-trade agenda.*

In setting out to sign trade deals, we should first of all never forget that the objective of a trade deal is to be true to the theories of competitive and comparative advantage, whereby we seek out deals that will provide great, cheap goods and services for the UK's citizens to enjoy. Using our good relationships with these countries will also persuade them to agree in turn that we can sell UK goods and services to them with as few barriers as possible.

Second, when we turn to helping our businesses export their goods and services to the rest of the world, it is essential that we realise how different the UK economy is from that of the EU – in particular, recognising that 80 per cent of our economy is in services, the second-highest percentage in the OECD.[55] The EU's internal-market regulations did not cover services, but, as the late Michael Burrage showed, that did not result in terrific growth of our world-class services to the EU.[56] Why? Because most of the large, established providers of services within the EU had collaborated with Brussels and their own national governments to construct the previously mentioned thicket of non-tariff barriers – for example, requirements to establish local offices; multiple local professional qualifications; complex local regulations.

Outside the EU, it's a different story. As already touched on, one of the tear-inducing consequences of our joining the Common

---

* An energetic free-trade approach (albeit one that has contained regrettable protectionist elements, such as the recent deal with Australia) has, since Brexit, been pursued by successive ministers and secretaries of state. Trade champion Crawford Falconer has been highly influential within the DTI. The more recent installation of EU-phile Lord Cameron as Foreign Secretary was more concerning but, thanks to Sunak's impulsive decision to hold an early election, was transitory. The new Business and Trade Secretary, the formerly Corbynite Jonathan Reynolds, seems open to trade deals – but appears to have a penchant for industrial policy, as well as a desire to placate the EU, which could make striking new trade deals more difficult.

Market in the 1970s was that it ripped us away from our ties with the Commonwealth, whose economy is now 10 per cent larger than that of the EU (and growing far faster than the EU, year by year). It is a prime potential market for Britain's services and its goods.

The Commonwealth is a key market for British services, in part because, as mentioned earlier, there are so many commonalities to our economies. This is an enormous competitive advantage that we are lucky enough to have inherited; one is left wondering what might have happened to our economic relations with these Commonwealth countries during the past fifty years had we not cut our ties to them on joining the Common Market. This is water under the bridge, but we now have the opportunity to painstakingly repair those former links. The CPTPP deal represents our first major opportunity to step towards that.

A further opportunity exists as we seek to get a visa programme with India that helps them get high-skilled Indian workers into the UK. (Note: in accordance with the comparative advantage argument, this would be a good thing for our economy as it would enable us to improve our advantage in high-value sectors.) We need to persuade India, in return, to open up its markets to British services. Again, in accordance with the theory of comparative advantage, this would be beneficial for India's citizens.[*]

To give an illustrative example (apparently small, but from which many consequences flow), a telling emblem of our continued relationship with the Commonwealth is the fact that dozens of

---

[*] This point refers only to the relatively small number of high-skilled immigrants who would potentiate economic growth per capita in the UK. It is not advocating continuation of the very large number of non-skilled or economically inactive immigrants that the UK currently imports.

Commonwealth (and indeed some non-Commonwealth) countries – Malaysia, Australia, Uganda, Botswana, Guyana, and Vanuatu, among many others – all use same the square three-pin plug that the UK does, as any tourist or business traveller to those countries will observe. This is a feature that signals that each of these countries uses a 240-volt electricity system; the apparently tiny fact of the square three-pin plugs means products and services developed for the UK's entire electricity ecosystem will also fit neatly with each of these countries' own needs in that sector, from generation to transmission to supply. This example, and indeed other more obvious examples such as the shared use of common law, point us to a better appreciation of the many different common standards and technologies that we still share with most Commonwealth countries – a clear signal pointing to the relative ease of selling goods and services to them, rather than to other countries.

Turning to the US, Rishi Sunak's trip there in June 2023 achieved some small but significant agreements to open up markets between the US and the UK – an achievement that could not have been accomplished while we were part of the EU. This points the way to a future where digital services such as AI could be an enormous export for the UK around the world. And the DBT's ingenious pursuit of trade deals at the level of individual states within the US – seven state-level deals and counting have now been signed, thus bypassing the Biden administration's self-harming reluctance to do an overall deal with us – will result in cumulatively closer trade ties between us and the more dynamic states of the US, resulting in greater trade between the UK and the US.[57] A US-wide trade deal is still elusive – but much less so than the complete impossibility that would exist if we were still in the EU.

Again, the argument as to what kind of trade deals we can accomplish as a standalone trading power in the world is bedevilled and confounded by the politics of Brexit. Some Brexiteers say we are now certainly going to be an exporting superpower. Many Remainers, having a mercantilist realpolitik view (even if they don't realise it – some of them bemusingly claim that trade freedom was achieved from being in the EU), take the opposite tack, and sneer that tiny Britain will be helpless before the trading juggernauts of the EU, the US, and China. When it comes to trade deals, Biden's people, in dogmatic ignorance of the facts on the ground, have seemed to discern some sort of Manichean choice between the EU and the UK – and thus they drag their feet when it comes to doing a deal with us.

Regardless – and if we're going to talk about realpolitik, bear in mind our leading position in soft power – we are already seeing significant export benefits, whether from our new independence or because of a new mindset among the British business community. In 2022, we saw a 23 per cent increase in exports to the Commonwealth and a 36 per cent increase in exports to Brazil (in cash terms).[58] These are just two admittedly outlier, but nevertheless indicative, examples.

Overall, if our trade negotiators continue to keep a cool head, are prepared to drop British tariff and non-tariff barriers to imports from other countries, and can focus on ensuring deals that will ease the way for services exports – for example, by mutual recognition of professional qualifications, mutual legal standards and mutual regulatory regimes – then significant growth in our economy can be achieved in the coming years, and major benefits for our citizens realised from such openness to trade.

THE UK MUST RECOGNISE PROTECTIONISM FOR WHAT IT IS AND AVOID IT

The prime reason for international trade faltering is growing global protectionism. This comes in many forms. Workers believe that their jobs are being taken from them by someone halfway around the world; farmers believe they should not have to compete with world prices; manufacturers would much rather not have to improve their game so as to compete with better or cheaper products from other countries. All those players are content for their country to erect tariff and non-tariff barriers, or lobby government to get subsidies to compensate for the lower competitiveness that results from expensive electricity or higher taxes – all the topics we discussed in Volume One. The EU is a master at putting up barriers, only semi-visible, to trade. A massively worrying example of a classic EU 'non-tariff' barrier (though it acts in practice as a tariff, disguised as a tax, further disguised in obfuscatory wording) is the EU's upcoming Carbon Border Adjustment Mechanism (CBAM). This, as *The Economist* pointed out,

> in effect taxes carbon-intensive imports [and] is seen in some quarters as a brake on African industrialisation. A recent study said it might reduce African exports to the EU by 6%. 'The EU and US are seeking to destroy our export potential,' says Mohammed Amin Adams, Ghana's Minister of State for Finance.[59]

The real issue with CBAM is that it will act to deprive the EU's citizens – and ours, if we adopt it – of cheaper and better products.

There is no need at all for the UK to follow – as it is currently threatening to – the EU's protectionist behaviour. We should ensure that, whether in this or with similar barriers, we go our own way and welcome reciprocal trade from across Africa, with huge benefits for both us and them.* The main reasons for implementing such a self-harming trade barrier as CBAM are ignorance of trade theory; a slavish desire to follow the EU; a worry that CBAM would nonetheless be mandatory in Northen Ireland (which it would be under the Windsor Framework), and that Northern Ireland would then kick up a huge fuss if it is subject to it without the rest of the UK. All this is turbocharged by the usual insane green virtue signalling.

Opposing such a melange of foolishness is politically challenging, but it must be done. This sort of obfuscation and wrongful thinking is why Britain took nearly thirty years, after Ricardo's compelling treatise in 1817, to abolish the Corn Laws, and it is why our recent trade deal with Australia will result in food prices in the UK being higher than they need to be for decades more – because in that deal, tariffs are not fully abolished for another fifteen years from the signing of the deal. Other countries have adopted the 'ripping off the plaster' approach in abolishing or massively reducing barriers to trade. These countries are the ones that have seen the greatest benefits from free trade.

In the studies listed earlier (Chart 3.16), country after country saw their GDP grow rapidly after they took the plunge. New Zealand, a farming country, abolished all farming tariffs in 1984–8. Despite forecasts of doom, New Zealand is now much richer, leading the world in many agricultural products. There are few New Zealand farmers who would argue for the country going back to its former protectionist ways.[60]

---

* Instead of putting up a border tax, we should cease subsidising green energy and thus simultaneously cease placing the cost of those subsidies onto our domestic producers – who could then produce in our country what we increasingly, though unnecessarily, now have to import.

THE UK SHOULD DEVELOP AND EXPLOIT COMPETITIVE AND COMPARATIVE ADVANTAGE

If we wish to grow the UK's economy, exploiting the opportunities for trade around the world, we must work our way towards doing the same as what New Zealand and other countries have done. For those sectors where we do not have competitive or comparative advantage, and don't think we can get it, it will be to the benefit of our nation to allow others to provide those goods and services to us, rather than producing them ourselves and selling to our citizens at higher prices than they would pay for the superior overseas goods and services.

To the issue of job displacement, it is certainly true that we must (and are currently failing to) control and manage our immigration policy, so that we do not overwhelm the labour market at the low-paid end and, at the same time, add to the already high demands on the country's vastly overstretched infrastructure. But today, Britain is suffering from labour shortages, not the other way round.[*] We have the opposite situation from what Remainers gloomily predicted.

We now need to look forward to a free-trade economy that is based around our competitive and comparative advantages. In the second half of the nineteenth century – as trade both into and out of Britain flourished, and as large amounts of grain were imported into the UK from around the world rather than being grown in England – agricultural jobs dried up, as less grain was produced in the UK, and farmers had to learn to be more productive to compete with overseas producers. Many tens of thousands of workers moved from the country to the towns, fuelling the manufacturing boom.

---

[*] Although much of that is a result of the dire 'mental health' epidemic discussed in Volume One.

LET FREE TRADE FLOURISH

The end result for workers was a much higher average wage – and for them and the economy overall, more jobs, all of which led to historically unparalleled prosperity. When there is trade liberalisation, just as in any time of technological change, there will be disruption of the workforce, involving regrettable individual difficulties and dislocation. But since the alternative to moving up the value chain is stagnation, and an eventual decline in job opportunities and wages for all, such challenges have to be faced head on.

The concepts of competitive and comparative advantage do not call for passive acceptance – rather, they call for active engagement. Comparative advantage works to the benefit of every country. In the UK, the building blocks of competitive and comparative advantage include our language, our common law, our academic and tertiary education excellence, our science and financial services capabilities, our fintech leadership, our success in attracting investment for and hosting high-tech startups, our many services skills.*[61]

In order to have continued long-term economic success, we have to continually build new competitive and comparative advantage, taking us ever-further up the value chain. Switzerland is a classic example of how to do this. As Switzerland does well in a particular field and resources are transferred to it, its finances improve; over time its currency appreciates (leading to short-term challenges but long-term benefit), wages go up and imported products become cheaper because of the stronger currency. Even just to stand still against competitor countries, let alone find new sectors to excel in competitively, Switzerland must continually upgrade its workforce's capabilities; its infrastructure; its general attractiveness as a country. Switzerland does all of that continually (*The Economist*

---

* A recent *Financial Times* article revealed that our largest subsector export was, of all things, management consulting.

recently revealed Switzerland to be the most innovative country in the world), so that its currency continues to appreciate, its wages continue to rise and the general standard of living of its citizens continues to grow even further, beyond those of all but a very few countries in the world. This is the path that the UK must look to take, in the same way that is also done in countries such as Singapore, Chile and South Korea.

Inevitably, this raises the issue for the UK of how to move up the value chain if we have a large swathe of our workforce as poorly educated as it currently is.[*][62] Creating productive citizens through an excellent education is entirely possible, as has been shown by the many schools around the UK that single-mindedly pursue educational excellence, discussed in Volume One.

In any event, the road to success is for us to create the conditions in our economy for the emergence of multiple types of competitive and comparative advantage, and then step back while our businesses build successful exporting enterprises, at the same time as our citizens enjoy cheaper goods and services imported from abroad. Unfortunately, under current governments, and throughout this poor-performing century to date, we instead interfere more and more in the economy, creating massive problems through distortive financial subsidies and incentives, with the imposition of punishment taxes, fines, consumer charges and other disincentives. This approach seems predicated on the assumption that centralised

---

[*] The recent PISA results show the UK, as a direct consequence of the Gove/Gibb reforms, shooting up the ladder of international comparisons, particularly in maths. But there are two caveats: first, our rise in the tables is to a large degree because other countries' results got worse during Covid, while our results stayed overall the same (of course, staying the same, despite Covid, is in itself a big achievement). Second, our schooling is now a tale of two 'cities' – the first, those schools that have embraced the reforms, and the second, the large swathes of schools that have not. The second, as discussed in Volume One, has resulted in an estimated 30–40 per cent of our schoolchildren leaving school either illiterate or innumerate (15–20 per cent of children are both), unable to function effectively in their adult lives as autonomous citizens. We *have* to turn this situation around.

direction of our economy will build winners. The remorseless and eternal judgement of markets, delivered against the many scores of centrally directed economies that sprang up around the world over the past century and more, suggests that the expected beneficial outcome from that is not going to happen. The prime outcome of this interference from the centre will be the waste of eye-watering amounts of money on fruitless fantasies: creating losers, not winners, and condemning our economy to low- or no-growth.

However, if instead we embrace and stick to the principles articulated in this chapter, we can usher in a new period of growth and prosperity for our country.

CHAPTER 3

LET SOUND MONEY PREVAIL

PRELUDE: QUANTITATIVE EASING AND THE DISTORTION OF THE ECONOMY

In recent decades, central banks have undertaken a massive, multi-decade experiment on many economies: quantitative easing (QE). QE is a financial market intervention conducted by a central bank, which puts what is essentially newly minted money into the economy. It is done by purchasing assets, mostly government bonds, from the market. Its long-term effects are only just beginning to be understood.

The unprecedented scale of QE by central banks worldwide over the past decade, including the Bank of England, kept interest rates lower than the level that would have prevailed in the absence of QE.[*] This was not why QE had been initially imposed; the original intent was to encourage lending and support economic recovery during the 2008–9 financial crisis by compensating for the massive loss of liquidity in the economy. That loss of liquidity was due firstly to banks no longer funding each other or the private sector, and secondly to banks being required to hold more capital than before.[†] But QE's biggest effect was to lower interest rates.

The effects of any liquidity flows – in this case, the surge of money

---

[*] In this chapter, when I say interest rates, I usually am referring to ten-year bond rates.
[†] See, for example, Tim Congdon (ed.), *Money in the Great Recession: Did a crash in money growth cause the global slump?* (Edward Elgar, 2017), https://www.e-elgar.com/shop/gbp/money-in-the-great-recession-9781784717827.html

caused by the central banks purchasing assets, mostly government bonds, in the open market – cannot last for ever. Nor, of course, can an asset-purchase plan the size of that 2010s QE programme.* In 2022, as the excess money created by QE in the UK started to dissipate – and, in particular, when the Bank of England reversed the money flows through QE's opposite, quantitative tightening (QT) – interest rates started to revert to a less distorted level.

The general rise in interest rates over the past three years, across all parts of the yield curve,† is therefore a long-expected, inevitable return to interest-rate levels that reflect reality more accurately, that more properly reflect perceived risk and that equilibrate the market's supply of, and demand for, credit. In the short to medium term, liquidity flows from or to one or another participant in the market can distort the price level of any asset, including the level of interest rates, but that can never be sustained in the long term – even for governments.‡

The Bank of England asserts that QE started in 2009 in the UK.[1] However, Japan employed QE earlier, in 2001.[2] Many count the start of QE as having taken place with the first major Federal Reserve liquidity intervention in October 1987 – the commencement of the famous 'Greenspan Put'. If they're right, then QE has been going almost forty years.[3] The idea itself had, of course, been around for many decades before that, but the QE interventions from 2008–9 onwards were orders of magnitude greater than in any

---

* The European Central Bank, in its purchases of not just government bonds but also corporate and asset-backed securities, is testing that statement almost to the limit. At the end of July 2024, it still owned over €3 trillion of purchased securities. See European Central Bank, 'Asset purchase programmes', https://www.ecb.europa.eu/mopo/implement/app/html/index.en.html

† The yield curve is the technical term for how interest rates in the market change over the maturity term of different bonds. For example, two-year government bonds yield a different rate of interest than do ten-year government bonds.

‡ The period 2010–22 did, admittedly, turn out to be a pretty long medium term, reflecting the fact that central banks, in theory, have access to unlimited liquidity – but sooner or later, even they run into the problem that printing money leads first to inflation and eventually to hyperinflation.

preceding programme. By the end of 2019, the Bank of England had purchased over a quarter of the UK gilts in existence at the time (£435 billion out of £1.616 trillion).[4] Then when Covid arrived, things really took off, with massive further purchases.

Chart 3.19 shows how interest rates have been gradually driven down over the past couple of decades or more by these programmes.[*]

Chart 3.19: UK Ten-Year Gilt Bond Yield, 2000–2024

Until Covid started subsiding, interest rates were being remorselessly driven down by central bank intervention in the long-bond market. After that, the withdrawal of intervention resulted in a return to less distorted market-level rates.

Source: FRED,[5] moyniteam analysis

As Chart 3.19 shows, the most visible result from QE was a substantial and ongoing reduction in long-term interest rates, over

---

[*] A useful and enjoyable lay review of these actions by central banks in the time of QE is Chris Leonard's *The Lords of Easy Money*. It's a compelling read about how QE and other easy money boosts have driven the US economy into problematic territory.

a very long period. Economists Tim Congdon, Ben Bernanke, Mervyn King and others offer persuasive arguments that a large QE programme was necessary to stop the 2007–8 recession becoming the great depression of the 2010s.* However, QE extended well beyond what was necessary to mitigate the impact of the financial crisis, and subsequently seems to have been used in a despairing attempt to boost sluggishly growing economies – a recipe offered by demand-side Keynesian economics, a school of thought that has dominated central bankers' thinking since at least the end of the Second World War. Critics of this approach, such as myself, counter that by lowering interest rates, the economy is stimulated not by increasing its productive capacity through needed productivity improvements, but by stimulating demand and thus keeping enterprises alive that would otherwise have failed. The economy becomes a zombie economy that needs continued propping up through ever-continued, ever-greater stimulus. This view does ignore the fact that excess money creation was needed because a draconian tightening of bank credit and capital rules, principally from the new Basel III regulations, had by 2011 led to a massive drop in the money supply.[6] Without that, QE might not have been needed – or certainly, wouldn't have been needed so much.

Anyway, as the chart shows, in the end you cannot push rates down for ever, however much you intervene to distort liquidity flows. Sooner or later, a more natural rate must reassert itself, reflecting true risk and return. As we would expect, and as Chart 3.19 shows, that is what has now happened in the UK.

The impact of these rate movements, with interest rates going down over many years and then back up over a rather shorter period

---

* Congdon is of the view that QE has little impact on bond rates. See *Money in the Great Recession*, p. 62. Many, including this author, disagree (for once) with him.

of time, is far worse than, at first sight, it might seem. QE hits both savers and borrowers; and each of these parties is hit twice – first when rates are on the way down and then when they are on the way back up. Let's review how that works for each party.

Savers get hit by QE in the first instance from what is called 'financial repression'. Retirees desire to purchase a steady stream of income for the period of their retirement, so they invest in safe, long-term, fixed-rate assets. During much of the period of QE, such investors received, in many cases, just 1 per cent a year, fixed for ten or more years, for the money they invested, rather than what they would have received in more normal times – which would have been anywhere between 3 and 4 per cent. Adjusted for inflation, that 1 per cent they were receiving was in real terms negative.

Many people, when reading that previous paragraph, tend to mentally shrug and tell themselves they wouldn't have done that; they would have invested their money in short-term assets or equities. They say this because they, like most people, are not yet at the stage in their life when they must look to purchase an assured stream of income. But most saved money is held by those aged fifty-five or older, and at that age – becoming increasingly pressing as one gets near to or beyond retiring – the prime concern of those individuals is for security in old age. That is best achieved, they are advised, through a purchase of long-term, fixed-rate assets – in particular, an annuity (which is usually structured to pay an agreed monthly amount until the holder dies, and it stops).

During the long period of financial repression, rates paid by annuities were pitiful – one third (or even less) of what a saver would more normally expect to receive. And advisers would have told their clients that they must not put off buying that annuity: they couldn't be sure that it wouldn't get even worse for them if they delayed the decision. Once they had bought the annuity, the deed was done. They wouldn't be getting more than the agreed rate from their annuity, ever. Think about that. For the rest of your life, your monthly income is, now that rates have dropped so suddenly, going to be a third or less of what you had expected it would be – and you were pretty much forced into making that low-return investment by the machinations of a central bank. There are probably hundreds of thousands of retirees now in those or similar circumstances.[*]

And that's only the *first* whammy for savers. Their second comes when, as some monetarist[†] commentators had in recent times warned persistently would happen, the excessive growth of money supply leads to inflation. Suddenly, after a couple of years of inflation, that already pitiful income stream from your annuity now buys (if we take the experience of 2020–24) only some three quarters of the already small amount you could get for your money when you originally purchased the annuity. You had, in the first whammy, been whacked by two thirds when interest rates came down; now you have been whacked by a further quarter as rates come back up. So now you're getting one third multiplied by three quarters – that is to say, just a quarter – of the income that you would originally have counted on retiring with.

The enormous impact that this has had upon hundreds of thousands of savers in the UK cannot be exaggerated; for many of them, it will have been pretty much catastrophic, destroying their dreams

---

[*] Similarly, no one seems to be remarking favourably on the considerably improved, life-long benefits now enjoyed by those purchasing annuities in the new higher-rate environment.

[†] Loosely speaking, a monetarist is primarily one who follows the views of Milton Friedman and others in believing that inflation is always and everywhere a function of – the rate at which new money is pushed into the economy. How that is measured and managed, and indeed whether the whole idea is true or not, is hotly contended among economists of various stripes.

of comfortable retirement. (It is amazing to me that, with all the careless talk in the media about the boomer generation scooping the pot, there is so little mention of how, to the contrary, so many of these boomers have been so badly hit.)

Borrowers also get hit twice – in an equivalent but reverse-order way. Financial repression leads to the value of assets (stocks, bonds, houses) shooting up during episodes of QE. So, when during this period an individual had to purchase a house, the price of housing had shot up, so they had to borrow significantly more money than originally expected to finance that house purchase. For the young families who bought their first home during the 2010s, the cost of the home was sky-high, which meant these couples had to borrow far more than they could have expected a few years prior. It was even worse in the UK because its stock of housing is so limited – and, worse, the population was (still is) growing rapidly, so demand increasingly outstripped supply and house prices went up even further. The large amount that people had to borrow ended up, for many of them, costing a huge proportion of their salaries, a cost which would persist over many years to come – far more than they would have had to pay had QE not led to so dramatic an increase in the price of property.

So, that high cost of purchase, leading to higher monthly payments, was the first whammy for borrowers. Their second was precipitated when rates went up in 2021–3. When they had bought their property, low interest rates meant that at first they could just about afford to pay the interest component of the large mortgage. Now, with the QE period coming to an end, that second whammy inevitably arrives, with the monthly interest rates on their mortgages doubling, or more, when the bank increased the rate. With an interest-only mortgage, if 25 per cent of the couple's income had been going on interest payments, now it might easily move up to 50 per cent.

For many borrowers, it could take a decade or more to get themselves out of the hole they now find themselves in from these two whammies. Currently, they hold an expensive home that may not even keep its value in the future, or that may require significant additional investment thanks to new government regulations – heat pumps, insulation etc. This home carries a huge mortgage that has to be paid off, with crippling interest payments on that mortgage. Most of this problem was created for them by excessive QE. The end result of this has been couples earning over £100,000 a year discovering they are now in dire financial straits.[7]

When there is some kind of financial crisis – what economists and central bankers refer to as a 'shock' – calls come from all sides to 'do something' about it. QE mostly came about, from 2008 onwards, to compensate for what was done when the call went up to 'do something' in reaction to the 2007–8 global financial crisis. The narrative among central bank economists was that the Great Depression of the 1930s could have been avoided had there been more stimulus from central banks. So, when the financial crisis erupted, and the collapse of liquidity in the banking market, along with draconian rules on bank lending and capital, threatened to shut the economy down altogether, central banks stepped in with a healthy dose of QE to provide that stimulus.

However, QE was then continued throughout the 2010s because it was seen as having successfully dealt with the 'shock'. But QE was massively overdone, and it might have been better to let the bondholders of the stricken banks sort those banks out without the government taking them over; or to have avoided imposing draconian Basel III rules, which shut down much lending.* Instead, they might have limited themselves to providing only enough QE to avoid the economy totally imploding. Given the general scale of economic shutdown at the time, it would have been a brave central bank that refused entirely to interfere – but it could be argued that any such intervention should have been confined to reorganising the banking market, and certainly not extended to a general QE programme that lasted more than a decade, and whose purpose seems to have been to goose the economy for an indeterminately lengthy period, far beyond what economic circumstances would have dictated. Without that long-term QE in the 2010s, there would have been no financial repression; without QE, or similar money-expanding actions, there would have been no (or, for sure, less) inflation.† And inflation is no small thing – as discussed earlier (and later in this chapter), it can destroy lives. It's worth noting that in the US, inflation was the number one reason that swing voters gave to pollsters in early 2024 for planning to shift their 2020 vote for Biden to a 2024 vote for Trump; it is still, at the time of writing, the major point of contention between Trump and Harris.[8]

As we can see, QE can create identical problems for a nation's economy as it does for its citizens: yo-yo interest rates and inflationary swings in asset values. Our nation as a whole is now in the same position as those house owners in the UK who took on

---

* On the first point in that sentence, Chapter 11 of the US Bankruptcy Code allows corporate restructuring to take place more easily than in the UK, as in the earlier savings and loans crisis there. In 2010, there was much talk of rewriting the UK's bankruptcy laws to achieve the same. That was quickly forgotten (and the US has not used that approach in recent times when it comes to failing banks). The collapse of Lehman Brothers was always going to be painful, but it was made far more painful than it need have been because it had to be sorted out in the UK over many years, before the liquidated assets were fully distributed to creditors. This created huge, value-destroying profits for the receivers.

† As Tim Congdon has laid out, the initial 2010–12 QE did not – despite the fears of many, including myself – result in inflation, because at the same time as QE was deployed, the balance sheets of banks were squeezed by central banks and by new bank regulations, thus lessening the quantity of money in the economy and so negating the inflationary impact of QE pushing money into the economy. But in 2021–2, when the level of QE swamped any shrinkage in the economy from Covid, inflation roared in.

variable-rate mortgages in the 2010s and have suddenly seen their monthly interest payments leap up to levels that they had never imagined would be possible. And just as mortgage holders wish they had converted to a fixed-rate mortgage in time, the UK's Debt Management Office (an off-shoot of the Treasury) must wish that it had issued even more low-coupon, long-term debt when it had the opportunity.*

QE's popularity among central bankers and governments was in large part due to its being not much more than an extension of how the neo-Keynesian view has, at least until recently, seemed to operate: always acting as if stimulation was needed. Both Alan Greenspan and Ben Bernanke, successive chairmen of the Federal Reserve, took the view that the pockets of the Federal Reserve, and indeed the pockets of any central bank with a money system such as ours, were almost limitlessly deep. Hence QE, the apparent success of which led to a long-running fascination, among those who should have known better, with 'modern monetary theory' (MMT, inevitably also dubbed the 'magic money tree').† MMT is the theory that because countries can control their own currency, operating a 'fiat' monetary system – where as much money as they wish to

---

* The author has a secret sorrow in this regard. When both Philip Hammond and Sajid Javid were Chancellors, he pressed each to push their officials into issuing a £100 billion, fixed-rate debt note, with a term of 100 years, which could have been introduced into the market at a satisfactorily low rate, somewhere between 1 and 2 per cent. My suggestions (and I was not the only one to make them) were responded to dismissively, but had the government done what was suggested, the nation's finances would currently be transformed to the tune of several billion pounds less of interest payments per year, for the next ninety years or more. The failure of our government to seriously consider that proposal at the time would be all very understandable, to be put down to the incompetence of the usual Treasury orthodoxy or whatever, except for the fact that at the time I and others made these suggestions, other countries actually did what we were suggesting. Argentina did (not so successfully, but still they did it) and Austria did so – very successfully, and twice. At the time I pressed the case for it in the UK, the Austrian bond, paying just 0.88 per cent on face value, was already trading well above par. That Austrian bond will be paying that 0.88 per cent for the next 100 years and currently trades at 33 cents. Not so great for investors who were foolish enough to buy it, but it has saved billions for the Austrian state's finances. A large-sized similar 100-year bond would certainly have helped the UK from having its financing arrangements questioned quite so rudely by the bond market in late 2022.

† For masochistic readers, the endnotes attached to the following two sentences (above) give a link to more detail on the delusive MMT view of the world. (These endnotes are best accessed through the QR code at the beginning of the book.)

print can be printed – all desired social projects could be paid for by printing new money without any negative consequences. The idea stemmed from a train of thought started in the early 1900s by Georg Knapp, eagerly embraced later by left-wingers such as Jeremy Corbyn, Bernie Sanders and their supporters.[9] It was extremely popular for a while, even though it was and is nonsense.[10] Following our recent bout of inflation, which showed that there are indeed consequences from issuing too much money, MMT has disappeared from view. But it was only the *reductio ad absurdum* of the neo-Keynesian embrace of excessive money creation through QE.*

QE is the latest wheeze of big-sized, high-tax, high-regulation, low-growth governments, whose fate is to have larger and larger deficits and bigger and bigger levels of debt, until the cost of government has expanded to such a size that it cannot be paid for through ever-increasing borrowing – because larger and larger debt cannot go on for ever. Managing the debt, worrying about deficits, worrying about the impact of taxes that prevent too-high deficits and worrying about inflation are all clearly crucial issues for any government. Experience shows that failure to control these variables properly will lead to inflation and/or a stagnating economy and, in the longer term, to economic collapse. Such a collapse for us would likely proceed slowly, gathering pace over decades, but the logical end result would be inevitable and devastating.

What fiscal and monetary tools are available to governments to prevent such undesirable financial and economic outcomes? A sovereign country, in capitalist systems such as ours, possessing those 'fiat powers' to issue unlimited amounts of its money, has enormous

---

* Greenspan, most definitely not an MMT proponent, nevertheless made a very MMT-friendly claim: 'The US can pay any debt it has because it can always print money to do that, so there is zero probability of default.'

– although not unlimited – scope. Most people agree that a sovereign country can influence:

- *its exchange rate*, by purchases or sales of foreign currency (or, although this is not anything I or most sensible people would recommend, by imposing capital controls).
- *its interest rates*, particularly short-term rates, by setting the overnight rate that it will pay commercial banks on reserves and by influencing longer-term rates such as bond or gilt yields, by buying or selling long-term assets in the marketplace, as in a QE programme. Changing long-term rates usually requires actual or threatened massive intervention. Such interventions can, in theory, and as discussed over previous pages, only work for a while.
- *its national surplus* or deficit and thus the growth or shrinkage in the overall level of national debt, through a combination of overall taxation and spending decisions. This is done through what is known as fiscal policy. The debt level is managed by borrowing money from the capital markets to pay for any financial shortfall in fiscal programmes.
- *its money supply*, by tightening or relaxing the constraints on, or interest levels of, lending by banks and other financial institutions or through using the central bank to purchase financial assets from the marketplace, 'creating money' out of thin air.
- *the level of inflation*, for example by altering the quantity of money circulating in the economy or by setting short-term interest rates.
- *the short-term rate of growth of the economy*, whether by financial stimulus (e.g. by changing tax rates) or indirectly through any of the other items listed here. (As I have argued in both volumes

of this book, while the government can certainly, through its actions, condemn an economy to poor or even negative long-term GDP growth, its best way of *improving* economic growth is to create an environment where entrepreneurs can flourish; and then step back and get out of the way.)

Of course, while most economists are in agreement that governments can and do set out to influence the items on the above list, there is a wide level of disagreement on how the mechanism of each does or should work, and what the level of impact of each is likely to be. Moreover, each of the variables above interacts with the others – which makes for a wide set of possibilities for policy programmes and for disagreement between economists as to expected outcomes.[*]

What are the indicated policies for an economy to enjoy a low level of inflation, appropriate rates of interest, high growth, balanced exchange rates and low debt? To answer this, I briefly review in the following pages the theories about each of these key economic variables, and our economy's actual experience of each, along with the various ways governments seek to influence each item, and to what extent they tend to succeed:

- managing the exchange rate
- managing interest rates
- managing the national deficit/national debt
- creating or combating inflation
- creating an integrated economic policy to ensure (or not) economic growth

---

[*] This is illustrated, for example, by the variety of often conflicting claims made by economists and bankers as to the causes of the high levels of inflation in the UK in recent years.

MANAGING THE EXCHANGE RATE

All the economic variables discussed in this chapter are interconnected with each other and each has to be carefully managed within the context of their 'interconnection'. Because of this, it's quite easy to debauch your economy and end up with a cratered currency. History has so many examples of nations that get busy spending more than they have, printing more money, creating inflation as a result, raising interest rates at the same time as capital flight takes place, and then seeing their currency fall further and further as an inevitable result of getting locked into that vicious cycle. Think Argentina, Venezuela and Zimbabwe. Nearer to home, Turkey has for the past three decades experienced this fate, with the incumbent government spending money it didn't have to get re-elected, creating hyperinflation as a result – so that now Turkey's currency, as Chart 3.20 shows, has lost as much as 99.99 per cent of its 1990 value. So, if you had put 1 million Turkish lira under your mattress in 1990 and kept it there till the present day, it would now buy the equivalent of what just 100 lira would have bought back then.

So, economic mismanagement can swiftly bring on an ongoing pathological failure of the currency. The impoverishment that results – with goods from overseas too costly for most to buy, and any domestic financial wealth destroyed by inflation – is, for most of the country's citizens, devastating.

But even in well-managed economies, currency management is not easy. How should it be approached?

In the previous chapter, we discussed the concepts of comparative and competitive advantage, and the way that countries with strong competitive advantage, and a willingness to focus on and facilitate comparative advantage, can move up the value chain. Let's look at a given country, country X, which as the years go by, follows that approach. It ensures it sells to the rest of the world only its higher-value goods and services, and therefore can see higher wages and increased productivity. Its focus on higher-value sectors leads to its not making goods and services of lower value-added, instead buying them from other countries – even if these other countries are less efficient than country X in those lower-value sectors. We discussed how Switzerland, the most innovative country in the world, steadily moves itself up the value chain, so that bit by bit its national wealth and the buying power of its citizens increases, in no small part because the value of the Swiss franc keeps rising. Since the 1980s, the franc has more than tripled in value against the dollar; in 2023 alone, it rose another 7 per cent.

Chart 3.20: Turkish Lira versus US Dollar, 1990–2024

Against the dollar, the Turkish lira has lost 99.99 per cent of its value since 1990.

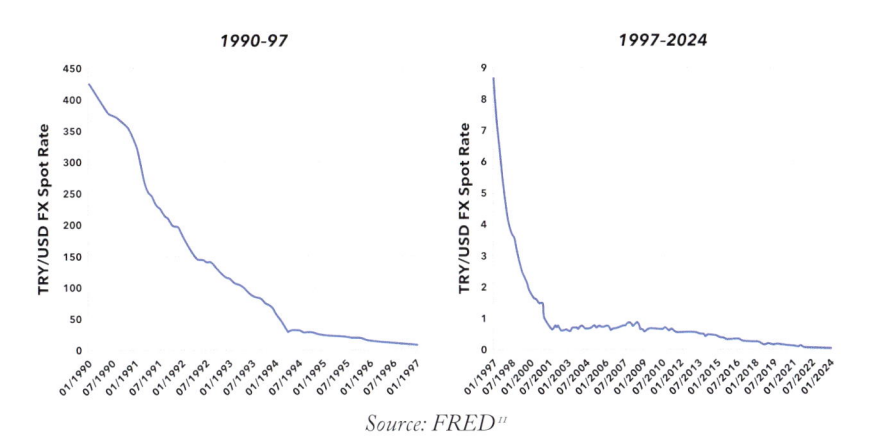

Source: FRED[11]

It is clearly in the interest of country X if its currency steadily increases, if that can be done without pricing its exports out of world markets. The most obvious reason why this process is good for country X is that its citizens can buy the goods of the world very cheaply – the Swiss can buy almost all the (dollar-denominated) goods that we discussed in Volume One of this book for around a third of what they would have had to pay had their currency not increased in value.

As mentioned, a too-high currency can make life hard on country X's exporters, making them constantly search for productivity improvement and competitive advantage. But to date, Switzerland's economy has risen to the challenge. If country X's currency increases to ridiculous levels, exports will tail off and the currency will then over time adjust downward – but none of that is an argument for a country to try to manage its currency down, in a process that can lead to competitive devaluation.[12]

So, the self-same strong currency that makes it a delight to buy cheap goods from the world makes it a very tough slog to sell that country's home-produced goods to the world. This is why exporters have a tendency to call for a weakening of the national currency. It also means that a country's home producers can get overwhelmed with cheaper imports from abroad – great, again, for consumers but not so much for your manufacturing base. And this is why a focus on both competitive and comparative advantage is so important. If your country is not able to develop further competitive and comparative advantage to replace sectors that are losing out to the cheaper goods or services from other countries, you will get unemployment and consequent unrest as a result of the rising value of your currency. In the UK, the continued rise of services is protecting the economy from losing out too greatly from our dropping competitiveness in manufacturing. In some parts of the US, they haven't avoided the crunch, so economic growth is more lopsided there and some parts of the country are being left behind (possibly as a result of misapplied welfare subsidies and the like, which slow down the necessary restructuring of the local economy). There is always a see-saw of need between exporting manufacturers and importing consumers, in an ongoing argument as to what the level of any nation's currency should be; a balance has to be struck between over-protecting no-longer-efficient sectors of the economy, versus moving up the value chain. A failure to innovate, to continuously create and exploit advantage, can lead to economic disarray.

Where would the free-marketeer come down on this issue? Starting at the abstract, theoretical level, we can argue, fairly uncontroversially, that the value of the nation's currency should be at some equilibrium level that is defined by a nation's true set of competitive and comparative advantages (taking into account supply and demand factors such as trade and capital flows, interest rate differentials, inflation rates and market expectations) at any given time. Based on our national strengths, there is an exchange rate that would, absent disruptive events, stay relatively stable as we traded with other nations (or, if our economic system was better than theirs in continually creating advantage, steadily rise).

Once a country accepts the idea that there is indeed a notional equilibrium level, even if we can never be sure what it is at any particular time, it becomes the task of the country (if it is seeking a better life for its citizens) to push its way up the value chain, increasing that equilibrium level – and as a result, increasing the value of the country's currency. This implies a free market for currency trading, so the exchange rate adjusts according to the economic circumstances.

But, in this theoretical circumstance, you can only see the currency move upwards if at the same time you move your economy up the value chain, thus growing your GDP by exploiting your competitive and comparative advantages.* In the worst-case scenario, a failure to be able to do that can lead to what Greece experienced, having failed to create or exploit advantage over past decades. The country's currency is the Euro so they cannot depreciate, and therefore had to go through massive unemployment, impoverishment and misery to restore their competitiveness. Ireland, to a lesser degree, had a similar experience post-2009.†

In the real world, of course, it gets more complicated than merely letting one's currency float. In the short term, like any other asset, the value of a nation's currency depends significantly on liquidity flows. As international markets move money into or out of a country, the currency's value will ebb or grow. For example, if imports get too much larger than exports, then the country's purchases of foreign currency (outflows, to pay for the imports) become too great, relative to the size of purchases by other countries of *its* domestic currency (inflows, which occur when it exports). *Ceteris paribus*, if the demand for our currency exceeds its supply because we are exporting more than we are importing, then the value of our currency is pushed up. If we import more than we export, then the value of our currency over the long term is pushed down. If there is speculation that our currency is going to appreciate or depreciate in value in the future (for instance, due to the expectations of higher or lower interest rates), then speculators jump into the fray, pushing our currency around, sometimes wildly (the most famous example being the time George Soros made several billion pounds in 1992 selling sterling short against the Deutschmark, which we were foolishly trying to peg ourselves against).

---

* If every country does the same, your currency will not appreciate – but all countries, including your own, will get wealthier nonetheless, by improving their productivity and moving up the value chain.
† Ireland's mature reaction to that shock has led to its national finances now being among the fittest in the world.

So, as interest rates and currencies move around, currency traders seek to make money in a further activity, known as 'covered interest arbitrage'. If two countries have different interest rates, the relative spot prices of their currencies should be a function of their expected future prices, discounted back by those different interest rates. One country with a higher interest rate than another will have a lower currency value now, relative to the expected value of its currency in the future, and any small variation in that number, away from what the maths say it should be, will allow the currency trader to make money by arbitraging away the difference. Sometimes, uncovered arbitrage takes place in what is called the 'carry trade', in which traders bet that the exchange rate won't move to the degree that the difference in interest rates currently predicts. (This is basically speculation; because of their riskiness, bets of this sort have been dubbed 'the widow maker'.)

All in all, a pretty bewildering situation for any country trying to manage its currency. All these different liquidity flows, arbitraging, speculators betting on your currency, the impossibility of knowing precisely what and how large your country's set of competitive and comparative advantages are, your exporters pressing you to keep the currency low – which, if you do, means your imports will cost more, creating potential inflationary pressures. Oh dear.

But free-marketeers have the answer: the best information about what level your currency should be is the information created from the actions of the millions of players in the market who determine these things. Not by governments. So, there's a simple rule: at first, keep your inflation down so you won't have to print money to the degree that your currency collapses. Then, *let your currency float free* and focus instead on doing the right things to improve your economy. Don't create an inflationary situation, don't attract speculators by attempting to keep your currency at an unrealistic level. Encourage your exporters, but at the same time recognise that imports represent a benefit to your country in terms of meeting both consumer and commercial needs and desires. Over time, if you do the right things economically – with good education, low taxes, small government and no protectionism – then your competitive and comparative advantages will increase and so will your currency. You have made the first steps in emulating Switzerland.

I try to sum all of that up in Chart 3.21.

Chart 3.21: How a Government Should Manage Its Currency

Governments should not target a given exchange rate but rather should embrace policies that, over time, will result in the steadily increasing value of their currency.

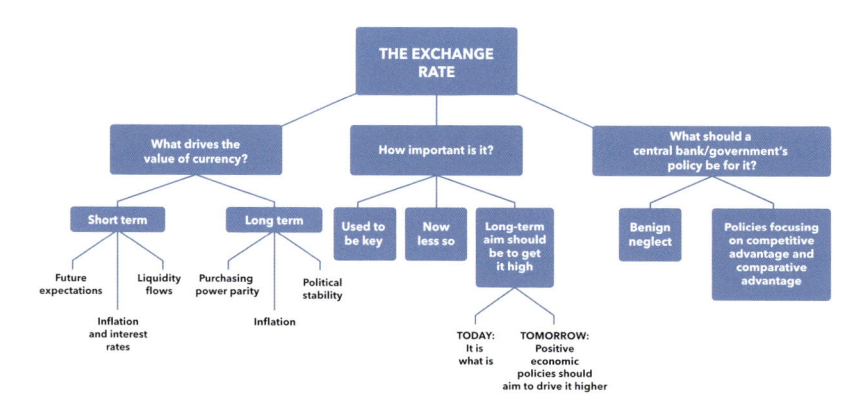

A crucial reason for benign neglect of your currency is that if a particular exchange rate is targeted in addition to your targeting some other economic measure – for example, inflation – then, at some stage, the two objectives will fairly inevitably clash with each other. As we show later in the chapter, this can be catastrophic (and lead to Soros-style events). Essentially, as virtually all economists now agree, you can't simultaneously manage exchange rates and interest rates unless you have capital controls,* which are highly inadvisable in a free society.† ¹³ There is a theory called the Mundell–Fleming trilemma, or the 'unholy trinity', which says that there are three options: an independent monetary policy, free capital flows or a fixed exchange rate. Any country must choose no more than two options out of these three; achieving a desired target for all three of them is unattainable. In the UK, we (rightly) go for options one and two. Individual European economies go for two and three. China goes for one and three. Because we target one and two, we need to allow the exchange rate to float.

If you don't care to manage interest rates, you can have a fixed currency rate or currency board (see Hong Kong). It's unclear how much that helps, unless you are strongly dependent on imports, because if you want to fiddle with interest rates, you need to float your currency. A stronger currency is the ultimate objective, and creates huge benefits for any country that can sustain that stronger level. However, a stronger currency is only reached in the long term through other beneficial economic successes.

There are always advocates who see the level of the nation's currency as some kind of totemic issue, with a 'weak' currency being seen as a blow to the nation's pride. Allowing such views to sway economic decisions can be destabilising; the market will know, better than such decision-makers do, what the level of the currency should be. If a currency sinks, it is either due to liquidity flows such as a speculative attack (in which case, since the speculation of that sort cannot last for ever, *ceteris paribus* the currency will recover),

---

* A capital control is where a company or individual is not allowed to make purchases abroad unless authorised by the government; and for individuals, they're not allowed to take more than a small amount out of the country for a holiday – between 1945 and 1980, the allowed amount in the UK was £50 only.

† Particularly because few will want to invest capital in your country if they're banned from eventually getting it, or its profits, out.

or because of deeper issues with the economy (in which case, it is those issues that should be addressed, not the currency). In certain cases, currency devaluation allows the country to restore its competitiveness and help recover the economy. This is what would have happened in Greece had it not adopted the Euro, most likely mitigating its painful decade-long adjustment through austerity and economic misery.

So, benign neglect for the currency. What about the other big financial and economic items? We move on to the next: the management of interest rates.

MANAGING INTEREST RATES

The interest rate set in any specific lending transaction will depend on a variety of circumstances and considerations, each of which have to be taken into account when setting the rate:

- The first consideration: the foundational, risk-free rate. What is the reasonable rate that private lenders would, in normal circumstances, seek to be paid when offering a short-term (overnight) loan to a risk-free borrower?[*]
- The second consideration: creditworthiness of the borrower. Lenders add on an additional rate called the 'credit risk premium' when lending to riskier entities. The amount added on varies with the level of risk of the borrower – the riskier the borrower, the more of a credit risk premium you'll want to charge.
- The third consideration: inflation risk. For the lender to be happy,

---

[*] The normally accepted definition of the risk-free borrower is an AAA-rated national government. As a given nation's economy becomes less sound, a credit risk premium is added on to the risk-free rate.

the interest rates the lender expects to receive over the life of the loan have to be 'real'; that is to say, the monies to be received have to reflect current and future expected inflation. The additional amount that a lender will expect to receive, as a function of existing and expected inflation during the term of the loan, is known as the 'inflation premium'.

- The fourth consideration: the additional risk of not being repaid if the money is going to be lent out for a longer period. This is called the 'term liquidity premium'. The longer you give your borrower to pay you back, the higher is the credit risk you are taking that something will happen with the borrower that results in the loan becoming unrepayable. The longer the repayment term, the greater is this term liquidity risk – and therefore, the more the borrower will be charged for the loan. At the same time, the borrower is prepared to pay the lender more, for not having potential problems from having to repay the loan in the short term.[*]

- The fifth consideration: the risk of having the interest rate you have to pay increased at regular intervals during the term of the loan. This is called the 'term repricing premium' – the additional amount a borrower has to pay for the interest rate being fixed for a lengthy period, rather than the payable interest rate repricing regularly during the life of the loan. (Think of a variable-rate mortgage versus a long-term fixed-rate one.) The loan itself may not need to be repaid for many years, but the interest rate you pay

---

[*] Mismatching the liquidity profiles of their assets and liabilities was what led to the collapse (a 'liquidity crisis') of the UK's building societies such as Northern Rock in 2008; their assets (loans, particularly mortgages) were long-term and therefore provided little or no liquidity, while their liabilities (e.g. borrowings from other banks) came due in the short-term. When the liabilities came due, there was no money to pay them. Therefore, collapse of bank. Note that these banks were only illiquid; they were not bankrupt (the value of their illiquid assets was greater than the value of their too-liquid liabilities).

for the loan can change regularly during the term of the loan.* This term premium is usually positive and is derived from the yield curve (discussed earlier) that prevails at the moment of issuance.

To understand the difference between the fourth and the fifth types of risk, consider that one can extend a loan to not be repaid for seven years (this defines the term liquidity risk) but arrange nevertheless that the rate charged to that borrower will be refixed every month (this defines the term repricing risk).

So, as long as no one (such as the government or the central bank) interferes, the rate which a lender will require they be paid when lending is the risk-free rate, plus the risk premium, plus the inflation premium, plus the term liquidity premium, plus the term repricing premium.

We know that the lower interest rates are, then the more economic activity we are likely to have in the short term – that's why QE was so attractive. But unless those rates are low for valid reasons (as opposed to being squashed low through financial repression), they will be temporary, while the economy will be distorted. For interest rates to be low, the risk of the borrower needs to be as low as possible, and above all, the actual and potential future levels of inflation need to be as low as possible.† And, if it can be achieved without too much expense, the average term of the country's debt load needs to be long, to avoid too much debt coming due at any given point in time,

---

* Mismatching the repricing profiles of their assets and liabilities was what led to the collapse of the US's regional banks, such as Silicon Valley Bank in March 2023; they had invested in long-term fixed-rate assets but were funding these investments with variable-rate borrowings, at which point interest rates shot up in 2022-3. The banks' margins went negative while at the same time the value of the assets collapsed.

† For some reason, it is generally accepted that any central bank's target level of inflation should be around 2 per cent rather than zero. The author has yet to find a plausible reason as to why that is a good thing – apart from the mildly enraging point that a bit of inflation reduces the cost of repaying the government debt without disturbing lenders too much. A few, such as Congdon, prefer 1 per cent. To the (admittedly not an economist) author, 0 per cent seems to be a perfectly good target.

favouring fixed rather than variable rates, so as to avoid a sudden large increase in the level of debt service, with a ladder of debt of different maturities, and some but not a lot of the debt index-linked (not too much, given our vulnerability to episodes of inflation).

Intervening in the market so as to push long and short rates away from the levels created by this list of considerations – seeking to distort the 'natural' levels of these rates – is mainly done through injecting new liquidity flows into and out of the banking system. If the central bank increases the money supply, rates go down (money becomes cheap) and vice versa. For short-term rates, this is done (putting it simplistically) by setting the rate the bank will pay for overnight money.* For long-term rates, this is achieved by buying long-term assets (QE) or selling them (QT). All such actions, seeking to impact interest rates, are essentially distortive. When the impact of the action ceases, interest rates will return to their 'natural' equilibrium levels. So, the more you try to fiddle with interest rates, the more they are likely to eventually boomerang back at you.

As we will see when we get to the section on inflation, actions taken to keep interest rates down that are too aggressive can lead to instability and, in the end, disaster. QE led to an apparently benign period of ultra-low interest rates and low inflation during the 2010s, but for all of that time, savers were, as discussed earlier, heavily punished by artificially low levels of interest and were, as a consequence, encouraged to spend more than would have been their true or natural propensity in the absence of financial repression. There was no way that situation could be brought to a benign conclusion.

---

* Market absolutists (with whom I have sympathy) believe that central banks can't, except for very short periods, control short-term rates, let alone long-term ones; the central banks are just town criers, announcing the result of what Mr Market has already decided. This argument has some power, although undeniably bank announcements and actions of various types do, in the short term, move interest rates.

Eventually, burgeoning inflation and the need to unwind huge stocks of purchased assets resulted in the inevitable policy reversal from QE to QT. Bond markets were roiled,* and the central banks of various major economies lost hundreds of billions by having to sell their QE-purchased assets for less than what they had paid for them.†

Low interest rates and freely available money also keep afloat 'zombie' companies: ones where it might, from the perspective of the economy overall, have been better if they were pushed into bankruptcy and restructured, with their assets and capabilities redirected towards more productive, higher value opportunities. Since the dot-com crash of 2001, there has been a lot of commentary regarding zombie companies inappropriately kept on life support by such tactics as QE.

The lesson from this? As with exchange rates, central banks should leave interest rates alone as much as possible. The less we interfere, the fewer negative (even if unintended) repercussions will occur down the line. Instead, we should focus only on growing money at the rate that is justified by the concurrent level of growth in our economy. If, after any boom (booms, especially artificially stimulated ones, will be less frequent under such a regime) and its inevitable subsequent bust, a somewhat deeper recession then eventuates, in which more zombie companies go under, the subsequent

---

* The Bank of England's QT announcement was much more sudden than that of any other central bank.
† Some people claim that no one has been the loser from that aspect of QE, since it only boiled down to money creation or destruction. But from another point of view, the economy became distorted and inflation was created. During QE, the government was initially able to show gains (in the bonds it had purchased), in a way that lowered the reported fiscal deficit. Thus, the government could, because no one argued against it, sneakily spend more than they otherwise could have. At the same time, the threat of deflation and recession grew because in order to choke off inflation, the central banks had eventually to tighten the money supply through QT. This meant that the purchased bonds showed losses. Because of the losses, the government's reported deficit increased, so the government can now spend less than it otherwise could. Sir John Redwood and others state that the bonds need not be sold off, but the losses are still there; it seems to me that dealing with that loss either way is just an accounting, not an economic, difference.

recovery from the bust will, Austrian economists would argue, be quicker, aiding a process that redeploys capital to more viable, future-proofed and economy-growing enterprises.*

Overall, the manipulation of interest rates is tempting to governments and central banks, but it results in only short-term gratification. Stimulating the economy by artificially depressing interest rates comes back to bite you in the bum; all that happens is that rates eventually go back up again, having distorted the shape of the economy in the meantime. Worse: for a while, the subsequent higher rates will most likely overshoot, to a level above the 'natural' level. That depresses economic activity and will enrage existing borrowers – especially those with variable-rate mortgages.

MANAGING THE NATIONAL DEFICIT AND THE NATIONAL DEBT

The national deficit or surplus

Fiscal policy is essentially a combination of how much the government taxes and how much it spends – ostensibly (as the IMF like to put it) to 'promote strong and sustainable growth and reduce poverty'.[14] In reality, however, governments of all stripes know that unless they are re-elected, they will not be able to implement any of their policies at all, so they use fiscal policy to target select political constituencies whose votes they are seeking, and as a result usually spend overall more than the country can afford. This is what leads – particularly in social democracies, whose ethos is based on redistributive policies – to high taxes and also, usually, to government deficits. Managing the annual deficit, and through it overall

---

* As I argue later, the economic programme I proposed in Volume One, of simultaneous cuts in expenditure and taxes, requires a lean to the (somewhat) accommodative if we are to avoid massive societal disruption. But that is only to a degree: we have already experienced what happens when the neo-Keynesians have their way.

government debt, then becomes the problem. When the handouts (and as very often accompanies them, the soft or hard corruption) get too great and the deficit gets too large, such as in the case of Argentina, Venezuela or Turkey, the economic slide gathers pace.

The way in which a nation's debt rises or falls in any given fiscal year is mainly a product of the difference that year between revenues and outgoings – which is mostly equivalent to tax revenues minus government expenditure. (Expenditure includes the cost of servicing the usually steadily increasing debt.) Roughly speaking, if the difference between expenditure and revenue is positive one year (a deficit), then national debt goes up. If it's negative (a surplus), then national debt goes down.

The policies that determine movement in the debt size are known as fiscal policies. The word 'fiscal' comes from the Roman word *fiscus*, which had two meanings: the public treasury and the emperor's private purse. The public treasury occupies multiple column inches in the media; forests die each year from the policy papers written on the topic, and it is *the* central issue for the UK's Treasury. Fiscal policy is a large subject, and different policies have very different effects. In particular, fiscal policies can be split into:

- *Demand-side policies* that are intended to incentivise increases in spending in the economy. Examples include lowering consumption taxes, such as VAT, or lowering income taxes so as to leave more in the pocket of the citizen – in either case, encouraging higher consumption and investment expenditure in the economy. Similarly, increasing the level of benefits paid out by the government can stimulate demand (although if you pay for the benefits by taxing other citizens, the overall consumption won't change – some will spend less and some will spend more. This stimulation

only works when the government borrows, which cannot be a forever strategy.) To the extent that there is a Treasury orthodoxy, then it includes a penchant for encouraging the demand side of the economy; but more through redistribution and borrowing, than by lowering taxes.
- *Supply-side policies*, which are intended to incentivise entrepreneurship and thus increase productive capacity, stimulating growth in the economy and the creation of new businesses and products – for example, making it more attractive to companies to allocate internal resources to innovation. Supply-side policies encourage investments and activities that lead to genuine growth in the economy, rather than just temporarily boosting consumption.

The subject of demand-side versus supply-side economic policies has, over the years, become massively politicised. Many demand-side advocates – those whose politics are usually to the left of centre – demonise supply-side economists, claiming that incentivising the growth of supply in order to grow the economy is incoherent or is 'tax breaks for the rich'. The unusually vehement attacks on supply-side economics from the left are in the main because demand-side economics are the heart of neo-Keynesian politics (this comes back to the old argument about dividing up the cake in different ways versus increasing the size of the cake). If the key to achieving sustainable economic growth in the long run is to incentivise entrepreneurs and businesses to invest, so that they take risks and thus grow the economy, then clearly being not overly horrible to the rich and to businesses has to be the sensible thing to do.

Supply-side advocates do, as accused, advocate lower top rates of income tax for the rich, because they believe that if a rich person chooses to exercise their God-given right not to participate in or invest in the country's economy, that's not going to help economic growth. Investors need to have a positive incentive to invest. Punitive taxes on rich people and anti-business regulations have, in the past few years, led to a mass (and continuing) exodus both of the rich, and of international companies, from the UK, as I showed in Volume One. That exodus has had a highly negative impact on our economic growth. And even if a rich person stays in this country, the higher the tax rate that they are required to pay on their income or their investments, the less they are incentivised to work or invest – instead, they sit on their cash and capital.

The impact of lower taxes on individuals is important, and lower taxes are equally influential in their incentivising effect on corporations. Tax credits, low corporation tax, low business rates for high street businesses, attractive capital gains rates for riskier investments; these are the things that lead to business growth. Volume One showed in great detail precisely why and how tax policies that focus on the supply side will massively improve the rate of economic growth in a country. So, supply-side policies work, and are more impactful on long-term economic growth than are demand-side policies.

In summary, managing the public treasury is in the first place a matter of (a yawningly obvious point) trying not to spend much more than you are going to raise in taxes. As we have seen, high taxes lead to low growth – so don't over-spend, and you won't have to over-tax. To the degree that you do spend, spend as much as possible on supply-side encouragement, not demand-side subsidy. The best way to stimulate the supply side is for the government not to spend so much; so confine economic activity as much as possible to within the private sector, and lower the taxes that inhibit and suppress business activity.

Getting it wrong, especially splurging on the demand side (for example, by giving large increases to public-sector workers without productivity improvements, as the new government has just done), can result in further deficits, the need for higher, growth-reducing taxes, and (for all these reasons) slower long-term growth. The worse you manage the public treasury, the bigger the deficit and the national debt and the slower will be the growth.

The national debt

Labour's Halloween Budget overtly espoused increasing the deficit, even though the moynicurve (see Volume One) means tax revenues will fall short and this will make the deficit even larger. So we will have to borrow more; much more. When does national debt get to be too big? What level of debt service is too great for a nation to be able to afford other necessary expenditures? Whatever the number, the first part of Volume One made it clear that we will, if we carry on as we are, find out.

Fiscal policy, including national borrowing, is an entire sub-branch of economics; hundreds of books, monographs and theses have been written on the subject. Obviously, I can't hope to replicate all that discussion, let alone come up with answers to these questions in this book. But – and beyond pointing out the obvious fact of how wonderful it would have been not to have, as we currently do, 11 per cent of the national budget devoted to servicing our national debt in 2023 – it is possible to get a general sense of what level of debt is supportable, at what level it is burdensome and at what level it starts getting dangerous.

In 2010, the economists Carmen Reinhart and Kenneth Rogoff made a seminal contribution to the discussion in a paper published in the *American Economic Review*, entitled 'Growth in a Time of Debt'.[15] The heart of their thesis was that, simplistically speaking, once a nation has increased its debt to above 90 per cent of its GDP, the country is embarked on a voyage of no return towards permanent low growth and ever-ballooning debt. They asserted that 'median growth rates for countries with public debt over roughly 90 per cent of GDP are about one per cent lower than otherwise'. Even at the time of publication, it was clear there could be issues with this view; then a student examined their paper and found a basic flaw in Reinhart and Rogoff's Excel spreadsheet.[16] Cue red faces. After the back-and-forth discussion that resulted, it became generally accepted that the Reinhart and Rogoff result holds *some* water, but their claim for a permanent negative impact from going above 90 per cent is not now as clear-cut as the original paper seemed to have discovered – a fortunate bit of news for the UK, as we currently have risen to around the 100 per cent debt-to-GDP level. Rather, we might say that at 90 per cent and above – i.e. even well below where we are now – the level of debt, already costly, becomes increasingly burdensome, taking up such a portion of the national budget that it constrains the country from spending on other, obviously more desirable things. (Infrastructure, anyone?) The higher and higher cost of debt service makes it more and more difficult to get the level of debt lower – an unsustainable, vicious spiral of debt and cost.

Regardless of the theoreticians, quite a few countries have approached – and burst through – that 90 per cent barrier, as can be seen from Chart 3.22 (also shown as Chart 1.26 in Volume One). Unsurprisingly, those high debt burdens belong to countries whose economic growth rates haven't been great. High levels of debt can be recovered from: our debt levels were about 200 per cent of GDP at the end of the Napoleonic Wars and the Second World War, and we gradually got them down. But those recovery periods involved considerable national austerity and hardship, which had to be sustained over very long time periods. So, the more we increase our debt, the more painful the eventual required recovery period will be – even if the electorate comes to agree to a long period of austerity.

Chart 3.22: General Government Debt as a Percentage of GDP
Advanced social democracies and hybrid economies, 2000 versus 2023

In the past two decades, many advanced economies have increased their level of national debt by enormous amounts. Debt levels cannot go on increasing at that rate for ever.

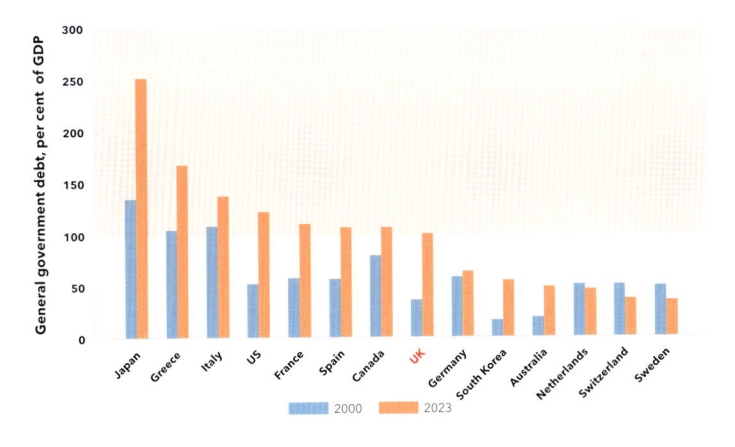

Note: This chart is also shown in Volume One as Chart 1.26
Source: International Monetary Fund[17]

The OBR has forecast that our national debt will rise to almost 300 per cent of GDP in less than fifty years if we carry on with the path we are on.[18] This makes my own warnings seem somewhat milquetoast, but in reality, if our debt started to run away from us towards the level of that sort, far worse things would happen to our economy than a bad debt ratio. The international markets would have called a halt to lending to us long before, and we would risk finding ourselves in a massive, austerity-fuelled depression, possibly accompanied by hyperinflation – an Argentina or a Turkey. At some stage, and the sooner the better, we have to get to grips with our current depressing and dangerous financial incontinence.

As can be seen from Chart 3.22, the UK is, like many other indebted advanced nations, already well above the Reinhart and Rogoff 90 per cent barrier. And when we extrapolate the UK's current levels of debt, deficit and GDP growth, our 'status-quo' model shown at the end of Volume One calculates that our debt will grow to some 150 per cent of GDP in fifteen years' time (the OBR, as discussed, forecasts worse). Now, the Reinhart and Rogoff thesis was clearly simplistic and to a degree flawed. In the UK, we piled up debt drastically during Covid – much of it to fund the costs of, I would argue, unnecessary later lockdowns. Will we now embrace the 'austerity' that is needed to repay that money, even if only at the mild level initiated in the early 2010s by George Osborne? That's not happening at present, given the proclivities of our new Labour government. Can we, should we, take on much more debt, as the new government's policies require? Spending even further beyond our means just to placate the electorate will result in ever-increasing debt. And yet, for the next five years at least, we most likely face ever-widening deficits and a greater prospect of national bankruptcy.

As we discussed earlier, debt-service costs for the UK in 2022/23 took up – it might be thought scandalously – over 11 per cent of the entire national budget. The cost of these interest payments was £128.4 billion.[19] One odd thing is that this shocking number drew very little attention in the media at the time – yet imagine how many hospitals, how many houses, indeed how many miles of HS2, could have been built with that money? Or by how much could taxes have been reduced, leaving our citizens richer than they are today?

Why was our cost of debt so high in recent years? One reason, hardly mentioned in most commentary, is the fact that the markets can't trust us not to generate future inflation, so they demand a higher interest rate from us than they demand from other countries. We discuss inflation a few pages on, but here I introduce the fact that during the Covid episode, out of all the major developed countries, we in the UK had *one of the worst inflation rates of all*, as Chart 3.23 shows. That chart also proves that the worse your inflation record has been, the worse your ten-year bond yield (a benchmark of what you have to pay bond buyers for the credit they extend to you) will be.

Chart 3.23: The Impact of a Country's Inflation Record on Its Cost of Borrowing

The worse a country's inflation record, the more it has to pay for its debt.

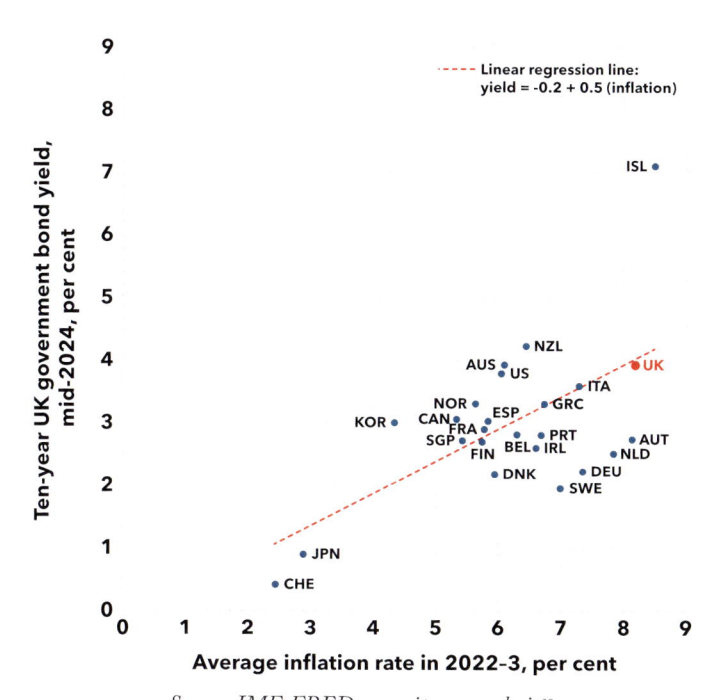

Source: IMF, FRED, moyniteam analysis[20]

Had we had less inflation, the cost of new debt would be considerably lower; as the chart shows, had we been merely in the middle of the pack on inflation, our bond yields would, indicatively, have been some 1.5 percentage points lower. This translates over time to an enormous saving: once all our debt has repriced, and if the situation remains as it is currently, we will be paying some £40 billion (1.5 per cent of £2.7 trillion) more a year, at the level of debt we currently have, than if we had achieved just the average (still uncomfortably high) level of inflation of the countries shown in the chart.

A further reason for the mammoth size of our debt service costs in 2022/23 was the fact that a great deal of the cost – some £57.3 billion, or 45 per cent of our total public-sector debt interest – was that year's payment to holders of index-linked government bonds.* In what was thought to be a terrific wheeze at the time, the UK started issuing index-linked bonds in March 1981.[21] At the time of writing, £608 billion, or almost 25 per cent of our national debt, is index-linked.[22]

At times, especially in the latter part of the 2010s, these bonds were eagerly snapped up, to such a degree that investors were prepared to accept a negative return on them for many years. (Not now, of course.) Issuing them seemed fine at the time; it met the needs of savers who wanted reassurance against any possible future depredations from inflation. But – another of those big buts – it was only a good idea for our country *so long as we could comfortably expect that inflation would be kept down*. Were inflation to flare up, the strategy would rebound against itself. Inflation did flare up, caused by reckless, feckless, monetary policy. The strategy has

---

* The payment was accrued and rolled up into the bond, thus increasing future years' payments and increasing the eventual amount to be repaid.

proved extraordinarily costly for the nation, with massive payments passed to the bondholders for each year that inflation has stayed up. It's not surprising that inflation was so high for a couple of years. As will be discussed, our policymakers at the time showed all the signs of having no clue as to what the underlying causes of inflation were. (One wonders if officials whispered to them that a sharp bout of inflation would do wonders to reduce the real value of the nation's debt. One hopes not.)

There has, bemusingly, been little interest in, and therefore very little review of, the retrospective desirability or otherwise of past years' issuance of index-linked bonds. Inflation has now subsided, but how certain are we that it will not return – spurred, for example, by another bout of money printing that could be necessitated by excessive public-sector pay rises and moynicurve-style[23] shortfalls in tax receipts?* Should we be risking any further issuance of index-linked bonds?

Of course, in real, inflation-adjusted terms, the government paid no greater amount of interest on these index-linked bonds than they were paying before inflation came, and for the country's non-inflation-linked bonds, they ended up, as a result of the inflation, paying *less* than when the inflation came. A fixed-rate bond is in real terms worth much less after a period of high inflation. In this way, inflation bails out governments from some of the consequences of their financial incontinence, but their citizens, as we have seen from the QE discussion earlier, suffer terribly. Those buying any new bond issuance then come to demand that even higher interest rates be paid on these new bonds, to compensate for the investors'

---

* See Volume One for a fuller explanation of the moynicurve.

fears that the UK government, already proven to be feckless on the inflation front, is likely in future to repeat those mistakes.

Chart 3.24: Share of Index-Linked Bonds in Government Debt Portfolio, 2023

The UK government has issued a large number of index-linked gilts since their introduction to the UK market in 1981. The larger western economies were more cautious than we were.

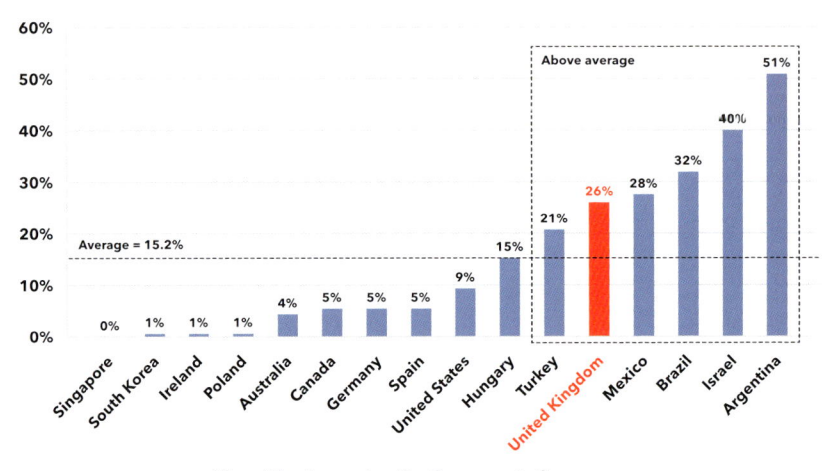

Country	%
Singapore	0%
South Korea	1%
Ireland	1%
Poland	1%
Australia	4%
Canada	5%
Germany	5%
Spain	5%
United States	9%
Hungary	15%
Turkey	21%
United Kingdom	26%
Mexico	28%
Brazil	32%
Israel	40%
Argentina	51%

Average = 15.2%

Note: The data point for Germany is from 2020.
Source: Bank for International Settlements,[24] National Treasury Management Agency[25]

But anyway, when we add all that up, it's probably not such a great idea to have had such a large amount of a country's debt be in index-linked bonds. If there's no inflation, it's cost you less for sure, but if there is inflation, you have to pay your bondholders the cost of that (which you wouldn't have had to do had the debt not been inflation-linked). The only country entitled to issue a lot of such bonds is that rare nation that has good reason to believe there will be no future burst of inflation. That's not us! Yet unfortunately, as Chart 3.24 shows, the UK holds much more index-linked debt than its comparator countries, with over a quarter of our debt in that category. From that chart, we might guesstimate that a more desirable – or anyway, prudent or typical – level might at most be between 10 per cent and 15 per cent, not 26 per cent as we have. That lower level should most certainly have been the more sensible choice if we are to accept that our central bank, the Bank of England, has failed to understand what causes inflation – and, therefore, is unlikely to know how to prevent it.

There is also the matter of the maturity and repricing structure of the debt in any nation's overall borrowing. Clearly, during the 'great moderation' (many years of declining inflation), it would have been advantageous to borrow as much long-term cheap money as possible. As discussed earlier, it is always good to have a large long-term component in your debt structure, and indeed, the UK did manage to do somewhat better than many in that regard by issuing a lot of long-term debt (albeit that much of our long-term debt is, negating that advantage, index-linked).

The UK, using the latest available statistics at the time of writing, has 30 per cent of its debt in short-term fixed-rate borrowing, 17 per cent in medium-maturity conventional gilts, 27 per cent in more long-term fixed-interest-rate debt and the remaining 26 per cent in index-linked gilts.[*] [26] There is not necessarily any such thing as an ideal structure, but the non-inflation-linked conventional UK debt has the highest average maturity among developed countries, which means that our interest costs are, beneficially for us, less sensitive to volatility in interest rates (although we have no 100-year bonds, which would make things even better). Now that short- and

---

[*] Short-term borrowing relates to gilts with residual maturity of up to seven years, medium-maturity gilts have residual maturity between seven and fifteen years and long-maturity gilts are those with residual maturity over fifteen years. The data is as of March 2024.

long-term interest rates have risen so much (even though they are now declining somewhat, they are still much higher than in the era of financial repression), and since the markets are still wary of the UK given its inflation record, when our debt eventually matures, we are bound to have to refinance at higher rates than we are paying now, so the cost of debt servicing will get even higher.

Most likely, an ideal structure for a nation's debt would spread the debt's maturity profile more evenly across time periods, and we would have fewer index-linked bonds. But beyond the question of how the ladder is structured, the chief issue is how to get the debt down and have a lower level of debt as a percentage of GDP. This can be accomplished by a combination of running surpluses rather than deficits, and growing the economy more rapidly – the latter being, arguably, easier to pull off than the former.

What sort of debt management policy should a country that has already reached a 100 per cent debt-to-GDP ratio be pursuing? Clearly, one wishes the debt ratio to start declining very soon. But if one immediately cuts expenditure, raises taxes, or both, so drastically that there is a budget surplus, rather than a (small) deficit, then one likely plunges the economy into a recession. That creates its own vicious spiral and would be difficult to emerge from. The conventional wisdom is that if there are too aggressive cuts in expenditure, the risk is of overshoot and the economy being shut down.* In 2023 and early 2024, there was a risk that that was happening. We are now, despite conservative rhetoric from the new government, entering a period with higher levels of expenditure (and the questionable claim of 'investment' as the excuse for some of it), even if

---

* Javier Milei, on the other hand, would disregard this point, saying that such cuts and the consequent pain are a necessity.

the economy doesn't grow; and therefore larger and larger deficits. We're stepping boldly down the rocky road of social democracy.

The 100 per cent debt-to-GDP figure has to be recognised as a result of cumulatively foolish policy decisions in the past; and now, in the present, a fact to be dealt with. In the next five years, it's almost certain to get larger. Turning the tanker of state around, under a more prudent government, so that the debt-to-GDP ratio starts declining, will have to be done with care. But it has at some stage to be done if we are to avoid a chaotic, impoverished future.

This leads us on to the question of what sort of policy should accompany the programme of expenditure reductions and tax cuts that I laid out in Volume One. In theory, since the reductions on both sides (tax and spend) go hand-in-hand, resulting in a balanced budget, there should be few concerns regarding inflation or over/under stimulation of the economy. It is possible, however, that the impact of the expenditure reductions will precede that of the tax cuts, given that any who are receiving less as a result of the expenditure cuts will pull back their own personal spending immediately, whereas those in receipt of tax-cut money will likely spend some of it but also save some of it. That combination may be contractionary on the economy, and there will need to be a major shift in employment patterns, out of public-sector-related work and into the private sector. This shift will also take time before its effect on the economy turns positive. Two implications for the economy there, and both in the negative direction.

This implies that the policies conducted during this time should be accommodative, rather than imposing further restrictions on the economy. Done wrong, or overdone, this would carry with it the danger of not only undesirably large deficits but also overstimulation. So, accommodative, while ensuring the money supply does not grow too fast, and only during a short period – between one and two years. The accommodation should be quickly dropped as soon as the stimulative impact of the supply-side changes takes effect. The long-term plan must be to get the level of debt – both absolute and relative to GDP – down.

Does a country need to have debt at all? There are various good reasons why a country needs to issue bonds – for example, to attract foreign investment, set a standard for interest rates for mortgages, for corporate and other debt, ensure deep sovereign debt markets that will support the country's liquidity and debt rating, which it always needs. The issue of how much debt a nation needs is similar to the puzzle of what debt-to-equity ratio a corporation should have. But the fact that a *gross* level of debt is arguably needed does not mean the country has to be a *net* debtor. Singapore, for example, has an entire ladder of sovereign bills and bonds, to a total value of slightly under US $1 trillion. Trade in those bonds helps underpin a number of other markets in Singapore and also funds the sovereign wealth funds that help grow Singapore's national wealth. Those sovereign funds have a total value greater than the debt, so Singapore's *net* debt is negative. Happy days! (Of course, this approach is something one can only advocate when, like Singapore, the country has achieved a low-spend, low-tax, high-growth economy.)

In summary, our debt in the UK is at this time rising steadily to undesirable levels. We have high debt-service costs that significantly cut into how much we can spend on our national needs. Our recent inflation added some very large additional costs. Even without more inflation, our increasingly large ongoing yearly deficits will add further to our debt pile, exacerbating yearly the cost of debt service. It is incontrovertible that we have got ourselves in a mess. Getting out will be painful.

Let's move on to the causes and impact of inflation, and how to avoid them.

CREATING OR COMBATING INFLATION

Inflation has an enormously damaging effect on an economy. It impoverishes people, it destroys wealth, it deters investment and ultimately it leads to the sea of catastrophe we already described as having happened to Turkey and other countries. Turkey grew rapidly under Mustafa Atatürk and was even, not so long ago, a candidate to join the EU – now, not so much. Argentina was, more than a century ago, the tenth-richest nation in the world. Venezuela, much more recently, was the richest country in Latin America. Inflation has destroyed the dreams of the populations of these and so many other countries. We have no special dispensation to believe that can never happen to us. Yet agreeing how inflation occurs, and how therefore to control it, is not something that economists have found easy.

Why and how does inflation arise? The answer is that inflation is caused by large, too-fast increases in the money supply, relative to the growth of the economy. The thesis was expressed most succinctly by Milton Friedman: 'Inflation is always and everywhere a monetary phenomenon.'[27]

This understanding has been pretty much universally accepted, yet in recent times it has become, it seems, ignored by most central bankers and economists (our Treasury abandoned the monetarist approach towards the end of the Thatcher era, and the Bank of England ceased even publishing the figures for monetary base M0 in 2006, with the obvious implication being that they no longer think that monetarist views had any credibility). The evidence is compelling that excessive money growth creates high inflation, and I don't know of any rebuttal of that.[28] (In the past year or so, it was interesting to see the Bank of England nonchalantly starting to talk about excess levels of money creation affecting the price level, as though that had been their view all along – yet their policy actions during the Covid years flew in the face of any such understanding.)

The implications of the monetarist (i.e. the correct) view of inflation are distressing for those who embrace neo-Keynesian economics, because it decries too-great stimulation of the economy. Keynesians have ruled the roost in government Treasury departments, in international bodies, and in academia for almost a century now. Even when apparently convinced monetarist Nigel Lawson was Chancellor in the late 1980s, he abandoned his original monetarist approach (apparently in part because he couldn't find a measure of money supply that would allow him to steer a monetary policy). But Keynesian advocates don't understand, or obstinately refuse to acknowledge, that what Milton Friedman's thesis, built on empirical evidence, actually implies is that the more you tinker with lowering rates, or indulge in QE-style behaviour, or incentivise financial institutions to lend more, the more you are likely to ignite inflation. And whatever short-term benefit you get from artificially altering rates, that benefit will have to be returned with interest (pun sort of intended) as rates push back over time to a more natural level (the level that is the clearing price between true demand and true supply for money). As the monetary economist John Greenwood recently put it:

> Every episode of sustained and substantial inflation in the UK has been preceded by a surge in money growth, and that is exactly

what happened in 2020–21 … though fortunately the money growth was not as egregious in 2020–21 as successive British governments had presided over in the 1970s and 1980s.[29]

There is an explanation for why this unarguable monetarist thesis still does not completely rule the roost (although the most recent bout of inflation means that the monetarists are now very much in the ascendant). The reason is that the thesis is a messy one. For a start, all are agreed that there is a time lag, after the increase in the money supply, before inflation starts, and that time lag can vary. Chart 3.25 shows that the lag between the egregious burst of money growth in 2021–22 in the UK, and the consequent rise in inflation, was some two years – a typical lag, but it can be a shorter or a longer time period.

Chart 3.25: Growth in Money Supply and Inflation, January 2013–June 2024

The sudden explosion in the growth rate of broad money between 2020 and 2022 led, with an approximately two-year lag, to a sharp burst of inflation in the UK.

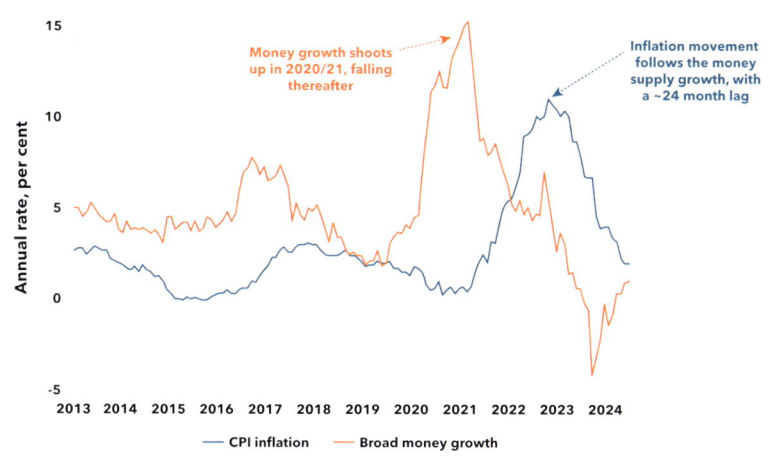

Note: Annual CPI Inflation versus twelve-month growth rate in M4 broad money monthly
Source: Office for National Statistics,[30] Bank of England[31]

A second issue is that there is a lot of argument as to how to define the money supply. Friedman favoured a narrow definition (mostly cash itself, plus central bank reserves), which in fact seems not to have worked well as a measure to predict inflation – something that may have led to Friedman getting less strident about, and Nigel Lawson abandoning, monetarism in the late 1980s. Tim Congdon shows that 'broader' money-supply measures (that include, for example, commercial bank deposits) do a far better job at predicting inflation.[32] That makes sense – after all, for those banks to lend out those deposits, with a consequent increase in bank lending, creates deposits, and thus money – and that point ties very nicely to Hayekian economics, which emphasises the key part played by financial institutions in the boom-and-bust cycle.[*]

Low interest rates, when artificially introduced, stimulate the economy through a variety of ways, in particular by straightforwardly creating money through QE, or encouraging borrowing. The Keynesian focus has always been on how to stimulate demand and thus give a boost to the economy, making sure to avoid any possibility of electorally unappealing economic decline, recession or depression. The supremacy of the Keynesian approach, adopted in the UK by left- and right-wing politicians alike over the postwar years, was transformed into a new incarnation in October 1987 when the head of the Federal Reserve at the time, Alan Greenspan, intervened in the 'Black Monday' market crash, pouring liquidity into the economy to reverse a sudden and startling collapse in US stock markets. Since then, the approach to dealing with market

---

[*] A story illustrating this can be told with respect to the causes of the global financial crisis. In 2009, Dirk Bezemer published an article in the *Financial Times* that reviewed which economists had models which predicted the crash. Bezemer quoted a number of economists who had, in fact, done so. Almost every one of their successful models incorporated, knowingly or not, Hayek's view of the crucial role of financial institutions. See Dirk Bezemer, 'Why some economists could see the crisis coming', *Financial Times*, 7 September 2009, https://www.ft.com/content/452dc484-9bdc-11de-b214-00144feabdc0

shocks that has reigned in the US and elsewhere has been strongly stimulative, coming to be known as the 'Greenspan Put' (discussed earlier). The approach continued in the US up to the present day. For example, in early 2023, a full rescue of several mid- to large-sized US banks, along with all their deposit holders, was put into operation.* The supremacy of the Greenspan Put has been bolstered over many decades by appointing a series of mostly Keynesians, albeit sometimes with monetarist tinges, as Greenspan's successors.

Chart 3.26: UK Short- and Long-Term Interest Rates Before and During the Greenspan Put

After the high-inflation days of the 1970s and 1980s, the reduction of inflation in the early 1980s, followed by stimulative policies but (initially) low or no deficits, ensured that both short- and long-term interest rates fell and fell. After the financial crash of 2007–8, massive QE intervention then brought rates almost to zero. With the return of inflation, short-term rates have now been jacked up and long-term rates are moving back up to more appropriate market levels.

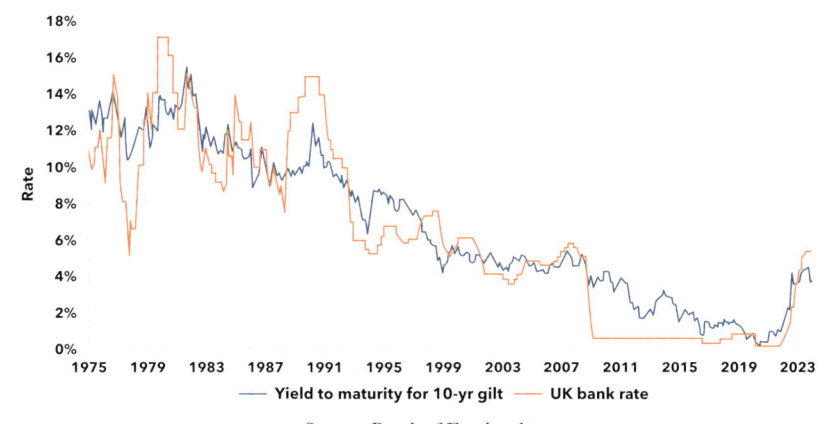

Source: Bank of England[33]

---

* Much of the resolution of this issue was accomplished through private-sector transactions (e.g. JPMorgan Chase purchased the failed First Republic bank). But the whole exercise was overseen by the Federal Reserve, and the Greenspan Put was in place, calming the markets and ensuring there were no ructions during the time it took to put the deals together.

The same approach as in the US has mostly been pursued in the UK. As Chart 3.26 shows, as a result of ongoing QE and other stimulative actions, the UK's short and long rates steadily fell over the more than three decades since 1987, the ongoing decline arguably leading to rates dropping well below an appropriate equilibrium rate – the outcome of an over-reliance on stimulating the economy. Eventually, for most of the 2010s, both short-term and long-term interest rates sank to almost zero. This created a distorted economy: frustrated savers, inflated asset values, goosed-up levels of consumption, and zombie companies – the number of which increases even now.[34]

Post-financial crisis (2010–12), the amount of money poured into the economy raised expectations that inflation sooner or later would have to take off. It didn't. Congdon had predicted that it wouldn't, because at the same time as the Bank of England took those easing actions on money, mostly through QE, it also took counteracting actions to suppress inflation by tightening bank lending conditions, and increasing bank capital and other requirements, thus significantly constraining the money supply.[*][35]

Mervyn King views the issue in a similar way, putting the initial agency onto market participants taking money out of the economy and fleeing to the safest assets – in particular, short-term US bills – and the central bank therefore having to stimulate the economy to prevent recession. He put it this way:

> First, the increase in the supply of money was matched by a sharp increase in demand for highly liquid reserves on the part of the banking system and the economy more generally. Second, the

---

[*] The main reason for those anti-bank actions was a vague sense of two things: that banks needed to be 'punished' for the risk-taking that led to the crisis, and that larger capital buffers would prevent future problems. (They didn't – instead, banks such as Silicon Valley Bank and First Republic took more risk. So, higher regulation had directly led to greater disaster.)

total supply of broad money, including bank deposits, rose only moderately. The 'emergency money' created by the Bank was necessary to prevent a fall in total money supply.[36]

Anyway, the net result of these various circumstances was that there was no burst of inflation in that post-crisis period; yet the economy was distorted, and asset inflation replaced the true economic growth that would have been spurred by greater business lending. And then, during the Covid era, the money supply ballooned and this time there was no countervailing flight to quality or tightening on financial institutions. So, inflation burst through – after the 24-month lag discussed earlier. With that, both short- and long-term interest rates started moving steadily upward – as is shown in the final months of Chart 3.26. Long-term rates are, as previously discussed, more difficult to control than short-term rates. As inflation increased, therefore, they responded to market pressure and drifted steadily up – and then rose even more quickly, as the Bank of England entered into an era that both retained some monetary looseness (keeping short-term rates relatively low) and yet promoted higher bond yields through quantitative tightening (QT: selling the gilts that had been acquired earlier through QE).

As our 2022–3 bout of inflation showed, there is a major downside to any reliance on flooding the economy with money, with the intention of keeping asset prices up and interest rates down. The more money pours into the market within a given time period, the more, in the short and medium term, interest rates are driven away from their equilibrium or natural rate. As discussed earlier, this 'financial repression' kills the savings and investment culture, while (but only initially) rewarding borrowers. In turn, that leads, among other problems, to further asset inflation (in shares, in bonds, in houses), and as discussed, to the emergence of a class of debt-ridden, ultimately unviable 'zombie' companies.

This phenomenon has been particularly pronounced in the EU, where the European Central Bank has purchased a large proportion of the entire stock of commercial bonds – that is, of debt notes issued by private companies. These purchases have helped to prop up those companies' bonds beyond what the market would value them at. (What could possibly go wrong?) Many of these companies should have and would have gone bust had they not been propped up by those central bank bond purchases. Fine for those with a short-term desire not to face the consequences of past economic policy, and bond investment decisions encouraged by loose money, but terrible for the long term, because the resources currently tied up in those 'zombie' companies need, for the good of the economy and economic growth, to be released (through bankruptcy) and re-deployed to more productive areas.

Financial repression also incentivises financial institutions into behaving in a dysfunctional way, borrowing too short and investing too long in their 'search for yield', due to the difficulty of getting a decent return in an environment of artificially imposed, ultra-low interest rates. This leads, as it did in 2007–9, to the global financial crisis – or, more recently, the tottering of the UK's leveraged LDI pension funds and the 2023 collapse of Silicon Valley, Signature, First Republic and other US banks.

Herbert Stein, a conservative economist, wrote in 1985, 'If something cannot go on forever, it will stop.' This is indeed what has now transpired. Incessant bond purchases from QE programmes led to bond yields plummeting; therefore, the price of bonds went up and up. But once inflation started, inevitably, bond yields steadily rose again – so bond prices dropped, initially over the first nine months of 2022, during the last months of the Johnson government. The Bank of England announced on 22 September 2022 that it was both keeping short-term rates low (encouraging inflation, although the bank appeared not to understand that) and, controversially, selling (QT) an enormous £80 billion of gilts into the market, discouraging inflation but creating significant short-term movement in the gilts market.[37] The combination of these two announcements sent bond yields even higher, as economic theory suggests would happen – one day *prior* to the mini-budget of 23 September 2022.[38]

More and more QE and money creation, lower and lower interest rates, higher and higher asset values – this could not go on for ever, so it didn't. The Hayekian approach argues that too great a focus on Keynesian stimulus only stores up trouble for the future, while making the eventual reckoning much more costly. The Austrian school of economic thought – which can be loosely described as focusing on supply-side and monetary considerations, while emphasising the role in the economy of commercial institutions over and above the role of the central bank – encompasses economists such as Hayek and Ludwig von Mises (both of whose ideas I subscribe to). It says it is better that market corrections should be allowed to take their course, if only to ensure that the economy is, by the end of any recession, populated only with productive enterprises. The neo-Keynesian tends to recoil from that, fearing human distress caused by the consequent (though temporary) higher unemployment and being concerned for the potential for the economy to get stuck in recession. Hayekians retort that propping up the economy both prolongs and eventually worsens the agony – in the end, drifting the economy in the direction of economic collapse.

A senior Bank of England official, Huw Pill, recently commented,

'People will just have to accept that they are poorer now.' This assertion is not 100 per cent right for *all* people. For a few lucky beings, the outcomes can be positive, although for most there are primarily negative outcomes from inflation. But Pill was, even if brutal, correct that people were poorer. In general, a high rate of price inflation imposes enormous pain across the populace (the 'cost of living crisis'). Inflation inflicts:

- sometimes terminal pressures on companies
- distorted investment decisions
- reduced investments due to uncertainty
- depreciation of the currency, making imports more expensive and thus increasing the cost of living even more
- increases (in the short term) in the cost of borrowing
- erosion of purchasing power, leaving almost all of us poorer
- drags income tax payers into higher income brackets

Regardless of the sagacity or otherwise of Pill's comment, the general assumption of the past few decades had been that the Bank of England knew what it was doing and that it knew what the causes of inflation were and how to avoid triggering it. In contrast to that assumption, though, the experience of the past few years has been quite conclusive: either the Bank of England has never known, and still doesn't know, what causes inflation or how to prevent it; or it does now realise that the cause was something it had itself done – putting too much money into the economy too fast – but it does not intend to admit or discuss that.

Given the bank's remit to control inflation, had it been looking at the broad money numbers (as it should have done), it would have been sounding the alert and taking steps to avoid (or at least warn against) such huge money-supply increases in such a short timeframe, as was done during the Covid pandemic. As we have already seen in Volume One (see Chart 1.24), money was issued to cover borrowing that was at a significantly higher level in the UK during Covid than in almost any other developed economy. So we had a Debt Management Office that issued the inflation-linked bonds that would predictably prove very costly if inflation were to erupt, but the Bank of England had, apparently, no understanding of the causes of inflation, no proper warning systems and too great a complacency deriving from the previous 'great moderation'. As a result, they were in no way positioned to prevent or mitigate inflation from happening. Eventually, those chickens had to come home to roost, and roost they did.

What do we learn from this recent history? First, the monetarist view that a large and fast increase in the money supply leads to inflation is correct. Second – again, a long-preached view of Tim Congdon – that it is *broad* money supply (i.e. money including the activities of financial institutions, not just of central banks) that determines inflation. (So, if you tighten on banks at the same time as you ease the narrow money supply, you will mitigate any pressures, but then, you will have somewhat defeated your objective of goosing the economy, so why did you do any of this in the first place?) Third, ballooning the money supply creates a distorted interest-rate environment.

How much better might it have been had there been less QE, less tightening on the banks, more willingness to let the Hayekian cycle take place, with a greater number of bankruptcies but ultimately a healthier economy?* How much better might it have been if the

---

* The US bankruptcy code is more flexible in getting bust companies and financial institutions back on their feet in short order (with new owners). The UK would greatly benefit from having a bankruptcy code equivalent to the US's Chapter 11. See Randall A. Heron, Erik Lie and Kimberly J. Rodgers, 'Financial restructuring in fresh-start Chapter 11 reorganizations', *Financial Management*, vol. 38, no. 4, Winter 2009, pp. 727–45, https://www.jstor.org/stable/40388692

Bank of England and the OBR had understood the implication of Friedman's, Congdon's and other monetarists' insights, and warned the government that their splurge of Covid cash for two years was going to have severe inflationary consequences?*

We appear to have – for now, at least – got ourselves out of the inflationary spiral. It could be much worse: persistent price inflation can become embedded, leading to the kind of economic collapse we have seen in other countries. It will be very important to watch the level of government deficit in the coming months and years, and it is worth noting (at the time of writing in September 2024) that while overall inflation is at the target 2 per cent, core inflation is still at 3.6 per cent.

Monetarist and Austrian economists believe that over recent decades, and across the western world, there has been a Ponzi scheme-style approach to the economy, whereby the stimuli that governments have decided repeatedly to apply have ended up creating a zombie economy, with more zombie companies and more zombie financial institutions… leading to the need for further intervention and the negative cycle repeating itself. The intention behind these stimuli was to prevent or recover from recessions – which, the Austrians point out, had been primarily caused by the stimuli. Both monetarists and Austrians predict inflation will be the consequence of over-stimulation of the economy. Too much of that, and the country gradually becomes extensively zombified at the same time as suffering high inflation, as in Argentina over the past century.

---

* It was ironic to watch Prime Minister Rishi Sunak, during 2023 and 2024, dodging the issue of how the actions of Chancellor of the Exchequer Rishi Sunak in 2020 had ignited inflation. The circumlocutions and blatant falsehoods that Sunak and his Chancellor Jeremy Hunt had to utter, blaming Ukraine (which happened after inflation took off) and other issues that were much less influential on inflation than was money growth, were painful to see.

So, continued over-stimulus is a politician's short-term drug that can only end either in addiction (inflation) or cold turkey (violent collapse). But what of the inflation of the past two years? The Covid years, and the policies imposed during them by most governments around the world, differ from the years 2008–10 in four important respects. First, the scale and rate of QE in the latter period was higher. Second, there was considerable further creation of money through debt issued to fund payments into the economy (such as the Covid-support payments of various types). Third, in the more recent episode, there were no counterbalancing capital/reserve constraints on financial institutions. Fourth, there was, more recently, less of a flight to safety by investors. So, there was no counterbalance to the monetary stimulus, and thus we got the consequent inflation.

As regards how market commentators and forecasters reacted to the Covid-era stimuli, this time a reversal of the 2010 forecasts took place. On the inflation-hawk side there was not nearly so much noise, even from monetarists, that inflation would increase – perhaps because so many Austrian or monetarist economists who had predicted inflation in the earlier period now felt abashed that inflation hadn't happened back then, while the neo-Keynesians had gained even more confidence from the fact that the QE programmes had resulted, for a considerable period of time, in both very low interest rates and very low inflation. The prominent economist who had so clearly predicted no inflation after 2010–14 was Tim Congdon. He then, as a pure and doctrinaire monetarist, got it right again, sounding the alarm in the Covid period and even going so far as to predict in late 2020 that inflation was going to top 10 per cent – in which prediction he was spot on. (Bizarrely, or perhaps because he thereby showed up so many other forecasters as being wrong, he has received very little credit for this.)[39]

RETURN TO GROWTH

Chart 3.27: Average Inflation Rate, 2022–3

The UK, having gone overboard with money creation during Covid, experienced higher levels of inflation than all but Iceland.

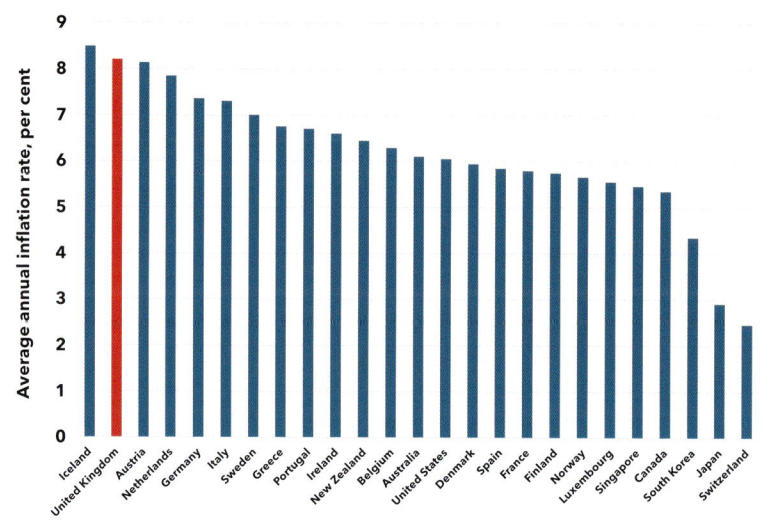

Source: International Monetary Fund[40]

As Chart 3.27 shows, inflation in the post-Covid period varied dramatically between countries. It is just not correct to say that inflation was a result of global factors; some countries suffered really badly, while others hardly did at all. The difference was in how much money was created in each. The UK was one of the worst offenders on that measure, and we suffered worse inflation over that two-year period than *every other major economy* – leaving aside the minor exception of Iceland. All this was a function of the policies each national government chose to pursue. Countries with smaller levels of government expenditure, that had not indulged in excess money creation, such as Switzerland or Japan, were relatively inflation-free – regardless of the increased global price of hydrocarbons, which both of those two countries had to import in large volumes.

(These hydrocarbon price increases arose both as a result of the 2022 invasion of Ukraine by Russia, and the anti-hydrocarbon policies adopted by many advanced nations, but these rises in price happened, in the main, well after inflation started to take off.) Because of their anti-inflation policies, the low-inflation countries were able to grow their economies without having to deal with the inflationary fallout from money growth or from a cost-of-living crisis.

So, as Chart 3.27 shows, countries who didn't go bonkers on stimulus had a less disastrous inflationary experience, regardless of global influences. As Friedman and others always say: control your money supply and you'll control inflation. In the UK, we had a problem doing that. By the end of 2021, inflation was above 5 per cent and was climbing rapidly – and then, as Congdon had predicted, it shot up to above 10 per cent. See Chart 3.28.

Chart 3.28: UK CPI Inflation, 2019–24

After the Covid-era money surge, inflation shot up in the UK.

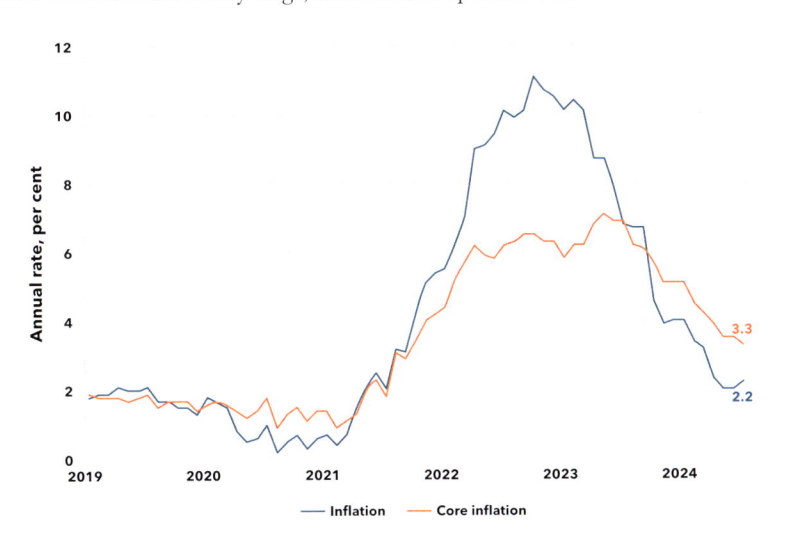

Source: Office for National Statistics[41]

What happened in the UK from 2020 through 2023 was fascinating. The monetarists and Austrian approaches predicted inflation, but the Bank of England didn't – even in late 2020, it was forecasting 2 per cent inflation for 2021. Inflation happened. The monetarists' solution to resolve inflation, finally though belatedly adopted by all central banks, was to tighten the money supply. The Bank of England, to do that, could not overtly say raising rates equalled tightening the money supply, because to do so would be to admit its previous fault. Instead, the bank followed the other central banks, who raised short-term rates. They did not raise rates as aggressively as the US Federal Reserve did, yet jumped aggressively into QT and ahead of every other central bank – 'making history', as the BBC gushingly and thoughtlessly put it.[42]

How to assert that you have taken measures to control inflation if you aren't acknowledging inflation and have not seen it coming? Simple, from their point of view – just take the sort of action that a monetarist would advocate to reduce the growth rate of money (e.g. increase interest rates) while pointing the finger at entirely different alleged causes of inflation, such as energy prices! After getting a rather rough ride in the House of Lords Select Committee, followed by an equally condemnatory debate in the House (in which I made my maiden speech), there seems to have been a change of heart. As Tim Congdon put it:

> An encouraging feature of the Bank of England's latest Monetary Policy Report is that it had six pages of analysis of money and its impact on the economy. These pages were very much in line with broad-money monetarism. They had no references to the monetary base and instead investigated in detail movements in different sectors' money holdings.[43]

This indeed was the case. Suddenly, the Bank of England was saying that they recognised that 'inflation is ultimately a monetary phenomenon (Friedman, 1963)' and, more cautiously and allusively, that 'developments in aggregate money growth can provide a signal about longer-run trends in activity and inflation'.[44] There was little tying of this sudden conversion to any mea culpa regarding the 2020–21 episode, nor was there any implication that the bank thought that Sunak and Hunt should stop blaming the world, Russia, Ukraine and energy prices for the drastic increase in prices.[*]

The likely longer-term consequences of this melange of conflicting views and ducking of blame are uncertain. The government, the Treasury, the OBR and the Bank of England all basically found themselves in a situation of hoping that inflation would somehow drop, but had, until very recently, no guidepost to tell them whether they would under- or over-shoot their target – because they were not using monetary data. The degree to which inflation will fall, monetarists say, depends on the amount by which the rate of growth in money is reduced. Because the Bank of England had ceased to look carefully at monetary figures and didn't publish or research much on the subject, it would appear that almost no one at the bank paid attention to how much money was circulating in the economy and at what velocity. Most agree that there are variables in the system that make it impossible to be precise on such issues; as Chart 3.25 showed, a useful rule of thumb could be to use first, around a 24-month lag and second, broad money measures. In any event, estimates could have been, and in the past had been, made.

While it is true that the money spigots were finally turned down by the Bank of England, we still need to have an ongoing feel as to

---

[*] The outcome of the election put a welcome end to all that nonsense, at least.

whether or not inflation will continue, and we need good data for that. As Congdon put it:

> Will the Bank continue to publish analysis of the behaviour of broad money and its bearing on macroeconomic outcomes? We have to wait and see. Much depends on the attitude of the Governor and the Deputy Governors, and to some extent of members of the Monetary Policy Committee. The inflation episode of the early 2020s should have taught the Bank to treat upheavals in broad money with respect. However, the same could have been said after the Heath-Barber boom of the early 1970s, the Lawson boom and later bust inside the European exchange rate mechanism in the late 1980s and early 1990s, and the Great Recession and its sequel. In the event, the latest cohort of top Bank of England officials defied the obvious lessons of history.[45]

Even if core inflation were to be returned back to a 2 per cent target level, nonetheless prices are now some 24 per cent above what they were pre-Covid.[46] Older people on fixed, non-indexed pensions have been massively impoverished by this, and those working-age people who did not receive a cumulative 24 per cent wage increase as a result of that period of inflation, i.e. the majority of workers, will continue to struggle with the cost of living. At best, we have had a highly and permanently damaging episode. At worst, we are embarked on a path of oscillating inflation, which could steadily wreck the economy. And we still don't seem to have a great ability to forecast inflation; the 2024 review of the bank's forecasting and communication processes by economist, Nobel Laureate and former chair of the Federal Reserve Ben Bernanke stated that the bank's forecasts had 'deteriorated significantly' in the past few years.[47]

So, as the discussion here shows, there is a major debate to be had as to how monetary policy should be run, whether in seeking to control inflation or in running the economy. Clearly, the prevailing economic orthodoxy, loosely termed by most as 'Keynesian', has singularly failed to give us a healthy economy or to control inflation. In future, careful attention has to be paid to monetary measures.

• • •

AN INTERLUDE: TREASURY ORTHODOXY AND THE FIGHT BETWEEN MONETARISM AND KEYNESIANISM

The preceding discussion on inflation has illustrated, I hope, the importance of controlling inflation, the lack of consensus as to how to accomplish that and the recent failure of the UK's institutions to succeed in that. Much of the problem, many critics assert, lie in the failures of what is referred to as 'Treasury orthodoxy'. The following interlude discusses that in more detail.

In modern-day discussions of the UK's economy, one idea seems to enjoy a general consensus: that there is a thing called Treasury orthodoxy. From the end of the Second World War onwards, all sides have said that it existed, and have offered their often widely differing views as to what it was, and whether it was a good or a bad thing.

Consensus is hard to find on the matter: there even seems to be very little agreement as to what Treasury orthodoxy actually consists of. Attacks on, and defences of, this 'orthodoxy' come from all sides of the political compass and are collectively hard to reconcile.

What are the dimensions of this Treasury orthodoxy controversy? In the following pages, I discuss three separate aspects:

1. the policies
2. the participants
3. the outcomes

The policies

A useful start is a recent speech by Lord Macpherson, the doyen of modern Treasury mandarins, titled 'Treasury orthodoxy: fact or fiction?'[48] (The title is a little bit of a misnomer, as he seems fairly settled in his mind that there is indeed an orthodoxy – although his is one that is dissimilar to the orthodoxy that the Treasury's opponents claim currently exists – see later.)

Macpherson believes that over the decades and centuries, the 'orthodoxy' has changed from one thing to the other and back. He says that originally, and up until 1931, the orthodoxy was Gladstonian; comprising free trade, limited expenditure (and thus low national debt) and the gold standard. As mentioned earlier, Tim Congdon, in a recent paper titled 'There is still no alternative to monetarism', lists exactly the same three items as the basis of the UK's policy roster throughout the nineteenth century.[49] So, with two commentators who are not normally bedfellows saying the same thing, we may assume some credibility to this view.

Some of that eighteenth-century orthodoxy, such as the gold standard, is now no longer possible (and I discussed earlier, and again a few pages from now, my own, not particularly iconoclastic, view that its modern equivalent, a fixed exchange rate, whether tied to gold or to the euro or the dollar, is not the right prescription for us). Macpherson and others believe now, as did Keynes at the time, that this original orthodoxy was, in its more stringent aspects, a mistake. A less draconian approach, they believe, would likely have lessened the impact of the Great Depression.*

Once an accommodative viewpoint became the norm after the early 1930s, the Treasury orthodoxy became that of Keynes. Then, throughout the post-war period, the UK, hooked on Keynes, had worse inflation than most comparator countries, until in the 1970s inflation really took off. Even then, monetarists were offering a critique of the UK's economic policy; in 1972 and 1973, Peter Jay, economics editor at *The Times*, accurately predicted, because of a sharp growth in 1972/73 money, 1975's major inflation.

The highly accommodative Keynesian monetary approach continued across most of the developed world until the mid-1970s. President Nixon had, in 1971, announced, with impeccably bad timing as he came off the gold standard and cemented the economy into an era of high inflation: 'We are all Keynesians now.' Then, the inflationary period of the 1970s put paid to that: nations agreed that too much Keynesian stimulus led to inflation. Jim Callaghan's famous speech to the Labour Party conference in 1976 was thought to have put paid to Keynesianism in the UK.

Macpherson correctly describes how, from Callaghan and his Chancellor Denis Healey on through to Thatcher, the Treasury orthodoxy changed tack for a while to an embrace of better fiscal discipline and monetarism. The supremacy of this viewpoint in the Treasury is said to have in large part come from Terry Burns, who, though not an outright Friedmanite, was inclined towards the monetarist view of the causes of inflation. Monetarism had been steadily championed

---

* To a degree, all agree on that point – but only to a degree. Not raising tax rates by a draconian amount would have been beneficial, and the stimulus need not have gone beyond being accommodative to banks with liquidity problems. The same point could be made about the recent global financial crisis of 2007–8.

by a small group of economists in the 1970s and assumed increased prominence, first under Healey (who at least theoretically embraced it, but then, nonetheless, proceeded to overspend) and then with the advent of Thatcher and her government. With great pain involved, Thatcher's governments initially defeated inflation, but experience was then to show that by the end of the Thatcher era, Keynesianism elbowed its way right back into pole position.

What seems to be less frequently discussed is that throughout the post-war period – indeed, for the entire twentieth century – perhaps the biggest focus of macroeconomic orthodoxy was on the exchange rate. Government after government lost its credibility by attempting to stand against the financial flows that washed through the global foreign exchange markets, driving up or down the value of our currency, sometimes for reasons to do with the balance of trade, sometimes because speculators were betting for – or, more usually, against – sterling.

The floating of our currency basically took away this issue by the early 1980s. Yet, in a madness-of-crowds moment, most of the key UK players in the late 1980s then decided that we should peg our currency to the Deutschmark, within the European Exchange Rate Mechanism (ERM). This put the exchange rate back at the centre of our policies – now on steroids, because we weren't even focusing on keeping our own currency stable, but instead we were trying to keep sterling stable against the specific currency of another country, and a country that had an entirely different type of economy from ours.[*] This nonsensical ERM peg idea turned out to be catastrophic, leading to 'Black Wednesday' in 1992, in which the Conservative Party lost, possibly for ever, its reputation for prudent financial management.

---

[*] As all are now agreed, exactly the same disaster would have occurred had the UK been foolish enough to join the Euro.

As Ken Clarke recounts, the agony of Black Wednesday was prolonged through the day of reckoning, far longer than it needed to be, with enormous financial losses accruing to the country hour by hour as the day wore on and politicians dithered.[50] The catastrophic loss to the Exchequer was thus made far worse as a result of Clarke, Douglas Hurd and Michael Heseltine initially insisting on not actually crashing out of the ERM until the decision had been submitted to and agreed by their EU colleague ministers in Brussels.

Much of the economic agony of this period – from the 1970s all the way through to Black Wednesday – was amplified by this obsessive concern with the exchange rate, which was seen as impacting our export competitiveness if too strong, and causing inflation if too weak. But that doesn't mean that it's possible to know what the right level for sterling should be at any time. An over-obsession with keeping our exchange rate at a predetermined fixed level can lead to disaster. As far as I know, since Black Wednesday no British government has attempted to manage the level of our currency through market manipulation. The estimated losses on the day were £3.3 billion – and at that time, a billion pounds was actually worth something. The Treasury, now fully led by Burns, claimed to have been forced into the position by three Conservative Chancellors: Geoffrey Howe, Nigel Lawson and John Major. These three are, certainly, collectively guilty for wandering down the currency-fixated ERM road, in opposition to Thatcher's principled resistance to it. Meanwhile, a failure to focus on monetary aggregates had resulted in yet another inflationary spike, followed by another economic recession.

The predominating influence of monetarism, as we have seen, had waned through the 1980s and had pretty much disappeared by the time Thatcher and Lawson were safely out of the way. It was – particularly following Black Wednesday – supplanted by 'inflation targeting' and by something that has until very recently looked suspiciously like the old Keynesian approach of continued stimulus, at times uneasily combined (selectively, depending upon the Chancellor) with some degree of Gladstonian frugality.

In 1997, Labour came into power with Gordon Brown as Chancellor; he and his officials added central bank independence to this new Treasury orthodoxy. The Bank of England was given the 2 per cent inflation target as its lodestar, but there was a still-lingering oddness to this: no one at the bank seemed to articulate a valid theory as to what actually creates inflation[*] and nor, therefore, was any policy applied to successfully control it. So, the Bank of England was required to target a 2 per cent level of inflation without there being an agreed way in which to accomplish that.

Macpherson's speech, which I referred to at the beginning of this interlude, can therefore be seen to be correct in claiming that the orthodoxy has changed over the decades. However, that orthodoxy, whatever it now is, cannot be said to have become any more coherent.

Several of the Treasury's policies, some small and some large, form the heart of where it is most criticised. For its opponents, the demerits of the Treasury orthodoxy are seen as going well beyond the issue of inflation. They include:

- Uber-Keynesianism in general (higher spending leading to higher deficits and higher national debt). Monetarism has been

---

[*] This is a slight exaggeration. A theory called 'new Keynesianism', encapsulated in Michael Woodford's *Interest and Prices*, dubbed the 'Bible for central banks', ruled the roost since the early 2000s up to the late 2010s. The approach encouraged the stimulative behaviour of that period. It is doubtful that, following the inflationary burst of the early 2020s, its exponents are nowadays vocal as to its merits.

forgotten, and mention of Austrian or (in particular) Hayekian economics is just greeted with puzzlement or derision.
- Attempted convergence with the EU's economies, despite the UK having a differently shaped economy and a different legal system to the rest of the EU.
- Static analysis that implicitly believes there will be little dynamic reaction to any tax or regulatory change – in particular, a disbelief in, and routine trashing of, concepts such as the Laffer curve.
- Relying on poor and usually inaccurate forecasting from the OBR. This can sometimes be recklessly negative.
- An outlier perspective on what the underpinnings of economic growth are; growth in the Treasury orthodoxy world seems to be treated more as a given, not as an outcome that will happen only if specific policies and actions are implemented.
- Economic forecasting that assumes all immigration is good, ignoring its impact on social infrastructure and assuming, with little data behind that assertion, that all immigration promotes growth.*
- Focusing on GDP, rather than GDP-per-capita, growth.
- Outsourcing responsibility and therefore blame to the Bank of England and the OBR; if things go wrong, Treasury responsibility can be denied – but the independent, arm's-length nature of those bodies means they also remain accountable.
- Little attention to the supply side, with an economic focus almost entirely on the demand side.
- Regulatory and policy actions that direct private investment into government bonds rather than private-sector equities.

---

* This particular assumption may be moderating as the evidence to the contrary becomes more and more irrefutable. I have seen it asserted, though, that the OBR model assumes that immigrants bring no dependents with them.

- Staffed by inexperienced and youthful PPE grads who have very little industrial or commercial business experience, nor practical understanding of how a capitalist economy works.
- Inattention to fraud (see, for one of many examples, the BCCI episode.)[51]
- Little focus on the economic impact and consquences of new regulations.
- Treasury as the boss, micromanaging other departments.

This is a long charge sheet. If only a fraction of it is true, we have a major problem.

There has in particular been fundamental disagreement among economists as to the role that should be played by one particular policy listed in the above charge sheet – namely, supply-side economics. The phrase was popularised by the journalist Jude Wanniski, and the economist Art Laffer, famous for the Laffer curve discussed in Volume One. The supply-side idea was particularly controversial because it was associated with 'Reaganomics', an approach to the economy that was, at the time, hotly condemned by many economists. (Much of the heat seems to have been a consequence of party politics, coupled with personal dislike of Ronald Reagan.)

Some opponents of supply-side economics claim that the supply-side approach is nothing more than so-called 'trickle-down' economics, the thought that if you make rich people richer, the benefits will eventually trickle down to poorer people. Clearly, as I have shown here and in Volume One, the supply-side approach is much more than that. At its heart is the obvious point, that just as demand-side actions alter people's propensities to *buy* goods and services, so do supply-side actions alter companies' propensity to *provide* goods and services. In Soviet Russia, the economy eventually collapsed, not just because people had no money to buy things, but also because there were no things to buy. Supply-side thinking is nothing magical or ridiculous; it merely says that for an economy to grow, you have to worry about suppliers providing as well as buyers purchasing (provision of new wonderful convenient products and services for consumers and businesses to buy, improving their enjoyment of life and self-fulfilment, is at the heart of what creates economic growth). A failure to think in supply-side terms has bedevilled post-war British economic policy, dominated as our economic management, our government, our institutions and our academia have been by Keynesian (demand-side) economists.

A second key policy area of disagreement is the issue of static versus dynamic modelling. Over the decades, so many have publicly derided the Laffer-curve concept that many assume that it is a busted, discredited idea.* But the Laffer curve is nothing but a logical extension of the concept of dynamic responses to changes in tax rates. These dynamic responses have been proven to occur over and again in recent decades, perhaps most obviously in the recent response of businesses in and outside the UK to our large rise in corporate taxes in late 2022 – which, as discussed in Volume One, resulted in many companies fleeing the UK, significantly depressing economic activity. Treasury orthodoxy clearly includes visceral dislike of the supply-side approach.

Criticism of the Treasury orthodoxy nowadays comes from all sides of the spectrum, even sometimes from the Treasury's key supporters; it is not confined just to the free-markets crowd. Even

---

* Laffer or dynamic modelling is, to be fair, now appearing in a few undergraduate economics textbooks, but in the media and popular mainstream discussion, it is still near-universally derided.

the venerable *Economist* has joined in, with a recent article asserting that 'the Treasury cannot be blamed for all of these problems. But its power means that its institutional flaws have a disproportionate effect. On three counts, the way the Treasury works makes Britain's problems worse.'[52] These three flaws, *The Economist* stated, comprised:

- *It is too frugal and puts too much value on short-term savings.* The Treasury argued that the M25 should be built only two lanes wide and that the Jubilee Line shouldn't be extended. Both would have resulted in catastrophically bad outcomes, had those arguments been accepted.
- *It does not prioritise growth*, with *The Economist* stating that 'over the past 15 years, it is hard to point to a strong record of pro-growth policies'.
- *It micromanages across government*; it has too much power and exerts control over other departments in a myriad of ways.

From the other end of the political spectrum, the *New Statesman*, there also comes an intriguing series of claims as regards Treasury orthodoxy.* [53] The post-war orthodoxy, they say, was a good one, comprising primarily the Keynesian consensus: 'Government spending was good and deficits were appropriate because they promoted demand.' The disaster of the 'Barber Boom' (which I discuss in a few pages from now), and the subsequent humiliation of Denis Healey by the IMF, led to a total reversal of the formerly Keynesian orthodoxy, the *New Statesman* claims, which now they say consists of:

---

* Note that those claims don't seem to have a great deal of fact-based backup to them.

- failing to follow the nostrums of Keynes
- adding in an inappropriate focus on monetarism
- privatisation, including selling off public-housing stock
- too much focus on the banking sector and the City

Certainly, the first two of these allegations are flat-out wrong, while the second two are, at the least, questionable. But anyway, for the *New Statesman*, the above list is what has created 'zero interest rates [and] a zombie economy … The bill for the crash … has now very much arrived.' This reversal of the orthodoxy happened, they say, in the 1980s, when Nigel Lawson was Chancellor. The *New Statesman* reviewer believes – I would say, against all the evidence – that this reversal, or 'settlement', that they say occurred then is still in place and has continued therefore for the past nearly forty years(!). I hope my earlier, more nuanced review of the history is more convincing than that suggestion.* Regardless, it's clear to see from this that different sides come up with violently different ways in which to roundly condemn the Treasury orthodoxy.

So, the Treasury's policies seem to come in for criticism, often in contradictory ways, from all sides. But the charge sheet is long: even when we necessarily agree that it's impossible for all these often contradictory criticisms to be correct, the list is cumulatively damning.

The participants

At the heart of the orthodoxy, we of course have the Treasury. But its grip is immensely strengthened by:

---

* As will be seen, some pages from now, I agree with the *New Statesman* on the malign impact of the Barber episode and a number of similar Conservative fiascos.

- *Two wingmen* – on one side, the Bank of England and on the other, the Office for Budget Responsibility. The Bank of England seems to hew to the same orthodoxies as the Treasury – and why not, if all four deputy Governors of the Bank of England are ex-Treasury? All three institutions are similarly stuffed with what the *New Statesman* – on this point, we must fully concede, correctly – refers to as 'PPE bluffers' or their equivalent. All three (the Treasury and the two wingmen) stick closely to, and collectively always come to a consensus on, the overall Treasury line.
- *Outriders* – these are staffed from the same pool as the Treasury and its wingmen. The IMF, the European Central Bank, the Institute for Fiscal Studies, the World Bank and other international financial bodies, plus most of the economics departments of the major universities – Oxbridge, LSE, Harvard, MIT and Stanford in particular. Again, they all have an eerie ability to come up with the same lines of thought.
- *Supporters* from the mainstream/centrist media, such as the economics journalists and editors of the *Financial Times*, *The Economist*, *The Times*, the BBC, Sky News and the *New York Times*. All have staff with the same educational background as the Treasury, its wingmen and its outriders. They move back and forth between the Treasury, its wingmen and outriders; all rely on carefully cultivated relationships with each other, as can be discerned from the swift yet uncannily uniform response from all of them to most financial events.[*] Maintaining status in this setup requires placing a premium on following the orthodoxy and on not rocking the boat; so our most prominent and respected media often fail to ask the hard questions regarding policies that even at the

---

[*] I call this 'the madness of crowded WhatsApp groups', because there are so many such groups that, removed from the public gaze, transmit the 'line to take' on any new economic event.

time could have been seen as questionable, resulting in outcomes that turn out to be undesirable.

Players in this network, a network that immeasurably bolsters the Treasury orthodoxy, are certainly not consistent in the way they play the game, but they come to each other's support with astonishing swiftness.

The global element of the network of participants leans (when it comes to the UK) in the direction of anti-Conservative and definitely anti-free-market policies:

- The IMF on Osborne: that he was 'playing with fire' for keeping growth in spending low.
- The IMF on Kwasi Kwarteng: criticised for *not* keeping growth in spending low.
- The IMF on Truss: that she should 'reevaluate the tax measures, especially those that benefit high-income earners'.

Oddly, they seemed to adopt an entirely different approach to Javier Milei's not dissimilar policies:

- The IMF on Milei: 'These bold initial actions aim to significantly improve public finances … Their decisive implementation will help stabilise the economy and set the basis for more sustainable and private sector-led growth.'[54]

As time has passed, the Treasury/OBR/Bank of England orthodoxy seems to have developed an ever-tighter grip on the UK's economic policy. The orthodoxy now seems to have bled into public consciousness as received wisdom, with these 'independent' (even though doctrinaire) structures and their assumptions being the accepted legitimate arbiters of government's political choices. The OBR now dominates the Treasury. The new Labour government has leaned into that approach, and the media in the UK seems recently to have adopted a rigid view that any government plan must receive the OBR's imprimatur – yet the OBR's assumptions seem to be static, left wing and social democratic in nature (even if recently unhelpful to Labour), while its forecasting record is erratically poor. (As was pointed out by David Smith in *The Times*, in 2022 the OBR's forecast was the fifth worst out of thirty-one major forecasters.)[55]

To take an example of why forecasts with a bias to static analysis can be expected to be so poor, let us take a forecasted fiscal outcome, which with the static model would assume that if tax rates were to go up, tax revenues would go up in direct proportion to the increase in rates. But as we saw in Volume One, for half a century the UK's actual tax take has remained largely stable, as a percentage of GDP. The Laffer-curve effect says that if tax *rates* are increased, tax avoidance and lessening of economic behaviour means that overall tax *revenues*, expressed as a percentage of the economy, won't increase by as much, and can even decline. If, to use an illustrative example, you impose a van levy, company owners who operate vans may no longer decide to grow their business by purchasing an extra van; or they may even shrink their business by getting rid of a few of their vans. Adjusting the economic forecast for such dynamic effects leads to a different out-turn from that produced by the static OBR model. The OBR's inaccurate forecasts are unchallenged by the vast majority of commentators, and the OBR is treated as the gold standard arbiter in media coverage yet they are by their static leanings biased to predict negative consequences for tax cuts; one of no doubt several reasons for the OBR's poor forecasting record.

A classic recent example is the Labour government's decision to abolish non-doms, a key part of their election manifesto. It is now accepted that this will yield at best zero (I would predict, negative) additional tax revenues – the flood of former non-doms leaving the country, along with other wealthy entrepreneurs and investors, continues.[56]

Another reason for static or other Keynesian models doing such a bad job of forecasting, beyond straightforward economic ignorance, incompetence or political bias, is that they fail to take into account the reverse side of the coin of punishing non-doms. This is the dynamic aspects of what would happen when tax rates were lowered. In Volume One, I gave an exemplary list of punitive taxes on business, all of which had been recently introduced. Were all those business-hitting taxes removed, there would be a rapid increase in economic growth – which would, in terms of tax take, deliver over time the greater tax revenues the Exchequer needs to fund more generous programmes.

The OBR's approach to economic modelling seems to assume significant benefits from high-tax budgets, and one-for-one drops in tax revenue from low-tax approaches, with assumptions built into the model that give almost inevitably negative predictions as outcomes from any steps to make the state smaller. The models assume that the more the immigration, the greater the growth; the impact of extra cost to social services is minimised. (Worse: the implicit assumption that employment among immigrants will be high does not appear to be data driven.)

The social democratic leanings of the OBR are not surprising, since it is now almost entirely dominated by émigrés from the left-wing Resolution Foundation, a think tank that focuses on redistributive policies.[57] The Resolution Foundation's mission is described by its parent organisation as seeking 'to improve the living standards of those on low to middle incomes'.[58] The long-time head of the Resolution Foundation until recently, Torsten Bell, was a special adviser to Alistair Darling and was then head of policy to the startingly doctrinaire Ed Miliband. Bell is now the MP for Swansea West. The OBR's head of economic forecasting Scott Bowman said in 2017, just before he joined the OBR from the Resolution Trust, that Jeremy Corbyn's economic manifesto, which included borrowing an additional £250 billion, had the potential to 'provide a significant boost' to growth and would 'provide much less of a drag on the economy over the next five years' compared to the government's plans.[59] (The OBR was brought into existence by George Osborne. At the time of its introduction, it was stated that it would be strictly non-partisan. Robert Conquest's second law: 'Any organisation not explicitly right-wing sooner or later becomes left-wing.')

Since the mini-budget incident, the OBR has held a steady grip on each subsequent Chancellor and the (not entirely unwilling) Treasury, whereby no economic initiative can be announced unless the OBR agrees that there is fiscal room to do so. But the OBR's estimate of available fiscal room tends to swing wildly back and forth, so that it's nigh-on impossible to articulate a coherent economic strategy, as Rachael Reeves has found out.

Nowhere is the OBR's political bias more evident than in its modelling on Brexit, where it forecast a drop in UK trade of 15 per cent relative to if we had remained in the EU. This would, by the way, have meant that our trade with the EU (about 42 per cent of our total trade) had dropped by 36 per cent. A carefully reasoned piece by Catherine McBride tears this absurd forecast apart.[60] (Further stunning newsflash: as shown in Chapter 2 of this volume, there has been no such drop in overall trade, whether with or beyond the EU.)

So, we have first shown an outline of what the Treasury orthodoxy is. This second section has shown how the Treasury, aided by its wingmen, outriders and supporters, have an iron grip both on the UK's economic policies and on how they are viewed within government, by the media and by the public. But what have been the outcomes of these policies, this orthodoxy?

The outcomes

There's no doubt that the Treasury has professionalised and improved over the years. In Lord Macpherson's speech he listed numerous improvements, particularly on the microeconomics side. Further, he made the case that the traditional micromanagement by the Treasury of other departments of state has lessened.

But the facts show that the uber-Keynesian view, which has dominated since the early 1930s, suffered only a brief reversal in the 1980s, and it has since returned full blast. Gordon Brown's spending when he was Prime Minister, and before that in the last few years of Tony Blair's premiership, was profligate, QE has been described as Keynes on steroids, and there must have been major complacency in the Treasury during Covid – and indeed throughout the Theresa May, the Johnson and even the Sunak years – to allow such incontinent levels of spending as have occurred, let alone the further increases promised by Rachel Reeves in her October Budget.

A momentary prim sobriety made a sudden appearance in late 2022; the OBR and the Bank of England played key roles in the Truss government's fall, abetted by other Treasury outriders such as the IMF, with the OBR raising the alarm about an alleged (and leaked) level of deficit that turned out to be exaggerated by at least £20 billion, probably much more.[61] The Bank of England then, during the LDI fund fiasco, declined to support the panicking bond market for more than a few short days – less time than was needed for the leveraged LDI funds to sort themselves out. This could be seen as a tactical and temporary stepping away from Keynesian complacency in order to eject a foreign body from the corpus.[62] Meanwhile, a more relaxed view on spending was the rule as the 2024 election approached, and we can confidently predict that the new Labour government, in the coming years, will steadily increase spending without having to endure much of the pearl-clutching from the OBR and the Treasury that was the response to the Truss mini-budget.[*]

This generally Keynesian and leftist approach is, I would argue, a hardwired feature of the Treasury orthodoxy. It will be incredibly difficult to remove. Even just since 1990, the list of disasters – in which features of the orthodoxy can be seen – is significant:

- the ERM fiasco and Black Wednesday in 1992
- the global financial crisis and, in particular, the failure of the Bank of England to spot it coming
- the expensive full rescuing of the banks in 2008–9, rather than allowing their bankruptcy (along with a haircut imposed on bondholders and other creditors)
- the outlandish forecasts during and after the Brexit referendum, with 'Project Fear' and the threatened 'punishment Budget'
- the failure to understand the causes of, or control, inflation – which has destroyed so much wealth over the past couple of years

---

[*] Labour have specifically raised the bar on further spending splurge under the rubric of 'investment' (Richard Partington & Kiran Stacey, 'How Rachel Reeves could release billions more for investment in the budget', *The Guardian*, 27 September 2024, https://www.theguardian.com/uk-news/2024/sep/27/how-rachel-reeves-could-release-billions-more-for-investment-in-the-budget). But a pound's a pound, and every extra pound spent will increase the national borrowing by that amount.

Whatever the driver of orthodoxy, whatever its specific characteristics at any time, it is plain that the Treasury's dominance has led to outcomes that have let the nation down. Without them, much national treasure could have been saved and much more economic growth in the UK could have been accomplished. There is a Treasury orthodoxy, and it needs major revision.

. . .

CREATING AN INTEGRATED ECONOMIC POLICY TO FACILITATE GROWTH

In the previous sections of this chapter, we have listed the economic measures that the Treasury departments of different governments find themselves wanting to, or having to, influence. We have also seen the range of so-called macroeconomic tools that governments use to achieve their desired outcomes:

- fiscal tools: taxation, borrowing and spending
- monetary tools: interest rates, asset sales and repurchases

There are also microeconomic tools: those targeted at impacting different parts of the economy, or creating incentives for consumers and producers. A lot of the levers available within the tax environment are essentially microeconomic (e.g. high-street business rates); regulation is the hardest-hitting microeconomic tool.

As we have discussed, both macro and micro tools break out into demand-side activities, such as unemployment payments and the like, or QE; and supply-side activities, such as changing business rates or the imposition of new regulations.

Chart 3.29: How Governments Should Manage the Economy
Ensuring coordination, not conflict

An integrated approach to all aspects of macro and micro tools is needed, so that rather than having independent, potentially mutually conflicting strategies, the government can oversee coordinated and mutually reinforcing policies and actions.

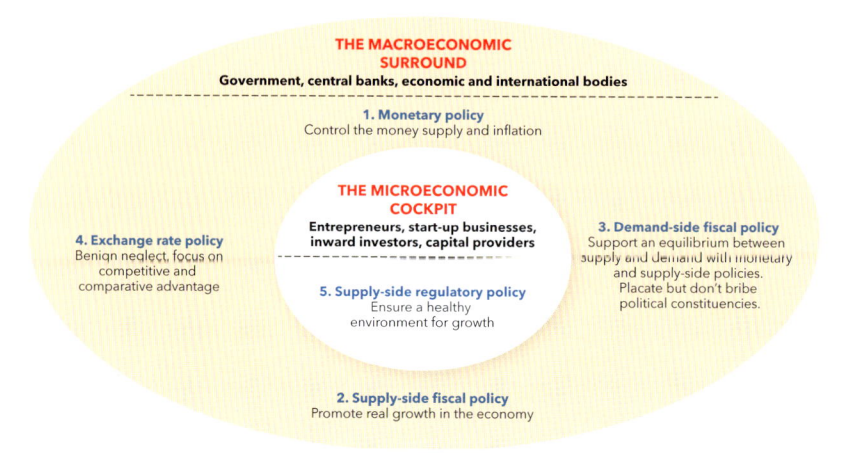

THE MACROECONOMIC SURROUND
Government, central banks, economic and international bodies

1. Monetary policy
Control the money supply and inflation

THE MICROECONOMIC COCKPIT
Entrepreneurs, start-up businesses, inward investors, capital providers

4. Exchange rate policy
Benign neglect, focus on competitive and comparative advantage

5. Supply-side regulatory policy
Ensure a healthy environment for growth

3. Demand-side fiscal policy
Support an equilibrium between supply and demand with monetary and supply-side policies. Placate but don't bribe political constituencies.

2. Supply-side fiscal policy
Promote real growth in the economy

Actions in these two different areas can have differing effects on the economy. Sometimes, the interventions can be countered by actions taken simultaneously by different parties in government, or by 'independent' institutions. It is self-evidently crucial that each member of the overall 'orchestra' of economic officials (discussed in Chart 3.29) should know, and be in accordance with, what the planned economic tune that the government is attempting to play should be – and equally crucial that the whole orchestra be conducted carefully, so that the separate instruments of government play together and harmoniously, rather than each playing a different tune – which could so easily lead to economic cacophony.

(Note that it gets potentially impossible to ensure that economic harmony, if parts of the orchestra are told that they are independent and can themselves decide what tune to play, and that they are entitled to ignore, or even play against, the tune that the elected government has decided on.)

Chart 3.29 takes a stab at depicting these different members of the 'orchestra', and their 'instruments' (the respective policy tools).

And here we get to the nub. In our modern democratic society, can a government conduct this orchestra, both policies and players, in a way that ensures that higher growth is achieved, in particular ensuring that all the players play the same economic tune? Is there a tune in the repertoire that leads, in a democratically acceptable way, to greater economic growth without overheating the economy, without incurring high debt or triggering inflation?

What we know for certain is that in the post-war years, most economic initiatives that 'went for growth' in the UK (almost all of these were put into action by Conservative governments) led quickly to tears:

- The Butler boom, 1955: Chancellor Rab Butler reduced income taxes. The resultant election was won, but consumers spent the extra money they got on imports, and a consequent balance of payments crisis forced a reversal of the tax cuts.
- The Heathcoat-Amory boom, 1959: Chancellor Derick Heathcoat-Amory again cut taxes, resulting again in an election win for the Conservatives. Again, a balance of payments problem resulted: inflation went up, interest rates went up, unemployment went up.
- The Maudling dash for growth, 1963–4: Chancellor Reginald Maudling removed income tax from residential premises. This created a widespread spending boom, which yet again led to a balance of payments crisis.
- The Barber boom, 1972: Chancellor Anthony Barber's large tax

cuts led to fast growth but, at the same time, to a major increase in the money supply – and subsequently, inflation, devaluation of the pound and the first recession since the Second World War.
- The Lawson boom, 1988–91: discussed earlier in more detail, but more of the same – Nigel Lawson's mortgage relief and taxation changes let the money supply rip, with the currency obstinately pegged to the Deutschmark. The result: Black Wednesday.
- The Sunak Covid chancellorship, 2020–22: under Rishi Sunak's tenure as Chancellor, furlough was a reasonable initial response to a flat-out crisis (although the 80 per cent of wages we paid was higher than that in other countries). Had furlough lasted just two or three months, it would not have been too damaging. But it lasted nineteen months, and its enormous cost, and other reckless expenditures, led to major inflation and a massive increase in our national debt.
- The Kwarteng mini-budget, 2022: Chancellor Kwasi Kwarteng's mini-budget was not even allowed to get off the ground before being knocked out by hostile institutions, by the unravelling of appallingly risky and incompetently supervised bets by the UK's pensions industry, and by that majority of MPs in the Conservative parliamentary party who were opposed to the entire Truss project.

Why did so many attempts to provide major stimulus to the economy end in tears? I argue that we can identify the following common elements:

- For all of these except the last, Keynesian demand-side, rather than Austrian supply-side, actions.
- For the earlier initiatives, an obsession with keeping a fixed rate of exchange while stimulating demand, which leads to greater

imports without immediately counterbalancing greater exports (in other words: demand-side rather than supply-side policies). The resultant money flows lead to balance of payments crises.
- Few microeconomic supply-side policies that would have encouraged investment-driven economic growth.
- The different instruments of the economic orchestra (the policies), as laid out in Chart 3.29, worked against each other.

Looking at these failed attempts at growth, it is clear that few, if any, governments at that time took Chart 3.29's integrated view on the macroeconomic and microeconomic players and levers that were available to them. They also failed to realise that if a government aimed simultaneously at two separate targets, such as economic growth *and* a fixed exchange rate, then the two objectives would as often as not be incompatible, as they were in all those cases.

Failing to get the economic orchestra to play the same one harmonious tune, going for two or more incompatible economic targets, ignoring the supply side: between them, these three policy confusions have created fiasco after fiasco in our post-war economic history, and it is depressing to see how often the Conservatives were to blame. (The accepted wisdom, now and then, is that post-war, both Conservatives and Labour pursued very similar Keynesian, so-called 'Butskellite' policies.) Taking the examples discussed here, we can see various Chancellors trying to play two tunes at once, indeed sometimes confused as to what the tune was.

Butler, Maudling and Barber all focused on the demand side by lowering taxes and made the fundamental mistake of thinking that they could create demand-led economic growth without accelerating imports – but that resulted in a currency drain before exports could take off. This in turn led – because at the same time, these

Chancellors sought to defend the level of the pound – to a balance of payments crisis and consequent attacks on the pound that eventually led to an unsustainable situation that required a policy reversal.

Although Lawson was one of the great supply-side Chancellors, he eventually attempted to outsource his monetary policy and his currency to the Bundesbank. He seems to have ceased paying attention to monetary aggregates, and having decided to target a fixed (fixed to the Deutschmark) foreign exchange rate, as well as targeting economic growth, he fell (by way of his successors, Major and Lamont) into the old problem of incurring an irresistible attack on sterling by speculators.

Osborne, with his Bank of England Governor Mark Carney, presided over a period of quantitative easing that kept markets buoyant, even as government expenditure (as a percentage of GDP) commendably diminished – although only slightly. Stocks, bonds, art, property: all rose, but they didn't budge the economy. The wealthy got wealthier, but apart from the tech sector, there was little of the innovation or entrepreneurial activity that would have led to growth, while small businesses struggled under more and more regulation and taxes.[63]

Sunak inherited as Chancellor a redistributionist economic apparatus whose individual players had long since stopped looking at monetary aggregates. He had to deal with an independent Bank of England whose primary objective was keeping inflation at 2 per cent – but they clearly had no idea how to do that. Both he and the bank were hapless in their failure to understand that the fiscal and monetary steps they took in 2020–21 were massively stoking inflation.

Then on to Kwarteng, who found that he had two members of his orchestra playing very different tunes from the one he wanted to be played. The first of these, the Bank of England, attacked the bond market with double-whammy announcements: first on interest rates, and then a very large, liquidity-threatening QT programme, the day before Kwarteng's mini-budget. The QT announcement made it predictable that there would be a rush by traders to sell their gilts ahead of the bank selling theirs; the expectation that the bank would, as announced, be selling lots of bonds was inevitably going to lead to a drop in bond prices and therefore an increase in interest rates.* This shows the folly of having one macroeconomic lever operated by the government and another operated by an independent central bank.† Then, finally, the bank shortly thereafter refused to support the market long enough for the leveraged LDI funds to be able to sort themselves out.

The second player, the OBR, adopted a static and almost wilfully pessimistic view of Kwarteng's Budget, not accepting that supply-side considerations should have allowed a more optimistic view on the mini-budget's potential future impact on the economy.[64]

It is clear that particularly difficult problems arise when different members of the orchestra are statutorily independent. Chancellor Gordon Brown made the Bank of England independent in 1997, and George Osborne founded the OBR as an independent entity in 2010. This might, conceptually, be fine, but as discussed, neither the Bank nor the OBR have remained (or possibly have ever been) *ideologically* independent. If, in the future, the nation democratically elects a government that wishes to adopt a monetarist, Hayekian approach, as advocated in this book, how could the two 'wingmen'

---

* The narrative that Liz Truss 'crashed the economy' depends on the belief that the crash in the UK gilts market was a result of the international bond market weighing in with a negative verdict on the creditworthiness of the UK's debt. But if that had been true (and even the Bank of England now says it was not true; they blame bad regulation and bad risk-taking in LDI funds) then as Patrick Minford points out, the price of credit default swaps on those gilts should have also moved sharply. It didn't. See Patrick Minford, 'Sunak and Hunt's economic policies have put Britain into recession', *Daily Express*, 22 December 2022, https://www.express.co.uk/comment/expresscomment/1712908/jeremy-hunt-rishi-sunak-economy-recession

† A recent paper from the Bank of England itself, referred to above and earlier, ascribes 66 per cent of blame for the crisis to the risks that had been taken in the badly regulated leveraged LDI funds market. The remaining 33 per cent can presumably be divided between, first, the Bank's interventions the day before the mini-budget and towards the end of the crisis, and, second, the mini-budget. So, perhaps just one sixth of the crash can be ascribable to Truss and Kwarteng's mini-budget.

institutions be compelled to adopt policies that aligned with the new government's objectives? If an institution has a particular in-built ideological economic bias that is opposed to the policies of the democratically elected government at the time, how can that opposition be modified or nullified?

We have seen in the preceding sections how a variety of policies are available to a government in its macroeconomic activity: exchange-rate policy, monetary policy, demand-side fiscal policy, supply-side fiscal and regulatory policy. Each of these economic levers has, when applied in different ways, multiple and far-reaching effects. All of them impact economic growth in different ways. Sometimes, simultaneously executed policies in different areas can, if not coordinated, cancel out or defeat one another. We have seen how after the global financial crisis, central banks around the world launched unprecedentedly aggressive QE in order to stimulate the economy. But at the same time, punitive new bank rules and other regulations constrained banks from lending. The first was stimulative demand-side policy; the second was depressive supply-side policy.

The result seems – possibly accidentally – to have kept the economy (through QE) from imploding, while keeping the growth in the quantity of money in circulation down (through squeezing the banks), thus supressing inflation. So far, so good, but that resulted in the QE programme punishing savers, zombifying companies and creating asset inflation – along with the inherently self-defeating circumstances of imposing two equal yet opposite policies at the same time.* But what if a government determined on a course of action that involved a less self-contradictory programme, only to

---

* In other words, if there had been less draconian new bank regulation, there would have been less need for QE, and the toxic consequences of QE could have been mitigated.

find that success or otherwise was at the mercy of one or more independent entities, who then proceeded to act in a way that went against the policy? This was the situation the Truss government found itself in during September 2022.

Clearly, what is needed is for all the institutions and their policies to be pulling in the same direction: all the instruments in the orchestra playing the same tune. An integrated review of all the economic levers available to a government should be undertaken at the beginning of any new parliament and a mechanism put into place to ensure that the overall economic policy of the government, whatever it is, is consistent across all these areas. (I would argue that this necessarily means that you cannot have, as we have now, institutions being allowed to operate entirely independently. Independence is important, but needs to be modified and channelled, so as to be in harmony with the policies and programme of a democratically elected government.)

Above all, creating these independent institutions has moved power, and the ability to make decisions, away from elected politicians and over to unelected institutions, whose lodestar is that very Treasury orthodoxy that is crushing economic growth.

What would an integrated economic programme look like? It would require enunciating an overview that took into account not only the macroeconomic but also the microeconomic tools – in particular, taking a supply-side view on regulation, and on the specific types and levels of tax placed on businesses and wealthy, mobile individuals. Above all, it would be one where all the institutions that make up Chart 3.29 are fully aligned.

What would this alignment look like, taking account of the current statutory independence of the Treasury's two outriders, the

Bank of England and the OBR? Three things would need to be aligned in particular:

- The first is the overall guiding philosophies of these institutions. The incoming government would need to have a clear understanding of its own philosophy and would need to audit the alignment or otherwise of those two outriders (and indeed of the Treasury itself). If the audit revealed too great a difference in philosophy, then some of the independence would have to be quickly removed, at least until the biases in those organisations have been dealt with. (Most easily, the OBR should be abolished and its useful competencies relocated back into the Treasury.)
- The second is the short-term actions of government and institutions. Never again should it be the case that the Bank of England can upset the apple cart of the government's economic plan by making a major announcement, directly opposed to the government's plan, the day before that plan is announced. At the very least, both sides should have a formal requirement to engage in two-way discussions of views and plans and agree intended actions, so that there is no major clash, as was the case in October 2022.* (It would certainly seem that there was insufficient interaction between government and bank during the crucial few days around the time of the mini-budget.)[65]
- The third is the long-term direction of government and institutions. The government should be expected to communicate and discuss its plans with the wingmen and outriders, and ascertain whether all are in alignment. They, in turn, should be given an

---

* The House of Lords report 'Making an independent Bank of England work better' reports the bank complaining that they had little communication from the government at that time. Regardless of the truth of that, what efforts did they make to warn the government about the timing and size of their own, unprecedentedly bold, QT plan and its likely destabilisation of the bond market?

opportunity and obligation to state where they have concerns. The government can then take whatever steps it sees as necessary to change things, if it thinks its plans are being obstructed. But the doctrinaire authority of the OBR in predicting the outcome of the plan – particularly given its staffing, its ideological bias, its antagonism to dynamic modelling and its poor forecasting record – should not be allowed to stay in place.

The Bank of England should always be required to attend to its secondary duty, already enshrined in statute, to 'support the government's economic strategy'. While respecting the bank's independence (if indeed it was decided to preserve that independence, which I argue would not necessarily be a good thing), the government could insist that the timing of any bank action or announcement should dovetail with the government's own programme and that the bank should – must – take the government's plans into account when deciding on its own actions.

So, aligning the institutions, so that every action taken on the economic indicators discussed in this chapter is harmonious with other actions, is crucial. If that could be achieved, the stage could be set for a harmonious orchestra of economic officials and institutions taking coherent, integrated steps, with in-tune policy instruments, to achieve a significant long-term increase in economic growth.

SUMMARY

Ensuring sound money involves growing the money supply at a rate consistent with the rate of growth of the economy, and thus not incurring inflation; balancing the budget; not trying to manage the exchange rate; and getting debt down to manageable or (preferably) minimal levels. All of this would lead to improved economic growth, through an integrated policy that aligns all the members and instruments of the government's economic 'orchestra'.

Accomplishing that is so tricky that since the Second World War, it has only rarely been successfully accomplished. The only exceptions, it seems, were the early Thatcher years, the final Major years and the early Blair years (in that last case, because Blair and Brown stuck with Major's economic policies for their first few years in power). The last fourteen years of Conservative governments were not at all successful in almost any of these respects, mostly because – inexcusably – the majority of those at the top of those governments seemed to aspire to being, at best, no more than the 'heir to Blair'. While economic growth can, clearly, be achieved through successful integration of these economic policies and approaches, doing so is clearly very difficult – and requires a detailed understanding of what *needs* to be done, combined with equally determined control of the various UK economic institutions. We need an insistence on breaking with the economic orthodoxy, while at the same time staying within the complex tramlines that I have reviewed and described in the pages of this chapter.

CONCLUSION

RETURNING THE UK'S ECONOMY TO GROWTH

Over the last 150 years or so, and up to a little after the turn of the twenty-first century, governments in western economies, including the UK, had maintained an implicit but nonetheless highly successful pact with their voters: the number of jobs in the economy would go up by around some 2 or 3 per cent each year on average, and the wages paid for any given job or position would also grow by a few per cent, over and above inflation.

In such an economic environment, even though there were bumps in the road, citizens could, in the main, confidently expect to keep their jobs or find new ones; they could expect there to be jobs for their children; and they could expect for there to be rising economic prospects for both them and their children. Those rising economic prospects would mean that each year, they would be paid more for their work, even when the work stayed much the same.

This pact meant most workers felt they had a stake in society and the economy, one that gave them a fair shake at realising their personal dreams and aspirations, and that enabled them to raise a family in a world that would give them the opportunity to succeed.

At the turn of the century, Tony Blair had just come into power with a new Labour government. That new government had promised to stick to the previous Conservative government's economic

RETURN TO GROWTH

spending programme for the first few years. The economy was in good shape, widely described as the best in Europe. GDP was growing rapidly. The social pact still existed. But now, a quarter of a century on, all of that has gone. As I write these words, the figures for the middle of 2024 have just come out, showing that our GDP stayed flat for the preceding months. Consequently, our GDP per capita has actually shrunk – because our population, thanks to immigration, is rising. And since growth in services was positive by a small amount, growth in the other part of the economy, manufacturing and construction, actually shrank (again).

It needn't be this way. Our GDP per capita has grown at 0.7 per cent per annum on average during the past twenty years – a pitifully low number, albeit one that we'd have been happy to see in recent months. The US was, at the turn of the century, already far richer than us; GDP per capita has since, in the US, grown at double the rate of ours – 1.4 per cent per annum in PPP terms.[1] So, as discussed in Volume One, GDP per capita in the US is now 45 per cent higher than ours. Workers are richer, and economic growth continues apace, widening the gap in both wealth and opportunity, year after year.[*]

As we have seen from Chapter 1, the richer the country, the more equally wages tend to be balanced between the well paid and the poorly paid. The more we grow, the richer all parts of society can become. If the UK had carried on growing at our turn-of-the-century pace, our GDP would now be some 60 per cent per capita higher than it currently is. Society in the UK would be transformed from where it is now. Wages would be higher, public services would be better and benefits could be far greater – yet the need for them

---

[*] I haven't been able to find any consensus on, or indeed much analysis at all of, the economic impact of the recent large influxes of legal and illegal immigrants into the US.

CONCLUSION

would be considerably less, because workers would be paid much better. So, taxes on those higher wages would be much lower, and take-home pay even greater.*

Economic growth matters, but as Volume One showed, over the past couple of decades, the UK spectacularly failed to provide it for its people.†

The purpose of *Return to Growth* has been to sound the alarm on how this has happened in recent decades to the UK economy, and to show that it need not have been so. In Volume One, we showed the significant increases to growth that can be achieved from drastic reductions in the size of government; the level of taxes; and the degree of regulation. In Volume Two, we have showed how to make the economy even more productive, through free markets, free trade and sound money, again using a validated version of a mainstream economic growth model to estimate the benefits to the UK that could be earned by making all these changes to the economy.‡

As discussed in Chapter 3, the UK's problems reach far back into the previous century. But the situation does seem to have worsened significantly since the year 2000. In that year, we had a government whose size (as a percentage of GDP) was not too far from what I propose in this book as an appropriate target. We had a faster-growing economy, so the size of government as a percentage of GDP continued to shrink. We had a budget surplus, so not only our debt-to-GDP ratio but also our absolute level of debt were declining.

By 2007–8, we had rapidly reversed these achievements. The Labour government engineered a rapid and massive increase in the

---
*   Assuming it shadowed GDP per capita.
†   The underlying problem has, of course, been going on longer than this.
‡   See Appendix B for a full description of that model, including the additions we made to it, which incorporates the further variables we have discussed in this Volume Two.

size of our state, resulting in a budget deficit, even in the good times, that meant we were totally unprepared for the global financial crisis that then took place. Since then, despite a change from Labour to Conservative (and now back again), we haven't reversed that poor position. We continue to worsen it, with a much-expanded state, ever-increasing taxes, nutty ideas about how the world works and above all, a strangulating, mushrooming web of regulation.

The year 2000 was only a quarter of a century ago. None of these worsening metrics have been to the benefit of the economy; they have crept up on the country by way of redistributionist social policies and extractive institutions; a press that amplifies the yelps of the indignation mob; and, sadly, a general attitude that says the government should be the route to solving all ills and that it is right for more and more money to be handed out to solve those ills.

But *there is no money*. Unless we spend much less, for a minimum of ten to fifteen years, and only then start to let up on the spending constraint, we will rapidly congeal into the mould of the mostly no-growth social democracies that make up the gradually disintegrating EU.

The policies – free markets, free trade and sound money – discussed here are not separate from the policies in Volume One. They are, let us say, the three 'angels' that protect the economy from those three 'devils' – large government, high taxes, and excessive regulation. If we cultivate and succeed in fostering these three angels, we will already be halfway to having small government, fewer taxes and fewer regulations.

So, the policies that have been discussed in this second volume are both enablers and enhancers of a sound economy. That enablement comes when ensuring *free markets* – because the specific things that one has to do to ensure them (enable competition, get rid of crony capitalism, protect private property) are the acme of *low regulation*. The things one has to do for *free trade* (remove tariffs and protectionism, have a mobile labour force, be outward facing) are key indicators of where and how to *lower taxes* and how to eliminate the negative impact of having subsidies. This comes from implementing *sound money* principles, which are central to having efficiently run *small government*, with fewer quangos and fewer non-democratic, only minimally accountable institutions. A sound monetary policy ensures that inflation will not arrive to cause disruption and damage to the economy. A country with lower debt and controlled inflation will be paying less debt-service interest, so has a smaller level of state expenditure. Small-sized governments will spend less on collecting and enforcing taxes, while low-regulation governments will need less officialdom, so will be smaller in size.

In estimating the overall likely impact on the economy of putting all our proposed policies in place, I was careful not to inadvertently double-count potential benefits (the impact of the variables we have reviewed in these two volumes can be 'confounding' to each other, so we made sure not to assume that the individual benefits from each were just additive). Even so, when we add the forecast for the 'angel' policies outlined in Volume Two into the 'anti-devil' forecast of Volume One, our model does show a further significant improvement in GDP growth rates and in national wealth, over and above the benefits from implementing the policies suggested in Volume One – even though in all runs of our model, we have been careful to be conservative when estimating the level of benefits.

The details of the modelled logic that led to these conclusions can be seen in Appendix B. We have used modest assumptions for some of the variables, making no extravagant claims for what could be achieved.* These levels of improvement are possibly pessimistic, at the lower end of potential additional benefits – but even so, they result in overall projected outcomes that, if achieved, would transform our country's economic performance, the wealth of our individual citizens and our country's opportunities to invest in both infrastructure projects and improvement of services.

In Volume One, we discussed how median take-home pay could, if the first three policy programmes were successfully put in place, increase over the modelled period from £31,500 to £48,000 a year. When we throw in the projected additional benefits from implementing the policies proposed here, GDP growth becomes (a conservative estimate) around half a percentage point a year higher; the expected improvements and opportunities become significantly greater. Government spend as a percentage of GDP declines faster, down to 33 per cent – not just because we spend less, but because GDP grows faster. National debt as a percentage of GDP declines even more.

Chart 4.1 sums up the modelled expected benefits from implementing the policies discussed in Volume One and Volume Two.

As can be seen from Chart 4.1, government spend in the final years of the fifteen-year scenario hits the 33 per cent line (and then we relax the spending constraint and let it continue at that level).† By the end of the fifteen-year period, our tax and other revenue take is (just) higher than our spend, so we are running a surplus. Our debt-to-GDP ratio, instead of rising to some 150 per cent, as predicted in our 'status quo' forecast, is projected to have already

---
* In particular, we avoided the over-optimism that could come from using recent higher-growth experiences that have been seen in developing countries around the world. Our modelled outcomes relied principally on data from developed countries and on the history of the UK itself, to ensure the feasibility and credible validity of our assumptions.
† Over time, an ambitious government may choose to reduce expenditures to lower than 33 per cent of GDP.

CONCLUSION

dropped to some 80 per cent, and will thereafter drop at an even more rapid rate. Our GDP per capita is predicted to have risen from some £40,000 a head to nearly £60,000 in real terms. And our economic growth should be around 3 per cent per annum on average – entirely feasible: achieved by us in the past; being achieved right now by comparator countries; achievable by us in the future.

Chart 4.1: The All-Policies Scenario

If all our proposed policies are implemented, income and wealth grow and the public finances improve dramatically.

	-1 2023/24	0 2024/25	1 2025/26	5 2029/30	10 2034/35	15 2039/40
KEY INPUTS (ASSUMPTIONS)						
Government spending as % GDP	44.5%	43.9%	42.2%	35.9%	34.1%	32.1%
Government receipts as % GDP	40.4%	40.4%	40.4%	33.5%	33.0%	32.5%
Annual productivity growth	0.1%	0.1%	0.1%	0.6%	0.7%	0.7%
Gross fixed capital formation as % GDP	18.4%	16.8%	17.2%	21.5%	27.0%	27.7%
Human capital index annual growth rate	0.2%	0.2%	0.4%	0.9%	0.9%	0.9%
Total population, million	68.4	69.0	69.6	71.4	73.0	74.6
Working population, million	35.8	36.2	36.9	39.1	41.2	43.3
OUTPUTS (RESULTS)						
GDP growth	0.2%	0.8%	1.8%	2.8%	3.4%	3.6%
Real GDP, £ trillion	2.7	2.8	2.8	3.1	3.6	4.3
GDP per capita	39,963	39,889	40,270	43,177	49,380	57,674
National debt as % GDP	100%	103%	103%	102%	95%	81%
Budget deficit, £billion	114	97	51	76	43	(16)
Budget deficit as %GDP	4.2%	3.5%	1.8%	2.5%	1.2%	-0.4%

Source: moyniteam modelling

I hope the reasonably exhaustive discussion in these two volumes has made it clear that, draconian as the policies proposed in this book may at first have seemed, they are not in the least exceptional. All they do is return us to what was the case just a short while ago. The UK seems, in the twenty-five years since the turn of the century, to have sleepwalked into an economic catastrophe of our own making. On government spend, all this book recommends is that we return to the size of government (as a percentage of GDP) that pertained shortly after Tony Blair took power. On taxes, all this book recommends is to return to the level of tax take and the simpler tax code that we had back then. On regulation, all the book recommends is to return to a time where we did not live in an ever-increasing and expensive thicket of regulation. Just a quarter of a century ago.[*]

Yes, so great has been our fall from economic grace in recent decades that now some large and painful steps will have to be taken. But there is a way forward. We have shown here a reasonable, sensible and achievable programme to make growth happen. If we step up to that programme, there is a bright, long-term future for our country and our people. We can return to growth.

---

[*] Note that, had we stayed at the spend, tax and regulation levels of 2000, our GDP would have by now grown so much more that we would have been able to afford a much larger government spend than we incurred in the year 2000. But that spend could be just 33 per cent of GDP; so much more money would be available for our citizens and for investing further to grow the economy – whether through improved infrastructure, more tax cuts, or some other way.

EPILOGUE

AND HERE'S HOW WE DO IT

TOWARDS A SMALLER GOVERNMENT AND A HIGH-GROWTH ECONOMY

The purpose of Volume One was to make the urgent case for taking the political and economic steps to return growth to the UK's economy. In particular, it tried to make clear the central importance of removing the three major obstacles to growth – our too-large state; too-high taxes; and a too-considerable amount of regulation. Volume Two set out to describe the overall framework that our economy should create to accomplish that growth: free markets, free trade and sound money. In this epilogue, I offer a proposed set of practical steps that we would need to take in order to reach those goals, so that the country can achieve the desired new, faster-growing economic setup.

To restore a dynamic level of economic growth to the UK, we need an action programme that will, over time, shrink both our government's expenditure and its tax revenues as a percentage of GDP, while preserving sound money. This, if accompanied by significant deregulation, particularly of the type that supported free markets and free trade, will unleash the entrepreneurial and productive forces that we have shown will lead to growth.

Somehow, all this has to be achieved while maintaining prudent fiscal and monetary policies, thereby avoiding inflation or financial disruption. For this to happen, we will need to reform the institutions of government. The end result will be a faster growing economy and greater wealth and fulfilment for our citizens. But to accomplish this, in the short term some politically difficult decisions will have to be taken, and a cooperative electorate will need to be convinced of the need for them.

. . .

It's the politically difficult decisions that are, of course, at the heart of why none of this has been attempted in the UK in recent decades (and why, in accordance with Wagner's Law, the situation has worsened year by year). But it is possible, if those proposing to implement such a programme communicate their intent with unflinching honesty and probity, to make and implement those decisions. After all, our electorate must surely be capable of being as sober as those of Ireland or Greece were when (as we will see later in this chapter) they accepted such measures. It is not impossible that Britons will vote for a modern-day Calvin Coolidge – who, as I show in a few pages, implemented similar measures in the 1920s with huge success – or the British equivalent of Javier Milei, who is implementing radical policies right now in Argentina.

We have seen how the UK has rapidly fallen out of that group of countries whose citizens can look forward to long-term, wealth-creating economic growth. We are now stagnating in that group of mainly social democratic countries whose economic growth has been flat (or in terms of growth in GDP per capita, at times negative). Our languishing position has led to all the problems discussed in Volume One: lack of personal opportunity for our citizens, budget deficits, high inflation, and an accelerating negative spiral of economic problems.

EPILOGUE

Our poor economic performance, a fate we currently share with our near neighbours, raises a host of questions that I hope I have managed to answer in these two volumes. How has our current situation come to pass? What specific decisions were made in the UK by policymakers of both major parties that led to it? How did those decisions reshape our economy so dramatically, abetted by the widespread belief that government is there to hand out money to meet every negative circumstance? There is, then, a further question that needs to be answered: how can the UK's electorate now be persuaded to elect a government that will focus on individual responsibility, taking the stringent actions needed to return to meaningful, sufficient, real wealth-creating economic growth?

The size of the changes now needed to reverse our problems clearly suggests that a comprehensive programme is needed. Necessarily, such a programme will take a good number of years to complete – although much of it can be implemented at the start of the process.* Here is my proposed sequence for getting the needed policies into place and working:

1. win the argument and get a democratic mandate
2. align government institutions with our objectives
3. deregulate as much as possible
4. cut government expenditures

---

* No political party in the last election proposed to implement a programme of the sort indicated in these volumes. Even if a centrist Conservative government had won the election, it would have been not much more likely to have sought to reverse the trend than our new Labour government is. It seems inevitable that it will take at least another five years of Labour's muddled and certain-to-fail economic mishmash programmes before there is even a chance of the electorate returning a party that advocates the kind of policies described in this book. Thus, any such programme would be unlikely to commence before 2029 and perhaps not till 2035, in which case the situation is likely to become much worse than it is today – both because of lack of economic growth, and because of implementation of the various 'moral panic' policies discussed in Volume One. There would then be up to ten years to wait before positive new policies could start to make a big impact. We by then have progressed to a dauntingly far-off 2040, or even later, for the wheel of fortune to have come around again in this country's favour. It seems inevitable that this is the best we can hope for. Depressing, but that does not mean we can't start planning for it now – indeed, we must.

5. reduce taxes

6. in parallel, ensure free markets, free trade and sound money

In the following pages, I elaborate on each of these steps.

STEP ONE: WIN THE ARGUMENT AND GET A DEMOCRATIC MANDATE

To be able to implement its programme, our new government must persuade the electorate that we cannot carry on down the social democrat road. We have to convince voters how crucial it is to resize the state, to allow deregulated and less-taxed free markets to return to working their magic, getting the country back on a path to growth. With a democratic mandate, such as the one Milei won in Argentina, the government will be able to get to work.

The path to being handed a mandate by a convinced electorate is, hardly necessary to say, littered with obstacles.

The first obstacle is the need for things to be accepted as being so bad that people understand that we can't go on as we are, that something has to change if things are to get better. While, in my view, the number of voters thinking that way is much larger than current media coverage might make it seem, there is no major party that understands what is wrong, and proposes to do something about it. Reform UK seems closest, but more so on tax and anti-woke policies than on spending – in the meantime, so long as Reform splits the right-wing vote with the Conservatives, it's highly unlikely that either could get into Downing Street. Of course, it's not that everything is seen by the electorate as full of sunshine and laughter right now; there is massive discontent across the country. The new government, in its opening months, seems to have been doing its best to do things that maintain or even enhance the pessimism.

EPILOGUE

But I would argue that in general, the kind of diagnosis I have tried to offer here is neither understood nor in general accepted. So while the situation is generally seen as bad – and I think we can expect that it will get worse over the next five years – there is clearly neither a consensus on what the 'bad' specifically consists of, nor a general feeling that there is a clear path to escaping from it.

So, the second obstacle is getting a general acceptance of the prime causes of things having got so bad. The second half of Volume One set out the stall on those propositions. Again, while the evidence is (I assert) convincing on that, and it seems that at least the two right-wing parties have begun to adopt my mantra – state too large, tax too high, too much regulation – neither of the two major parties went to the electorate with a detailed platform based on that. Just about all parties currently assert that the most important thing for the economy is to get it growing again, but neither the Conservatives nor Labour offered any hard, convincing proposals as to what to do about it. Perhaps Kemi Badenoch will prove better.

We somehow have to achieve a sufficient level of understanding among the electorate that until we restructure the economy and the state, we won't get the growth that will eventually make enough money available to fund the kind of country that our social justice campaigners demand, and we need a better awareness that some of those demands should never be met, given that they encourage many in society not to contribute their abilities and energy to the economy, but rather to find ways to live off society. There are considerable incentives in the current welfare system for citizens to seek payouts, rather than developing self-reliance by getting and keeping a job.

Towards the end of Volume One, I discussed the extraordinary demonisation of business and entrepreneurship that a notionally conservative government had indulged in while it was in power; I don't think we can hope for Labour to be particularly better on that front. The media, in the main reliably anti-capitalist, have done their bit to vilify businesses, and we now have children coming out of school ill-educated, indoctrinated with woke nonsense and filled with the dysfunctional 'be kind' approach, as opposed to the needed 'face the facts' perspective – as discussed in Appendix D of Volume One. Yet there is light at the end of that particular tunnel: we are told that Gen Z children, reacting to all that nonsense, are turning much more (twice as) conservative in their views than millennials.[1] The human race, and particularly Britons, did not achieve their present-day circumstances by allowing fancy to overrule fact, and we can hope that a good look by younger voters at what they are being indoctrinated about means that there will be an inevitable backlash.

Thus, if we believe that a consensus is beginning to emerge both as to the size of the problem and its causes, then we come to the third needed outcome: finding the politicians who will articulate and communicate a programme of what needs to be done. In these two volumes, I have proposed a way to get us to our desired economic structure for the UK, but I will be first to admit that while I believe my diagnosis is correct and my plan the right one, I am no silver-tongued politician who can sell it all to the people. (The tragedy of Boris Johnson – who would have been so able to do that, and had the mandate for it, but was surrounded by magical thinkers who led him down the delusionary garden path of net zero and other fantasies – shows both what could have been, and at the same time how easy it is for things to go wrong. The Truss premiership experienced the opposite problem, in that she had the right prescription but did not have the support.) It is, again, not clear, when at the time of writing Kemi Badenoch has just been elected leader, whether the Conservative Party will embrace what needs to be done; clearly, we need a united right-wing movement that will do all the above, including convincing the country to vote for it.

This requires, fourth, achieving a voting coalition that gets into power. These two volumes have, apart from this epilogue, stayed away from how that can be achieved; it was task enough to say what was wrong and what needed to be done. I'm not a politician, so I am not the one to find the way to achieving electoral victory. Set against such a programme is the voting coalition that social democrats rely on to keep them in power: extractive institutions such as crony capitalists; civil servants; other public-sector workers; beneficiaries of the state – those who get more benefit from the state than they pay in tax. Overall, it's a formidable combination. We have always relied on the three left-wing parties (Labour, Lib Dem and the SNP) splitting, and thus letting in a Conservative government. The tables are now – for now – turned. A single right-wing party has to emerge, and that can be done only through one of three ways: the two parties merge, or Reform destroys the Tories, or the Tories destroy Reform. They must then elect a leader for that party who can (miraculously) work their way through these many obstacles.

The key to winning the needed mandate is to draw public attention to the negatives that so many are feeling, but about which there has not been enough reporting. When that happens, the electorate would need to be persuaded that the benefits of the programme would be far greater than the costs of its implementation. In these two volumes, my intent has been to provide the material that would allow a future political leader to embark on getting through the obstacles described above.

When elected, a new government would expect to have laid out in its manifesto the targets the new economic plan would be seeking to achieve. It would need to lay out a timeframe encompassing a ten- to fifteen-year period, but with the emphasis on the first few months and years of the programme. The diagnosis from the two volumes of this book is, I hope – now you have masochistically read this far – clear. I have shown numerous reasons why our growth rate has collapsed. Increasingly, our status as a free-market economy is being dented as the government interferes more and more, in sector after sector. A lingering protectionist view of trade policy, in great part a legacy of our fifty-year membership of the EU, will have to be gradually overcome, as our traditional openness as a country reasserts itself. However, the work on that has only just started and our progress could easily be reversed.* And as a final concern, our overall economic strategy continues to be compromised by the strong influence of the nation's Keynesian institutions.

The biggest short-term problem is that we are spending at a far higher level than where a dynamic economy can flourish, with the welfare state denying personal agency, and government after government throwing money at more and more societal problems without (as the example of the NHS shows) getting the success that was expected. As we have seen across two volumes of this book, we are spending more and more money that we don't have. That is clearly not going to work out as a long-term strategy.

Chart 4.2 is the development of a chart from Volume One, Chapter 6. We have not reached the heights of high expenditure per capita that equivalently rich EU social democratic countries such as France now spend, but we are moving in that direction. What

---

* At the time of writing, the new government is engaged in discussions with Brussels. The fear is that they will come to an agreement that shuts down trade with the rest of the world.

we share with those social democracies is that we are spending as if we were much richer than we are. By the estimates of this chart, we are spending some £112 billion more than the average country that has the same wealth per capita as us is spending. Just to get the UK back in line with the hybrid (not even with the free-market) economies shown in this chart, that have equivalent wealth per capita to us, would require expenditure reductions of that much – some £112 billion.

Chart 4.2: Living Within One's Means

The UK is spending £112 billion beyond what other economies with equivalent levels of wealth per capita are spending and £300 billion more than a 33 per cent of GDP target.

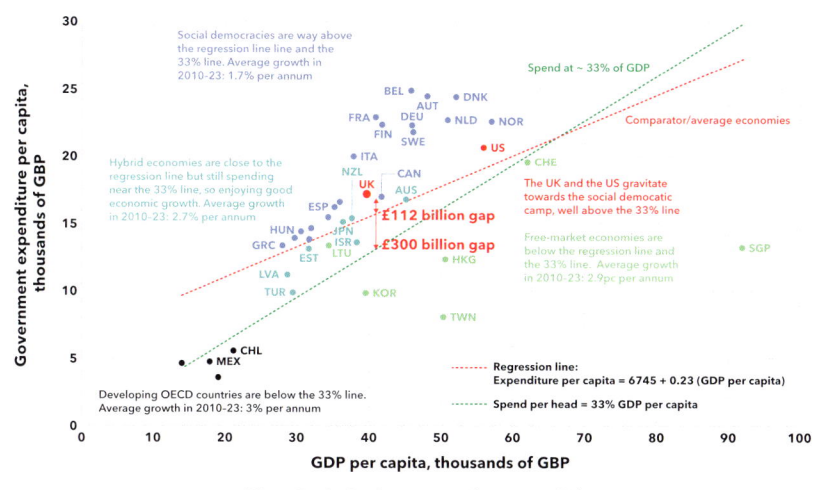

```
[Scatter plot with GDP per capita (thousands of GBP) on x-axis (0-100) and Government expenditure per capita, thousands of GBP on y-axis (0-30).

Annotations:
- Social democracies are way above the regression line line and the 33% line. Average growth in 2010-23: 1.7% per annum
- Hybrid economies are close to the regression line but still spending near the 33% line, so enjoying good economic growth. Average growth in 2010-23: 2.7% per annum
- The UK and the US gravitate towards the social democratic camp, well above the 33% line
- Free-market economies are below the regression line and the 33% line. Average growth in 2010-23: 2.9pc per annum
- Developing OECD countries are below the 33% line. Average growth in 2010-23: 3% per annum
- Spend at ~ 33% of GDP
- Comparator/average economies
- £112 billion gap
- £300 billion gap

Country markers: BEL, DNK, AUT, FRA, DEU, NLD, NOR, FIN, SWE, ITA, US, CHE, NZL, CAN, UK, AUS, ESP, JPN, HUN, ISR, GRC, EST, LTU, HKG, SGP, LVA, TUR, KOR, TWN, CHL, MEX

Legend:
- Regression line: Expenditure per capita = 6745 + 0.23 (GDP per capita)
- Spend per head = 33% GDP per capita]
```

Note: Includes Singapore (not OECD)
Source: International Monetary Fund,[2] moyniteam analysis

This £112 billion is a whopping 9 per cent of our current national budget. Yet even were we to succeed with that reduction in the short term, that would only get us down to an expenditure level of around 41 per cent of GDP. The £112 billion is, however, only a small part of the overspend; overall, our expenditure is over £300 billion per year more than if we were to meet a growth-promoting government spending target of 33 per cent of GDP, as I proposed in Volume One (with tax plus other revenues at about the same).

Chart 4.3: Reaching the Target of 33 Per Cent of GDP

Government expenditure will drop to 33 per cent of GDP in thirteen to fifteen years under the moyniteam scenario.

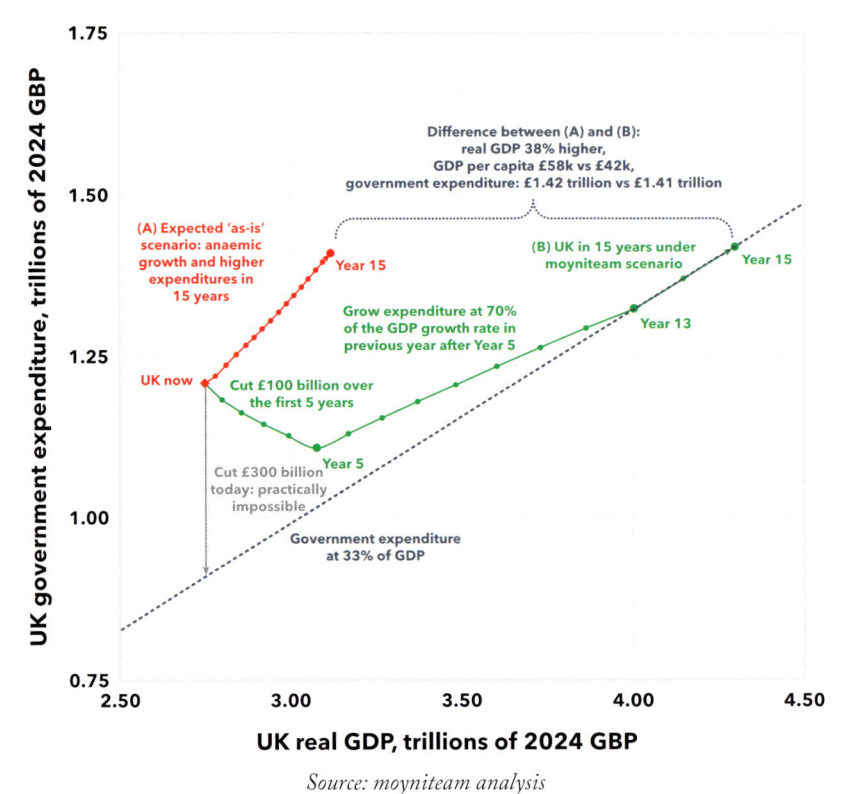

Source: moyniteam analysis

To get down to a growth-promoting state that's sized at a third of

GDP, we need to be spending a full £300 billion less – 33 per cent is what pertained just two decades ago, in the early Blair years. It's a sensible, perfectly achievable target. We could in theory get there almost instantaneously by cutting £300 billion overnight – around a quarter of our over £1.2 trillion budget (the grey line in Chart 4.3). We could get there more slowly, over a few decades, with only low, bit-by-bit increasing, levels of growth, freezing the current level of expenditure in real terms; but the electorate would run out of patience. A scenario that is somewhere in between those two choices is the best way (the green line in Chart 4.3). This would be a process requiring significant cuts, both up front and over time. The growth-promoting benefits, as we got nearer to target levels, would increase steadily over time.

If the UK had the GDP per capita of the US, then we could afford considerably more than just the level of government expenditure that we have now. But entirely because we have chosen to spend above our means for decades now, we no longer have that fiscal room – so, for a while, we have to cut our spending drastically. (Much of our spending is anyway, as I have shown, unnecessary and often counterproductive.)

In Volume One, we showed how the estimated spending cuts that could be achieved during the new government's first term in office were some £118 billion, slightly under 10 per cent of current national expenditure. This would reduce national spend to between 40 and 41 per cent of GDP, which is still significantly above the ideal level of 33 per cent of GDP that we have targeted. If we are to reach that 33 per cent, it will have to be done by constraining future cost increases carefully, and growing significantly faster (in terms of GDP per capita) than the rate of increase in expenditure.

How to ensure that? I have suggested that we create a constitutional (or quasi-constitutional) limit on increases in expenditure – no more than 70 per cent of the previous year's growth in GDP. This limit should be in place until expenditures have reached 33 per cent of GDP; thereafter, spend should be no more than the GDP growth rate in the previous year. This rule would have to incorporate a variable rate of welfare payments, so that if in any year the welfare rolls increased but GDP did not, then the level of individual payments would have to be adjusted down by the appropriate percentage.* Ensuring that GDP grew as fast as possible would depend on two things: first, the £118 billion of reduced expenditure that would provide the crucial fiscal room to create a more attractive environment for business to grow and entrepreneurs to return to the UK and flourish, implementing a considerable but carefully targeted set of tax cuts similar to the saved expenditure. This would need to be accompanied by, second, a swift and massive attack on regulation, so as to make it easier for corporations and entrepreneurs to set up, invest in and successfully grow businesses.

This discussion, on how to get overall government spending down to 33 per cent of GDP, may seem overly aspirational, but I have written this book to answer the questions of how we got to this situation, and how we get out of it. The approach of recent decades – to gain electoral popularity by spending more and more on increasingly dysfunctional programmes – has been an utter failure, even in its goal of providing for its intended beneficiaries. How we get from where we are to where we need to get to is at first sight complex and difficult, because the problems have become

---

* This goes directly against the concept of increased welfare payments during recessions being 'automatic stabilisers' for the economy. Discussion of this and other such Keynesian concepts is beyond the scope of this book, but the Keynesian approach to economic management must surely now be seen to have had its day.

entrenched and, in the eyes of many, intractable. But as I show here, other advanced western economies have accomplished far more aggressive reductions than I propose here, once their electorate was shown, and had accepted, the inexorable necessity.

Conservative policy solutions can be implemented successfully in the UK, just as was done under Margaret Thatcher in the 1980s. As I argue here, the examination of the causes of the UK's decline into stagnation, laid out in Volume One, leads us to the conclusion that it is perfectly possible for the UK to return to a faster-growing economy, despite the enormous institutional resistance that will emerge against the needed changes – but only if it is accepted that difficult steps will have to be taken.

Creativity is needed if we are to move from a low-growth, high-regulation, big-government, high-tax social democrat model to a free-market structure. In late 2022, *The Spectator* published a seventeen-page plan that the Truss government, during its brief life, had created, as part of its attempt to create a faster-growing economy.[3] That interesting document, which received almost no notice in the political world, offered numerous positive ideas. Other political manifestos from around the world, such as Javier Milei's approach in Argentina, will likely add to those perspectives.[*][4]

The tedious length of the two volumes of this book – which nevertheless describe only a fraction of the many economic issues

---

[*] At the time of writing, the impact of Milei has been successful, particularly as regards inflation; as this book goes to press, Argentina has celebrated its first month of zero inflation in food prices in three decades. One can expect bumps in the future, no doubt, but the success so far indicates that an aggressive approach can work. Milei, of course, spent twenty years as an economist and had used the long period of time before he came to power to prepare a plan, which, on reaching office, he could put straight into effect. His approach makes the policy changes that I have suggested in these two volumes appear wimpy: he has slashed expenditure to the bone and achieved a budget surplus in a year. He proposes to reduce spending to 25 per cent of GDP – which, if I thought it was realistically achievable, I would indeed suggest for the UK. (Perhaps we can get to 25 per cent in the *subsequent* fifteen years.) He proposes reducing taxes to the same level, while requiring a non-negotiable balanced budget. He is reforming the pension system. He is making private property sacrosanct. He is deregulating so as to open up exploitation of the country's national resources – drillers and frackers are now pouring into Argentina.

that face our country – shows what a fiendishly complex web of problems needs to be solved if we are to return our economy to faster growth. Worse, as all would agree, the 'how' to do it is equally as difficult and complex as the 'what' to do. Before embarking on a transformation of our government and our economy, the new Prime Minister and their team would have to square the electorate sufficiently during their first term to win the next election after five years had passed – defeating bogus allegations, Keynesian bully boys and the 'something must be done' crowd.

With this in mind, how quickly can the economic environment in the UK be altered? Given our five-year electoral cycle, change has to be seen and experienced by the electorate in a relatively short timeframe. As events in 2022 showed, however, moves that are too fast can lead to resistance and destabilisation from the many institutions that, it would seem, have more power than the government.

As discussed, before economic growth can increase, both the business and regulatory environment will have to change. We have to make a new environment, one that is attractive to wealth creators:

- *The self-employed*, who need particular encouragement since they are the initiating basis for entrepreneurial activity. Exemplary steps would be to repeal IR35 rules, lessen national insurance contributions and implement other measures discussed in Volume One.
- *Entrepreneurs*, who need lighter and less regulation and low business taxes.
- *Wealthy and high-earning individuals* who have fled overseas, and who need to be attracted back to the UK with their capital and their business know-how, as well as their own considerable spending power and the tax revenues we'd get.

- *Small businesses* who need low employee taxes, low business rates and less regulation (SMEs encompass 60 per cent of all employees in the UK).
- *Large domestic companies*, who need less product regulation, low employee taxes and less regulatory and compliance intrusion.
- *International companies*, who need an attractive business regime, low and stable corporate taxes, low energy costs, low production taxes and a cast-iron promise that there will never again be such foolishness as an 'excess profits' tax.[*]

So, the very first thing to do is to secure an environment where:

- government-spending programmes, particularly welfare, can be reduced significantly
- taxes, as expenditure drops, are steadily lowered
- regulation becomes less draconian

To energise the business community and attract overseas capital and know-how, the plans would have to be publicised in detail; understood by business, the markets and the electorate; and ready to go. The detailed programme would then need to be implemented as soon as the new government came to power.

In laying that out, the government would need to:

1. Set out a long-term shape of government, one that spent mostly on 'core' and 'productive' expenditure, while de-emphasising 'unproductive' elements.

---

[*] The imposition of this tax in 2022 dealt an enormous blow to Britain's long-standing reputation as a business-friendly country, which it will take a great deal to recover from. A government wishing to attract business investment back to the UK will need to provide compelling reassurances that all has changed before foreign capital is likely to flow as freely into the country as before.

2. Publish an upfront, realistic plan envisaging a series of progressive changes, some of which would only be implemented once certain milestones are reached.

The inexorable growth of the size of government in the UK (see Volume One, Chart 1.2) seems to have led to the UK government ratcheting up its expenditure to an unaffordable level, and then not being able to find a way to reduce it down again. We began to see how very difficult it is for large governments to shrink back to a size where a higher level of economic growth can be hoped for.

Chart 4.4: Public Perceptions on the Responsibility of the Government

UK share of adults replying that the government definitely should…

Big government is all the rage among voters.

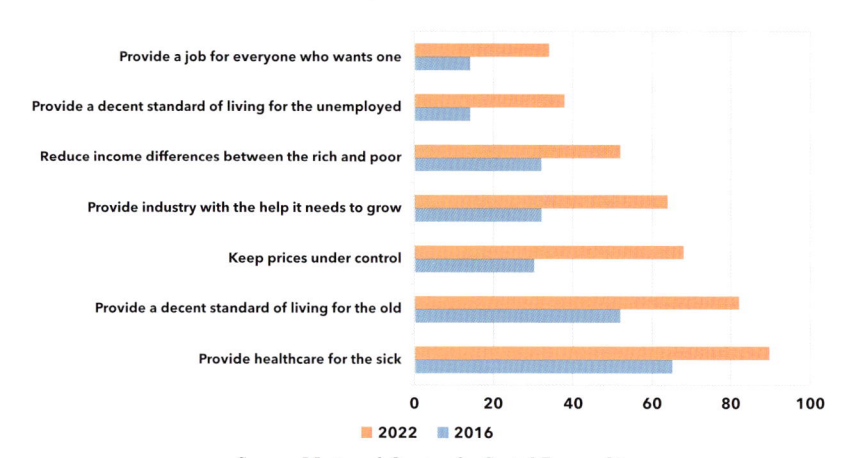

Category	2022	2016
Provide a job for everyone who wants one	~33	~15
Provide a decent standard of living for the unemployed	~37	~15
Reduce income differences between the rich and poor	~52	~30
Provide industry with the help it needs to grow	~63	~30
Keep prices under control	~67	~30
Provide a decent standard of living for the old	~82	~52
Provide healthcare for the sick	~88	~65

Source: National Centre for Social Research[5]

And let's be frank, if we want to shrink the UK's government, we are swimming against a strong tide. Several generations have been taught that there's no problem that can't be solved by the government bunging out lashings of cash; that the government is there to meet all needs. Chart 4.4 shows how the problem has significantly worsened post-pandemic. But, as discussed, these views are unaffordable; they fly in the face of what actually happens to socialist states as economic growth slows and the economy ultimately implodes. We can only hope that, as discussed earlier, the common sense of the British people reasserts itself.

There's more than pure size of government to consider. We saw in Volume One how the *shape* of government, not just its *size*, is highly influential in accelerating or slowing growth. So, the long-term proposed shape of government, emphasising core and growth-promoting spend, needs to be articulated and laid out in those terms.

Once a democratic mandate for overall change has been won, the detailed programme that needs to be sold to the electorate (using 2024 as an example, but the numbers will be different in future years) is for significant one-off cuts of about 9 per cent of total expenditure during the new government's first term of office. Tax cuts can then match reductions in expenditures. Assuming no violent global disruption, there should be enough success from that for the government to be re-elected after five years. The longer-term targets should be reachable within ten years, fifteen at most.

STEP TWO: ALIGN THE INSTITUTIONS WITH OUR OBJECTIVES

Step one demonstrated the need to plan, and communicate that plan widely; emphasising the democratic approval already obtained from the electorate. By doing this, the aim is to reduce the impact of any potential hostility to the plan from those in charge of the institutions discussed in Chapter 3, many of whom are currently instinctively opposed to a free-market approach. For some of these institutions, it will inevitably need to be not so much an issue of *reducing* hostility, but one of *ensuring* cooperation. This was, in some commentators' views, the main cause of Liz Truss's downfall: that key institutions were not aligned with her plan and indeed were actively opposed to it. Certainly, the Bank of England announcing £80 billion of QT the day before the mini-budget, and the leaking of the OBR's alleged £70 billion 'black hole' in the mini-budget, must have served to destabilise both markets and the government – and, more importantly, public opinion and approval.[6]

To avoid any similar problems in future, the key economic institutions, that are there ostensibly to support the government, must be aligned with it. Chart 4.5, an extension of Chart 3.29 in Chapter 3, shows the activities related to those institutions that have to be taken into account, and how.

Chart 4.5: How Governments Should Manage Institutions
Ensuring coordination not conflict

The institutions need to be aligned with the plan so that they support, rather than derail, government policy.

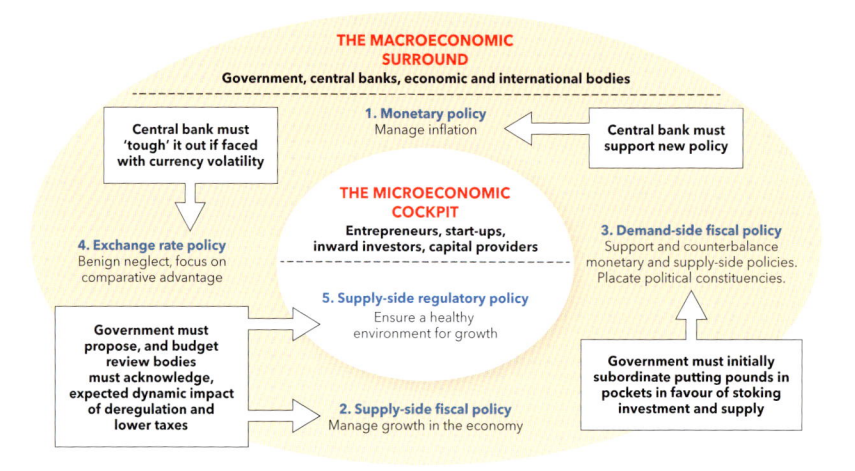

THE MACROECONOMIC SURROUND
Government, central banks, economic and international bodies

1. Monetary policy
Manage inflation

Central bank must 'tough' it out if faced with currency volatility

Central bank must support new policy

THE MICROECONOMIC COCKPIT
Entrepreneurs, start-ups, inward investors, capital providers

4. Exchange rate policy
Benign neglect, focus on comparative advantage

5. Supply-side regulatory policy
Ensure a healthy environment for growth

3. Demand-side fiscal policy
Support and counterbalance monetary and supply-side policies. Placate political constituencies.

Government must propose, and budget review bodies must acknowledge, expected dynamic impact of deregulation and lower taxes

2. Supply-side fiscal policy
Manage growth in the economy

Government must initially subordinate putting pounds in pockets in favour of stoking investment and supply

EPILOGUE

As shown in Chapter 3, it's essential to have an integrated approach between all the players in the various parts of the macroeconomic arena, and the government's initiatives in the microeconomic arenas. In recent decades, there has been a major shift in responsibility away from government ministers, and towards heads of autonomous or quasi-autonomous bodies. The most perilous aspect of this abdication of control is in the economy, where the Treasury has been hollowed out. The Bank of England pursues policies that can work directly against the elected government's views and policies, and the OBR has at times adopted a defiant approach that is bound to clash with that of any growth-seeking, free-market promoting government. Over and above all that, the civil service has mostly abandoned its principles of impartiality and now is a formidable obstacle to any classic liberal economics programme.

At the time I write this, the Bank of England and the OBR are independent from the elected government. While the arguments to give them that independence were accepted at the time, what was missed was the iron rule that all such 'independent' bodies, over time, drift leftward. If their independence is maintained, a pro-growth, free-market approach will be difficult to pursue. The OBR model forecasts positive economic growth from higher immigration, and de-emphasises dynamic responses to changes in taxation and regulation. Meanwhile, the Bank of England has been getting worse at forecasting. It seems not to understand the causes of inflation, has a Keynesian bias and has succumbed to being overly enamoured with quantitative easing (QE).

To succeed in implementing a free-market economic programme, we need to ensure an aligned response from the Bank of England, and remove any redistributionist influence from the OBR. In doing so, we would not want to rely on current Treasury forecasting capabilities, which have been hollowed out – Treasury officials now defer to the OBR, itself no great shakes at forecasting. Instead, we should build a new, modern modelling capability, ensuring improved economic forecasts that are tied to the government's objectives and that properly capture dynamic responses.

Aligning the institutions also requires a complete transformation of the government's relationship with the civil service. This encompasses responsibilities and rights:

- *Responsibilities*: It cannot be that civil servants should be the ones to formulate policy. Civil servants in their professional capacity should not be allowed to exercise significantly opposed views from those of their political masters, whose policies they should be implementing.
- *Rights*: Any future government determined to push through free-market policies absolutely has to grasp the nettle, and put paid to the current situation whereby politicians are at the mercy of entities and processes that have been set up to regulate their conduct, administered and often even staffed by civil servants. If a politician behaves abominably, we already have a process to remove them. It is called an election. Politicians are appointed by the electorate, and it is the electorate that should be given the ultimate choice as to whether to remove them from power or not. The incoming government should create new laws to abolish the many current lines of defence, such as the 'Ministerial Code of Conduct'.

How to make the public sector more like the private sector? Where to start? The main answer surely lies in major structural reorganisation of the civil service, so as to create an institution that is not able to evade its responsibilities, to both the public and the elected government, in the way it seems to do now. As detailed in Volume One, the self-regulating civil service is overlarge, overpaid, unproductive, politicised and obstructive. Its lack of productivity is a major component of the UK's failure to attain the economy-wide productivity levels seen in comparable countries.

A new structure should define the respective jobs of the government and the civil service, and make sure that both understand what their proper role is, with the civil service focusing predominantly on delivery, not policy formulation or disputation. This does not mean the civil service should be entirely cut off from policy. If a government wishes to seek suggestions from its civil service, then it is, of course, entirely free to do so. If it wishes to create policy units within the civil service, on top of the non-civil-service Policy Unit in Downing Street, it can do so. But government should be the one to decide whether to do that or not, and the civil service should be in no doubt that its fundamental job is to make the manifesto happen, as directed by the government. If it acts too slowly, or in opposition to the manifesto, it should be shaken up through sackings, transfers or demotions – just like any private-sector organisation would be.

Lowering the headcount of the civil service will likely prove impossible until we separate the HR function from the main body of the civil service, in particular to ensure that the new, independently run HR body abandons the civil service's current absurd infatuation with woke practices. Previously, whenever cuts in civil servant levels were achieved, the numbers bounced right back – to even higher levels. The price of a more lean, productive civil service is perpetual vigilance by the politicians. This can only be achieved by making the HR function independent from the main body of the civil service. The HR function would be told to put a stop to promoting all woke nonsense; told that its prime job is to maintain and pursue the vision of a small, shrinking, and ever-more productive civil service workforce.

Every manager who has had to survive in the more competitively demanding private sector knows that a target of 15–20 per cent of staff reduction is, for any organisation that hasn't recently gone through a reduction in force (RIF) exercise, a minimal target. When Elon Musk bought Twitter (now X), he fired 6,000 people out of its 7,500-strong workforce – a full 80 per cent of staff. People cried woe betide and that X would fall over. It didn't.[7] Musk announced a similar RIF, of more than 10 per cent of jobs, at Tesla in April 2024. Within weeks of Musk's move, Meta, Amazon and Google all announced plans to cut tens of thousands of jobs; the bloated monopoly tech companies all began to realise that force reduction was not just achievable, but also imperative, for them, too.[8]

So, a smaller, more productive civil service *is* possible, just as has been proven possible across the private sector and just as a few (a very few) ministers in the past have achieved inside their own departments. But it will take reformation of the entire civil service structure to accomplish that.

Once the change of terms has been accomplished, a change of activities can be put in place. Overall performance improvement is urgently needed. In the private sector, that is easily accomplished because the HR function reports ultimately to the CEO and thus through to the board. In the civil service there is no such constraint. Civil servants manage their own workforce. Many departments don't even record whether each employee is performing well – let alone do they have a programme to ensure better performance. Over the years, this has led to greater and greater problems. There is now

EPILOGUE

an overwhelming focus in the civil service on process, rather than outcomes. There is a culture of impunity, and a lack of the necessary accountability that in the private sector would lead to sackings and demotions. Civil servants are promoted and moved around at the whim of internal HR, regardless of the impact of their departure on the unit they have been serving.

One perennial complaint that I hear from ministers is that as soon as they have finally persuaded a civil servant to actually hunker down and get something done, that civil servant is transferred, or goes on sabbatical, or sickness leave, or whatever. Very often, in the end, absolutely nothing gets done on the piece of work the politician wanted done because the political imperative eventually moves on before anything has actually been implemented – which, of course, may well have been the civil service's plan all along.

Targets would have to be set and implemented for the number of civil servants in each department, initially to cut numbers by some 70,000, back to 2019 levels, as was attempted (albeit feebly) by Chancellor Jeremy Hunt in 2023.[9] (Boris Johnson had in 2022 tried for 90,000 – again, without discernable result.[10]) After that 70,000 reduction had been achieved, more stringent cuts could lower the total by a further 20 per cent, accompanied by changes in working conditions. Defined-benefit pension schemes (see Volume One) should be replaced by defined-contribution schemes. Civil servants should be required to come into the office five days a week.[*]

Moved or demoted civil servants would not need to be treated brutally. A hiring freeze could take place for a year or two. Talented individuals who had lost their jobs could be 'parked' in a talent pool

---

[*] Volume One provided plentiful evidence that working from home, four-day weeks and the like were all productivity destroyers and should all be banned.

for a while, and either offered new positions as they came up over the following months, or assisted with a transition to the private sector. All of this is standard process in the outside world, even if it is somewhat unknown within the civil service.

Alongside making civil service units smaller and leaner, a complete review of grades would be necessary, with the objective of returning to the prior proportions of senior versus junior grades that existed pre-Covid. This alone would save an estimated £3 billion. (See Volume One.)

One way to ensure more appropriate skills and attitude among the civil service's workforce would be to administer psychometric testing, designed to ensure a healthier proportion of 'thinkers' in each department – most importantly, wherever policy was being proposed or implemented. Proper planning could ensure that teams were in place that would *remain* in place for the period of a government or ministerial appointment, with the objective of delivering the new government's manifesto. If the political leadership finds a particular civil servant or team unsatisfactory, or failing to deliver, then that could be swiftly dealt with by the new arm's-length HR department, rather than having to go through the tortuous and usually ineffective process that currently exists – or, in some cases, going through no rectification process at all. Promotions could be done based upon proper assessments of capability and achievements, rather than political conformism. All this can be achieved just by taking HR out of the insides of the civil service, and making it a separate, independent and professional organisation, reporting to its political masters rather than to the mandarins.

Reducing the number of civil servants will also be easier if HR and managers crack down on the public sector's abuse of sick leave policies: nearly 1.9 million sick days taken in 2022.[11] In the private sector, many people take virtually no sick days throughout their entire working life. Employees often exhibit a different attitude in the public sector, taking numerous sick or 'duvet' days. It is often a matter of attitude, not actual health problems. The civil service should be as intolerant of those who take advantage of their employer as any private-sector firm would be, and reducing the number of sick days to a fair level would allow a smaller and a more efficient workforce.

All DEI, ESG and similar activities should be dumped. Activist staff should be told to do their political organising elsewhere, outside of office hours. One of the major changes that would result would be the abolition of all political and identitarian activity during work time. Similarly, there has for many years been talk of not paying union representatives to do union work on government time. Successive governments have sworn they will stop it, but they haven't.[12] They should. The TaxPayers' Alliance estimates that the annual cost is some £200 million.[13]

'Away days', 'team-building sessions' and all other such claptrap activities should also be banned; if teams wish to celebrate, build or have a moan session, they need to do it on their own time, not the government's. The days of going down to the pub at Friday lunchtime, staying there for the rest of the day and badging all that as a 'team-building session' – a fairly frequent activity among civil servants from what the author has been told in the past – would be over. The new, independent HR organisation would need to become adept at enforcing proper behaviour in the workplace through appropriate disciplinary actions. Many dysfunctional private-sector businesses in the UK had to go through the same kind of behavioural changes during the 1980s and 1990s and it is time for the civil service to do the same.

Over and above all this, there should be better ongoing and overall review of the performance of the civil service, just as there is with any other major body of public servants. 'His Majesty's Inspectorate of the Civil Service' should be created, with regular reports on efficiency/productivity made to Parliament and the government.

In the private sector, the role of the CEO is to be strategic, looking out over the entire horizon of the organisation to understand what needs to be done. As a check to anyone having too much power, a chairman and a board oversee the private-sector CEO, who is expected to lay before the board what the primary objectives, intentions and deliverables of the organisation are for the coming years, and whether or not they are being achieved. The board first approves (or otherwise) the objectives and then regularly reviews the performance of the organisation against the deliverables. There is then the COO, who is responsible for making sure that the operations of the organisation are effectively run.

Transposing those concepts onto the civil service, we can say that the Secretary of State's (SoS) function should be as chairman of the organisation. Our departments of state already have boards (a relatively new innovation) allocated to them, but the agendas for those boards are prepared by the civil servants in the department, so mostly the board discussions end up having nothing to do with either the political manifesto that should be setting the objectives for the department, or with any proper list of deliverables that were created from that manifesto.

Who should be the CEO of the Department of State? I argue that the CEO should be appointed by the chairman (i.e. the SoS) as the chair's representative, there to ensure that the SoS's and the board's desires and instructions are being implemented. The CEO should be an outside appointment (civil servants would be welcome to competitively apply for the job, but they would have to show their considerable independence from the existing civil service structures). These outside CEOs could bring entirely new, and far more effective, standards to the civil service: removal of overly precious rules, elimination of woke and identitarian nonsense, a proper work ethic, abolishing working from home and swiftly moving on those staff who fail to live up to these new standards.

The permanent secretary (the top civil servant in the department) should have the function of the COO, there to make policies happen, rather than to propose different policies. Their appointment must be approved by the SoS and they must be a compatible individual who would fit in with the political team, rather than one who might offer resistance to the programme.

The top team would, with the agreement of the CEO and the COO, be kept together for the duration of an administration, with a sense of urgency around their mission to deliver the policies on which the government was elected. In this new civil service, HR would report centrally to a Cabinet-level minister in the Cabinet Office, with dotted-line reporting within each department of state.

A detailed proposal along similar lines has been laid out by the Effective Governance Forum, a self-described non-partisan group.[14]

All this could also be done for local government, thus strengthening our elected local representatives (namely, councillors), many of whom are currently under the thumb of local government officials.

In particular, and as mostly discussed in Chapter 3, four key areas need to be brought back under democratic control:

- *The Treasury*: the office needs to be staffed at senior levels by monetarists/free-marketeers. If none are to be found in the civil service, they must be brought in from outside, to bring in welcome private-sector expertise.
- *The Bank of England*: the quality and background of officials must be improved. In particular, we need individuals who are aware of, and prepared to publicly discuss and address, the causes of inflation. Monetarist and Austrian thinking should play a large part in the Bank's decisions. Any activity that goes beyond the Bank of England's monetary policy mandate to keep inflation at target and its requirement to support the government must urgently be removed – in particular, its current absurd focus on social justice-style campaigns and climate change.
- *The OBR*: should be closed, with its modelling resources (but not its modelling biases) transferred to the Treasury.
- *The civil service overall*: a public sector that is generally indifferent to improving, and has no incentive to keep costs down or become more efficient, must eventually break either itself or the state. A future UK government seeking growth must immediately adopt a multi-year programme that challenges and requires every part of our public sector to reform, in a way to make it emulate the competitively responsive private sector.

With these changes, we might stand a chance of a responsive, effective, productive civil service emerging from the current disastrous present situation – not to mention the £40 billion that could be saved annually by such changes, as shown in Volume One. This, coupled with alignment of other institutions, would create an environment where a small-government, low-tax, regulation-light economy can be created.

EPILOGUE

STEP THREE: DEREGULATE

Deregulation has the opportunity to get the economy moving much more immediately than do cost and tax cuts. To the degree that a better regulatory regime can be swiftly installed for key parts of the economy, significant new investment and entrepreneurial activity could result:

- *in housing and construction*. For Labour, who have declared their intention to remove obstructive planning regulation, this is an historic opportunity. The various Conservative governments of the past fourteen years made a mad bet on being kept in power by an elderly NIMBY generation. This made meeting the younger generation's need for new housing increasingly impossible. The result has been that there are no houses for that younger generation, which consequently became united in its desire to throw the Conservatives out. Which they did. It may be that, if Labour grasps the nettle of planning reform, the house-building and rental markets will be freed up and the economy will be given a mighty boost.[15] We will have to wait and see.[*]
- *in nuclear energy*. So convoluted and expensive is the planning regime for nuclear that despite decades of official positivity, all we have to show for it is the world's most expensive nuclear station still under construction, with nice-sounding plans for small modular reactors (SMR) still going through impossibly expensive planning cycles and no actual SMR as yet in sight. A more streamlined permissions and planning regime, along with

---

[*] In stark contrast to the vindictive anti-landlord actions taken by the previous UK government, Javier Milei abolished rent control in Buenos Aires: the number of apartments available for rent almost tripled, while inflation-adjusted rents dropped by 40 per cent. Free markets are not just a theory!

aggressive promotion of sites and benefits for such, could result in development of world-beating capability in small modular nuclear.
- *in employment.* Bill Clinton's employment reforms of the late 1990s were seen as draconian at the time, yet the result was that a large number of previously long-term unemployed entered and stayed in the workforce. The key was the tapering off of benefits after a fixed period of time; the unemployed individual was helped over a generous time period, but they knew that it was essential that they get a job before the end of that period, because their benefits would be coming to an end.[16]
- *in licensing and credentialling.* A perfect example – one of so many – is the foolishly restrictive requirement that nurses must have a university degree. It would be far better to have different ranks of nurse, with different levels of responsibility and different levels of pay.

Overall, there are innumerable reforms (mostly supply side) that a government could make, which would provide growth in the economy. Regulation is the biggest stultifier of growth, and therefore it is the true ideological battleground between those who seriously want the populace to prosper and be happy, versus those who want to keep a tight grip of control on the economy and the people. Both Javier Milei and Donald Trump (each in their own separate ways) understand this; the massive spurt in economic growth during Trump's presidency was (as he himself has said) in large part due to his administration's rapid and aggressive series of deregulatory actions. Milei is also moving fast to remove as many restrictions as his minority government can push through.

Giving businesses room to breathe and freeing entrepreneurs, small and medium enterprises and large businesses alike to compete and grow, requires a vast deregulatory programme. In order to kick-start growth in the economy, this major programme of deregulation must be planned and ready to go on day one of the new liberalising government finally taking power.

For the past several years, a great deal of work has been undertaken, and many proposals have been made, as to how to go about deregulating the UK. There is general agreement that government should modify its current approach to deregulation, changing it back from EU prescription and stultification towards the traditional British laissez-faire, common-law approach.

How and in what direction could that deregulation take place? As Volume One showed, the subject is vast. We need to:

1. *understand* where quick deregulatory wins can be achieved
2. *examine* and prioritise deregulation opportunities
3. *legislate and train regulators* to adopt facilitating, rather than prohibiting, regimes
4. *ensure deregulation happens* in as quick a timeframe as possible

We review each of these in the following pages.

Understand where quick deregulatory wins can be achieved

Even the briefest review of the status quo reveals opportunity after opportunity to deregulate. Borrowing from the many publications and reports that already exist on the topic, we quickly find the opportunities to:

- reform excessive EU data protection rules (in the main GDPR), which have a disproportionate impact on small businesses and

disincentivise tech investment, new market entrants and innovation and competition.
- take a grown-up, common-sense, personal-responsibility approach to health and safety.
- replace overzealous, expensive EU rules with guidance.
- reduce, or exempt where appropriate, the application and processing costs for environmental and waste disposal licences, permits and surveys for small businesses.
- revive deprived coastal towns, economies and communities by reversing the unfair hand dealt to British fishermen over the last fifty years by the Common Fisheries Policy. While protecting fish stocks, make the centralised imposition of quotas less onerous, restrictive and unrealistic.
- deregulate and simplify employee support requirements for small businesses, to incentivise business expansion and reduce reliance on underpaid or zero-hour contractors.
- liberalise administrative procedures for public contract tendering to increase accessibility of the public sector to efficient businesses, thus rewarding and encouraging public-sector competitiveness while reducing costs for taxpayers.
- reform road transport regulation to support businesses that depend on our road network.
- reform food and plant labelling rules, rejecting one-size-fits-all approaches and taking into account consumer shifts towards online purchasing.

Examine and prioritise deregulation opportunities

The City of London is one area where there is (still) a desperate need to deregulate. Bit by bit, individual sub-sectors are transferring to less-regulated financial hubs such as New York, the UAE

EPILOGUE

and Singapore.* In the 2023 spring Budget, some steps were taken in the right direction, but many proposals were not taken up. A step in reversing the destruction of the London Stock Exchange would be to revisit the 2004 Pensions Act, which did so much damage in pushing pension funds to invest such a large portion of their monies in government bonds (as shown in Volume One). Incentives should be crafted for UK pension funds to invest in UK equities rather than gilts, which would result in better returns for the pension funds and mitigate the incentive for them ever again to invest foolishly, such as in leveraged LDI positions. Non-distortive incentives could include removing stamp duty for UK-listed shares.

Healthcare is a second area where Britain is rapidly losing its former worldwide pre-eminence in the arenas of drugs, devices, gene therapy, GMOs etc. Again, the government made a few steps in the right direction on this in its 2023 Budget, but it is unlikely that those few steps will be enough to reverse the recent rapid drain of investment from major pharmaceutical and other companies out of the UK, until a more facilitating regulatory (and tax) environment is brought back.

While recent governments have paid good lip service to the need for deregulation, the requisite actions haven't resulted. One reason may be that there is no clear locus for deregulation in the government. A Department of State for Deregulation should be set up, for a fixed term of, say, five years, with the Cabinet-level appointment of a Secretary of State for Deregulation. This individual, reporting regularly to the Prime Minister, should have the right to insist on deregulation happening in all departments and in arm's-length

---

* Admittedly, other parts, such as Lloyds of London, are flourishing. It is reasonable to hypothesise that these are the less tightly regulated sectors.

regulators and quangos, also blocking the introduction of all but crucial new regulation.

Legislating and training regulators

The government needs to modify regulators' attitudes to regulation, changing it back in the direction of the traditional British common-law approach, rather than the constricting Napoleonic Code approach that has infiltrated our country from the EU. We have succeeded over the centuries by letting our citizens live and act freely – not by codifying and confining more and more of their day-to-day lives and activities.

It is easy to get into a mindset where the answer to every issue is to regulate the populace and particularly the business community. We have an increasingly absurd and factually incorrect narrative, where capitalism is depicted as bad for the human race; businesspeople are basically crooks, so *of course* they need to be regulated; the more regulation, the better.

But while that anti-capitalist view has been getting great play in the media and academia, somehow when it comes to elections the great British people have in the past often managed to sidestep this clearly bonkers view of the world. In 2019, following that trend, we elected an allegedly conservative government with a considerable majority; unfortunately, that Conservative government eagerly embraced mostly left-wing approaches, jumping on the bandwagon (that had already been merrily ridden by Theresa May's government since 2016) of greater and greater regulation. It would seem that the urge to regulate – to 'do something' whenever a problem arises – has in recent times been overwhelming, so that it is now a formidable task to get ourselves a government that is prepared to reverse, in any way, the regulatory onslaught. That reversal will need a change in approach overall to regulation and regulators, not just a dab at winkling out the most egregious regulations. I argue in this section that we need to:

- reverse the proliferation of regulators
- train the remaining regulators to think differently
- constrain regulatory overreach

Reverse the proliferation of regulators and regulation

In the UK, a regrettable tendency has developed in the past ten to twenty years: 'If there's a problem, let's create a regulator.' We've recently had the risible (and economically damaging) announcement of the football regulator, and now we have the Office for Environmental Protection. Of course, in this latter case, there were no doubt many reasons put forward for why we should create this environmental 'watchdog'. But the mindset underlying its creation assumes that every new regulator is necessarily a blessing; no negatives are imaginable. Where exactly has that approach got us? Where is it taking us to?

Whenever the government interferes in any situation, for however worthy a reason, the new rules and regulations will, necessarily, always have some negative consequences. Worse yet, regulators imagine that their job requires them to create and enforce new rules with every new year. All those rules and regulations, increasing year by year, further constrain what our citizens and businesses can do. The economic and indeed moral harms from this constraint will almost always swamp any presumed benefit – never mind the further limitations on personal freedoms.

The problem starts with this proliferation of regulators and regulations, so we need to reverse it. Action one: stop introducing new regulators. Action two: introduce a Secretary of State and a Department for Deregulation. This new deregulation department should embark on a systematically managed review of the regulatory state:

- Require each existing regulator to justify itself, both in terms of showing a real societal need, and of proof that the regulator has the capability to meet any such need. For regulators that don't pass those tests, close them down – quickly. For those we decide to keep, cut their funds in half nevertheless, and set them to work both harder and smarter, focusing only on essential stuff.
- A team of civil servants should be asked to trawl through correspondence from our past twenty years of EU membership pertaining to all Brussels directives, pulling out every instance of where the government or the department had opined that this or that directive was not good for the UK but that it had to be implemented, due to EU law. Then make sure each such regulation is dumped under the Retained EU Law Act.
- A comprehensive review should be undertaken for every deregulation proposal that has been made by every business entity, think tank or academic in the past twenty years. Swift, decision-oriented consultation should take place, deciding on which to implement and taking into account both ease of implementation and potential impact.

There is, in fact, already a conscientious and not unfruitful exercise ongoing withing the Department of Business and Trade to clear the backlog of unneeded EU regulation, with regular reports being produced. These make it clear that there is a lot of work to do. The government offers screenshots showing the well-organised work that civil servants are doing to push the project along.[17] Alas, the plan to sunset all retained EU law, put in place by Jacob Rees-Mogg, was abandoned by his successors. As a result, far less deregulation can now be expected to take place, whatever the efforts of those few good-hearted, hardworking civil servants.

Train the remaining regulators to think differently
In my various business experiences with regulators over the years, I have observed that there has been a gradual but general transformation of their attitudes, in the direction of hostility rather than cooperation. This applies to many parts of the regulatory world – in recent years, for example, HMRC seem to have changed from a usually collaborative approach to a more frequently hostile one.

Worse is the attitude of the quango regulators. From the Electoral Commission to the Charity Commission to the Information Commissioner, and on, the attitude seems to be: 'Our suspicion is that you are doing something wrong; you will do as we say.' Alan Halsall's book, *Last Man Standing: Memoirs from the front line of the Brexit Referendum*, recounts a nightmarish four-year experience at the hands of a regulator who referred him to the police (wrongly of course) for having performed a needed public duty.[18]

A different viewpoint needs to be instilled. The vast majority of citizens are law-abiding and well-intentioned. Regulators should understand that and assume innocence in the first instance. A light touch, at first, is always better. Will the proposed steps that the regulator is suggesting improve outcomes over the long-term? Is the malfeasance that the regulator suspects has taken place worth going after – or is it trivial or accidental? Addressing these issues should start with giving training to all regulators and members of quangos to help them understand what they are there for. Regulators should be taught to have that light touch, constantly thinking about how they can help citizens, who they should be taught to think of as their 'clients'. So:

Action three: regulators should be trained to restrain any dysfunctional suspicious nature and understand the benefits of a light-touch approach.

Action four: the Secretary of State for Deregulation should ban any zero-risk-based application of the precautionary principle and insist that regulators make judgements that are based on the balance of risk.

Constrain regulatory overreach

It is said that if you give someone a hammer, they will see every problem as a nail. Thus, regulators who are given powers over organisations impose more and more new rules and regulations on those organisations, year after year. We routinely see regulators saying that their problem is that they need more powers, more money, more reach into the organisations they regulate. To argue for that is as natural to them as breathing. But the opposite is the way to go. If we are to give our economy a chance to compete in the world, it's crucial for us to find ways to *loosen* the constraining grip of regulators, rather than relentlessly increasing their powers.

A solution could be to consider whether any regulated area or business sector could be divided into two: one part requiring regulation and the second part not requiring it, or requiring less. For the second, less regulated part, there could be an explicit warning to ensure that those engaging with any organisation in that category are happy to accept the higher risk involved. This is already done to a degree in the financial world, where the rules regarding how a financial institution should deal with its customers vary according to whether the customer is 'sophisticated' or not. As a non-business example of this, take the Charity Commission. Why could it not be that we divided all charities into two segments? Members of the first segment would be overseen by the Charity Commission. The second segment would be allowed to opt out of supervision by the Charity Commission. If organisations in that second segment broke the law in any way, they would still be subject to the same criminal prosecution, in all the usual ways that any organisation faces, but they would not offer their donors the putative comfort of Charity Commission supervision. That would reduce heavy-handed regulation by quite a bit in that area; it's an approach that could be applied in many areas.

Action five: require all regulators to state what opportunities there are for narrowing the spread of the activities that they regulate. Fire the boss of any regulator who replies 'none' or gives an unsubstantiated, box-ticking response.

Action six: announce the new government philosophy on regulation. Say that we espouse a sceptical view of the need for draconian regulation, recognising that not all regulators and regulations are a net good. Acknowledge and incorporate the traditional British common-law approach of 'if it's not explicitly forbidden, then it's allowed'. Require regulators to offer an in-depth, cost-benefit analysis of any new proposed regulation, and only implement those regulations that carry a large potential net benefit.

Action seven: create a code of conduct for regulators that ensures they have a more customer-oriented focus and that they worry about the overall impact of their activities and impositions, rather than seeking to stamp out every possible infraction of the norms. Make them report on their compliance with that code of conduct every year.

Action eight: audit behaviours by regulators. Require that all regulators and quangos conduct a one-time exercise on themselves, which examines whether their actions have been in accordance with the new philosophy and code of conduct. Get them to report on the results of that audit. Get it reviewed and critiqued by the Department for Deregulation. Replace any regulator who has failed to take the exercise seriously.

An important point, for any government wishing to ensure that no useless, self-harming, virtue-signalling policies are adopted, is to impose, possibly through legislation, a firm rule banning any anti-business policies that have no direct effect on the agenda of the government of the day. Take hydrocarbon energy as an example of what needs to be done:[*]

- Levies on energy customers to pay for subsidies on green sources of energy should be abolished. This will ensure that the manufactured goods are no longer driven out of the UK, adding to global pollution rather than lowering it because now they are being made in countries whose energy carbon footprint is worse than the UK's. A clear benefit would be the large drop in energy prices that come from not having to pay for these subsidies; so for example, there would be no need for winter fuel payments or other supportive handouts.
- Prohibitions on drilling for gas, particularly the ban on fracking, have had an enormous negative impact on both the UK's economy and its carbon footprint, and should be reversed. Because fracked gas has low greenhouse impact, the UK's carbon footprint would go down. And, as discussed in Chapter 1, the fracked gas we use

---

[*] Some of the damage that I rail against here was done more through legislation than regulation, but the same principle applies.

comes, as a result of the domestic ban on fracking, from Texas, having been subjected to a transportation process with itself an enormous carbon footprint. Its very use makes our ban on fracking gas ourselves both absurd and hypocritical. Almost all of that unnecessary carbon footprint would be eliminated were we able to create our own fracked gas instead.

And through our continued failure to learn the lessons of 2022, where Europe was caught napping because of its overall dependence on Russian energy, we continue to face the possibility of further energy price shocks and shortages. We import a large portion of our electricity from France. If there were a sudden Europe-wide crisis and consequent shortage, would France give what spare electricity it had to us or to Germany? There is, always has been, and regardless of Brexit, a pretty clear answer to that.

While fracking and North Sea hydrocarbon production would only address the issue of potential national shortages, rather than being enough to prevent any Europe-wide or worldwide price shocks, it would be possible to mitigate the effect on the UK of any such price shock if a positive drilling and fracking policy were to be adopted.

Specifically, we could adopt the approach that the Dutch government used when granting licences to the commercial companies who exploited the Groningen 'gas bubble' in the 1970s and 1980s. This could look something like the following. First, we would grant licences that allowed the British government to have the right of first refusal on oil or gas. This would ensure security of supply for the UK. Second, a revenue-share deal could be agreed as part of the upfront licence contract. Drilling companies would be allowed to cover their costs before being taxed. Then, any revenues above that would be shared between government and producer, in a way that allowed an expected healthy profit for the company but, in times of higher gas prices (like now), plenty of revenue for the government. When the price of oil or gas went down, the share of revenue that the government took would go down, to ensure the company covered the underlying costs of production. If the price of oil or gas went up, the share that the government takes would equivalently go up, so that the benefits of higher world prices were split between the nation and the production company.

This, while not a perfect free-market approach, would deal with any ludicrous accusations of 'profiteering' or the like. It would result in drilling companies offering (and paying) less for the right to drill, because their upside would be diminished. But it would give them predictable cashflows under different price scenarios, thus allowing them to bid rationally for those drilling rights. Above all, it would offer a way to address local and national resistance to fracking, with some of the government revenues donated to those communities that allowed fracking in their backyard.

What we've outlined here is a detailed, doable approach to deregulation, showing a top-down strategy, a process approach – and a detailed look in just one area. With this sort of approach, economic dynamism would be unleashed and growth would be boosted. Similar methods could and should be applied to many other areas.

Ensure deregulation happens

The problem with our current amount of excessive regulation is that even when we have managed to elect a government that wishes to deregulate the economy, there will still be an insufficient number of politicians to be found in that government who have the understanding, fire and zeal to go about, Milei-like, slashing so many regulations. So, the deregulation imperative should be given to one absolutely committed minister, with extensive overriding powers.

A whole new approach would be needed for a major deregulation initiative to bear fruit quickly. A programme that covers deregulation across the entirety of government should be set in place, with a Deregulation Czar, who reports directly (and regularly) to the Prime Minister, running the previously discussed Department of State for Deregulation with a government-wide remit. The new government should quickly commence a major, systematic process of ongoing deregulation that would cover all quangos, regulators and regulations.

In order to get deregulatory wins on the board, the initiative should not, of course, wait for the process to be perfected before being put into train. And it should not propose merely a few headline changes while ignoring the longer term, wider needs. A three-phase approach for a complete process would yield valuable results:

Short term: implement the best and easiest ideas that the process uncovers, to give quick impetus to improved economic growth.

Medium-term: have all departments, regulators, and quangos continue the self-audit I proposed earlier, and the work on eliminating unnecessary or counterproductive regulations that were imposed on our country by directive from the EU.

Long-term: commence a major deregulation programme that spreads across the whole of government, reviewing the entire regulatory arena and finding ways to make it more responsive, less intrusive and more pragmatic. If the current situation is to be changed significantly, then a systematic, multi-year, piece-by-piece approach to deregulation has to be created and implemented. The process should comprise, at a minimum:

- *Nominate that powerful Secretary of State for Deregulation.* This Cabinet-level minister should have powers to make enquiries in all departments, to require and publicise reports on progress in each department, to demand specific actions and publicise where they have not been taken, and to demand replacement of obstructive or non-compliant regulators.* Deregulation should be seen as one of the top five most important activities in the new government.
- *Create legislation* that makes it more difficult for regulation to be so ubiquitous and to have metastasised so much. For example, a 'one in, two out' law should be created that applies to each department; sunset laws for regulations should become the norm, with blocks against circumvention of any agreed sunset; and a regulatory ombudsman should be appointed, with powers to question the conduct of regulators and quangos and make far-reaching recommendations to the Deregulation Secretary.
- *Commence a major process*, under the remit of the Deregulation Secretary, to review every regulator and quango. Each should be asked to respond to questions, as discussed earlier, and as here:
  – What are the intended beneficial purposes of this entity?
  – Are the intended beneficial purposes being properly met? What proof is there that that is the case?
  – Is there a disruptive change that could be brought to this entity that would allow it to achieve its beneficial purpose with less intrusiveness?
  – What failures or errors has this entity caused in the past five to ten years? What lessons were learned from those failures? Do

---

* Some might claim that this goes against the constitutional principle of sovereign Departments of State; in which case, legislation might be needed to ensure other Departments of State cannot hide behind that principle to avoid action.

those failures indicate that the entity is not, as structured, fit for purpose or that it should possibly be closed down or defunded?
– How can the entity pursue a lighter touch at half the cost?
– What changes should be made to the entity, in light of the responses to these questions?
- *Eliminate* one third of regulators and halve in size the remaining two thirds. Ditto for quangos. The Cabinet and the Treasury to monitor this.
- *Create* a project team with the power to implant project managers within departments, to make ministers and senior civil servants accountable, and to make recommendations for major changes when obstructions arose.

An alternative way of accomplishing this would be to incorporate this team into a wider programme of change that included not just deregulation, but also expenditure and tax reductions. We review those two additional areas in the following sections.

STEP FOUR: CUT GOVERNMENT EXPENDITURES

In Volume One, I proposed a two-stage process to reduce expenditure as a percentage of GDP. First, cut £118 billion from the overall budget over a few short years, and second, restrain expenditure to 60 per cent of the previous year's GDP growth rate, until expenditure as a share of GDP reaches a 33 per cent target. Thereafter, allow expenditure increases of up to 100 per cent of the previous year's GDP growth rate. In Volume Two, after incorporating the free trade, free markets and sound money approaches, we relaxed that 60 per cent constraint by allowing an increase in spend (after the initial large cuts) of up to 70 per cent of the previous year's GDP growth rate, rather than 60 per cent. After thirteen to fifteen years overall, the size of state expenditure would, according to both models, end up at 33 per cent of GDP.

But how easy would it be to achieve such cost cuts and that overall cost constraint?

Since the size of government expenditure grew by 20 per cent (in real terms) between 2019 and 2022, we can be confident that a number of early opportunities exist to remove some of those increases, while devising a clearer road map to achieve further cuts in the medium to long term.[19] However, given that there have been many strenuous yet pretty much unavailing efforts to cut costs for at least the past three decades, we can assume there would be considerable resistance to such an initiative. What would we have to do to ensure such significant reductions? The difference this time would be to begin with the process described in step one, and achieve a general level of democratic agreement that getting costs down to a much lower share of GDP is absolutely essential if we are to grow the economy and thus the individual wealth of our citizens. Cutting costs must be seen as an imperative, not just an electioneering slogan.

To those who would claim that the level of cuts we are discussing here – getting down eventually to 33 per cent of GDP, a reduction of some 11–12 per cent of GDP over fifteen years – are impossible, there is an easy rebuttal. Country after country in the EU, when faced with an internal crisis, succeeded in cutting their government spend by a multiple of that target, resulting in surpluses and massive reductions in overall debt as a percentage of GDP – as Chart 4.6 shows.* In contrast, in the UK we have failed to take the issue

---

* These were mostly the smaller, more downtrodden countries, such as Cyprus, Ireland and Greece. France would be a different proposition. Germany has cut costs somewhat, but much less than the others on the chart.

EPILOGUE

seriously enough; we seem somehow to have decided that we will just go on recklessly spending.

Chart 4.6: Largest Public Debt Reduction Episodes in the EU

Once the urgency of lowering expenditure is accepted, countries find the strength to get costs down, enabling them to reduce the national debt considerably and thus improve their public finances.

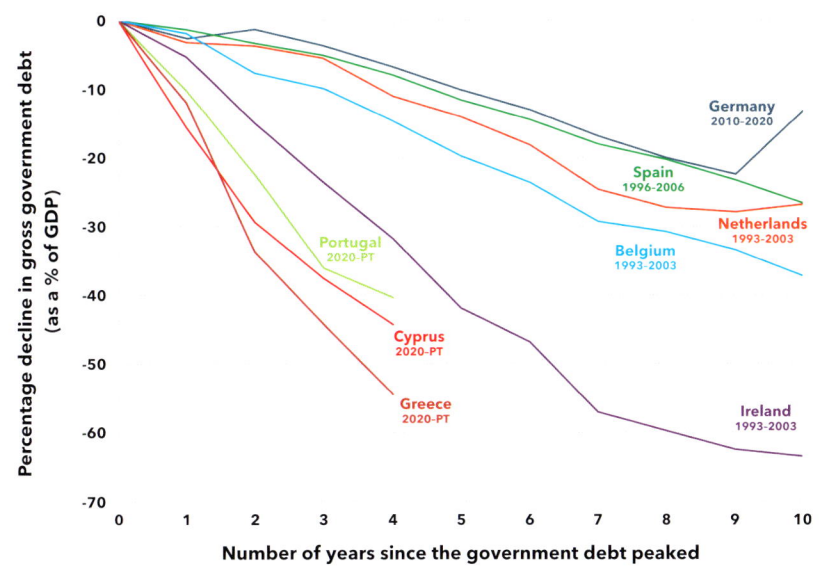

The values for Portugal, Cyprus and Greece for 2024 are IMF estimates
Source: International Monetary Fund,[20] moyniteam analysis

So, in establishing a successful programme for shrinking expenditure, a new government would need to:

- establish a consensus that the level of current expenditure is not viable long term
- state its priorities for expenditure reduction
- implement a rolling programme of cost reduction and cost containment

- publish an upfront, realistic plan

Let's look at each of these in turn.

Establish a consensus that the level of current expenditure is not a viable way forward

No government can afford to give its citizens everything they would like; choices have to be made. This country saw in 2022 a catastrophic political *degringolade*, where the right prescription was derailed by the leveraged LDI crisis. In consequence, the argument for small government and low taxes is frequently now vilified, with the questionable assertion that the free-market approach had been 'rejected by the markets'. In the face of this, how can any pro-free-market government not only persuade the electorate that the generally accepted narrative was incorrect, but also ensure that it can stay in power while implementing its economic programme? The Truss government was catapulted into power with only days to prepare, with much internal opposition from Tory MPs, and with only some two years to go before they would need to fight an election: these were possibly decisive factors in her government's failure. Fortunately, in future circumstances, a political party seeking election as a proponent of cutting expenditure is likely to enjoy more preparation time than that. During that preparation time, they must:

- Establish a consensus that an ever-expanding government is not a viable way forward and that even at our current size of government, we are squashing economic growth flat. The recent expansion of the state must be reversed.
- Agree the priorities and targets for expenditure reduction and

how those cuts in expenditure would be compensated for via economic growth that would offer new jobs and opportunities for those previously dependent on welfare.
- Show how changes in the tax and regulatory regime will increase economic growth, leading to improvements in disposable income for most households.
- Have a plan to ensure the institutions support the government, as discussed earlier.

How much wealth a country can afford to spend on various social programmes depends upon its level of economic development. The majority of the world's population lives in countries whose economies don't generate enough income to offer anything like the level of unemployment payments, pensions, healthcare and other benefits that richer countries like ours have come to believe we can afford (but in our case, can't). The failure of the UK to grow its GDP per capita by much in recent decades was compounded by a needlessly rapid expansion of expenditure. This has led to the UK spending over £100 billion more than what the average country, at a similar level of wealth as the UK, spends (as shown in Chart 4.2). As I have demonstrated in these two volumes, only a significant increase in GDP per capita will safely allow us to offer our current level of benefits to citizens – although, as I have also pointed out, with much higher incomes there would be much less need for the current level of handouts to be given.

That's not the entire story, of course; almost all countries care for their citizens, and whatever the stage of a country's development, the intelligent use of available money will ensure a better impact on a country's citizens' lives than will foolish squandering.

As an example, South Africa, the first major country to be hit by the Omicron variant of the Covid virus, concluded after careful scientific analysis that Omicron was not nearly as dangerous as was being touted by other countries or by global organisations. South Africa therefore was able to adopt, even with far less available funds than more developed countries, a sensible and beneficial approach to Omicron – while in contrast, most other countries squandered many billions on unnecessary and constricting precautions, at the same time creating massive disruption to its citizens, and especially its children, with these draconian policies. Focusing on the reality of available money and resources leads to more efficiency and less spend.

State priorities for expenditure reduction
Sensible politicians understand that they have to pick what benefits to offer, out of a near-infinite number of possibilities. Obviously, the lower is a country's GDP, the smaller are the tax revenues that can be extracted from the population and the fewer are the benefits and services that can therefore be offered. Considerations that thoughtful countries have to take into account include:

- How to provide all 'core' services, and as many 'productive' services as possible. These should clearly take priority over welfare-style benefits and other redistributionist programmes.
- How to avoid paying out benefits that actively discourage citizens from being productive, income-generating, tax-paying members of society. The 'mental health' crisis is perhaps the most egregious example of this.
- How to keep expenditure low enough to ensure that GDP per

capita is growing, so that in turn the levels of services and benefits the country can provide to its citizens will also grow.
- How to balance the various needs of the sick, the unemployed, the young, parents and the elderly. There will always be an understandable pressure to increase expenditure in all of these areas, but there is unlikely to be enough money, however fast we grow in the next few decades, to do so universally. The electorate should be offered a transparent review of the overall amounts available in this area, and an explanation of whatever choices are made. In theory, the unemployed are the most obvious area in that list to spend less on. In the case of healthcare, it might be better to spend more on early life (ante- and post-natal care) than at the end of life.

Implement a rolling programme of cost reduction and containment
In Volume One, we came up with an initial programme of cost reductions that amounted to £118 billion. How quickly and easily could that programme be implemented? Depending on the degree of electoral and administrative resistance, the steps taken would be as follows.

First, create the enabling steps, including any needed legislation, to allow the programme to commence:

- Appoint a cost reduction and efficiency czar at Cabinet level, with powers across all departments and across local government.[*] Introduce targets and, potentially, financial incentives to meet those targets.

---

[*] This individual could at a pinch also be the same person as the Deregulation Czar.

- Restructure the civil service, in particular creating a separate HR body outside the service, which reports to the czar.
- Pass laws permitting this czar to impose transfers or terminations across the top three layers of the civil service.
- Implement a project-management style approach to cost reduction across the entirety of government, ensuring there are no protected jobs, reporting monthly to Cabinet on progress.

Next, announce the cost reduction programme:

- Announce specific steps in specific areas: eliminate approximately one third of all quangos, cut funding in half for those that remain, cancel all spend on sock-puppet charities, ruthlessly prune all virtue-signalling aid programmes, get rid of the dysfunctional target for overall overseas aid spending.
- Announce general steps across all areas: ban and eradicate all ESG/DEI activities inside the workplace and require all areas to reduce headcount by a further 15–20 per cent *after* the 'specific' reduction activities have taken place.
- Cut the welfare bill over a number of years: reduce out-of-work benefits, make sure all benefits are means-tested, cancel the triple lock in pensions, raise the retirement age to seventy.

After five years, the new government should have completed phase one of the needed reduction in government size. These cost cuts would, of course, not be sufficient; we would need the additional deregulation and tax cuts discussed in Volume One to get growth moving optimally.

After being re-elected, the government would then be in a position to take the steps needed to preserve and extend the cost savings achieved from phase one. In the meantime, the economy should have grown enough to lower the overall cost ratio to an acceptably small slice of the economy (our model predicts spending to be just over 34 per cent of GDP by year ten – the end of the second term). A more efficient, leaner and motivated public-sector workforce will be a help, but at the end of the first five-year term, a rule must be agreed to ensure that each year, public-sector spending rises at only 70 per cent of the previous year's growth rate.

Publish an upfront, realistic plan

The issue that in the past bedevilled Argentina, and other economies like it, was that responses by, or even a totally unrelated disturbance in, the capital markets (or an intervention of some sort from, say, the IMF) could instantly threaten to destroy any plan for reform. This fact must always be a consideration when planning the shape of an economy. It will be an increasingly important consideration for the UK in the next few years, as our financial situation worsens. Certainly, when a country runs out of money as Greece did, the havoc wreaked on the citizenry by the subsequent abrupt collapse, and then the cleanup, can be enormous. Getting our house in order, before all that is imposed on us, is crucial.

Communicating the plan requires both good timing, and bringing many participants on board, some of whom may be ideologically averse to the proposed direction of travel. Argentina can point the way on this: despite Javier Milei's chainsaw-wielding bravado, the IMF has, after careful discussion, enthusiastically bought in to his proposed programme.[21]

What timing sequence should be employed? Which participants need to be addressed? Chart 4.7 suggests the steps that would need to be followed.

Chart 4.7: Communicating the Plan to Stakeholders

Both timing and keeping the markets calm (as much as possible) are key.

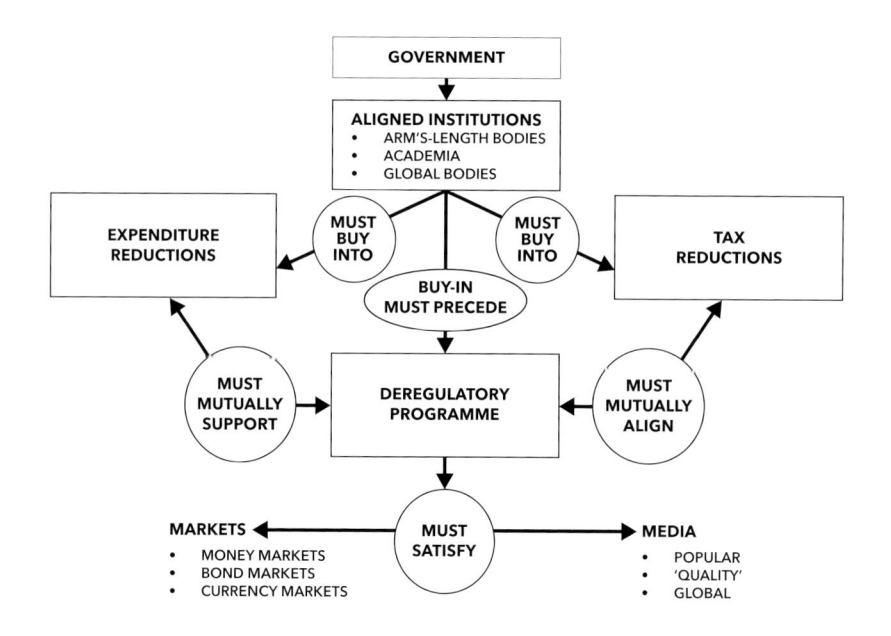

[Diagram: GOVERNMENT → ALIGNED INSTITUTIONS (ARM'S-LENGTH BODIES, ACADEMIA, GLOBAL BODIES) → MUST BUY INTO → EXPENDITURE REDUCTIONS and TAX REDUCTIONS; BUY-IN MUST PRECEDE DEREGULATORY PROGRAMME; MUST MUTUALLY SUPPORT / MUST MUTUALLY ALIGN; MUST SATISFY → MARKETS (MONEY MARKETS, BOND MARKETS, CURRENCY MARKETS) and MEDIA (POPULAR, 'QUALITY', GLOBAL)]

STEP FIVE: REDUCE TAXES

I hope I have managed to be reasonably convincing that taxes must be far lower, and more friendly to economic activity, if we are to have growth. High income and corporation taxes hit growth worst, while high consumption taxes do the least damage, and other taxes (such as capital and production taxes) lie somewhere in between these two poles. Yet in recent years, many Conservative governments, perhaps being led by the nose by anti-business Treasury types, or perhaps with too close an eye on opinion polling, have seen it as virtuous to take more and more individuals out of the tax net, and encourage multiple exemptions to consumption taxes (especially VAT), while at the same time increasing taxes on business. To work our way back out of the

EPILOGUE

growth-destroying trap, we badly need both a lowering of taxes *and* a restructuring of the mix of taxes.

In Volume One, I set out a series of tax cuts, amounting to some £113 billion in the first five years, with a further £82 billion to be implemented once the economy grew enough to support those additional cuts.* The mix and timing of those cuts was prioritised accordingly: business cuts first, cuts to attract wealthy investors back to the UK second, taxes on individuals cut thereafter; and only then reductions on consumption tax rates (while broadening the consumption tax base).

Is this proposal fantastical? Not at all. The cuts are achievable and, so long as they are accompanied by sound money policies, could spark tremendous growth in the economy.

An episode from history backs up that view: the Harding/Coolidge tax cuts of the 1920s in the US. Warren Harding and Calvin Coolidge were consecutively President through most of that decade, while Andrew Mellon, the driving force behind those tax cuts, was their Treasury Secretary. Under Woodrow Wilson (the President before Harding), the prevailing top rate of income tax, 77 per cent, had kept back economic growth. Harding, Coolidge and Mellon cut that top rate from 77 per cent down; first to 44 per cent and later to 25 per cent (briefly to 24 per cent). As Chart 4.8 shows, even at an income tax rate that had been cut to less than a third of what it had been, the government ran a surplus for the entire 1920s. So, even with those low tax rates, national debt as a percentage of GDP halved, down to a ridiculously low (by modern standards) 16 per cent.

---

* Beyond that, a further £59 billion of tax cuts was identified as highly desirable, but under our sound money policy could only be considered after the economy had grown enough to accommodate those extra cuts.

RETURN TO GROWTH

Chart 4.8: US Government Budget Deficit, Debt Ratio and Top Marginal Income Tax Rate, 1918–1933

The record of the 1920s clearly demonstrates that low tax rates can go hand-in-hand with budget surpluses and can therefore result in significant improvements to the level of national debt. Conversely, high tax rates in the 1930s went hand-in-hand with budget deficits.

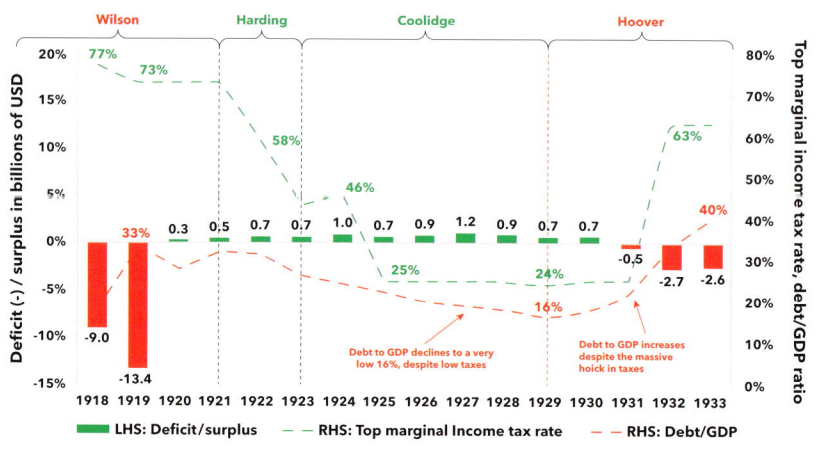

Source: Tax Policy Center, International Monetary Fund and The White House [22]

Enter the 1930s. With Coolidge departing, Herbert Hoover, the next President, arrived just at the wrong moment, with a fanatical insistence on balancing the budget. In a widely accepted analysis by Milton Friedman, a mild recession precipitated by the 1929 stock market crash eventually led, in 1931, to the first fiscal deficit in a decade.[23] Utilising money-supply sadism, Hoover and the Federal Reserve together implemented an acceleratingly contractionary monetary policy. Hoover increased taxes substantially in order to 'balance the books', and the Fed let over half of the 25,000 banks in the US close their doors, rather than acting as lender of last resort to them. As Chart 4.8 showed, the deficit ballooned, and the

250

EPILOGUE

debt-to-GDP ratio shot up, from 16 per cent to 40 per cent – all in a brief four-year period.

Chart 4.9: The US in the 1920s
Tax Rates Low and GDP Growth High

The 1920s saw an extraordinary economic boom in the US, prior to the Great Depression in the 1930s. It is now generally acknowledged that the depression was caused by a panicked Federal Reserve withdrawing liquidity as local banks across the US failed, originally precipitated by a mild recession being compounded by Hoover's massive tax increases.

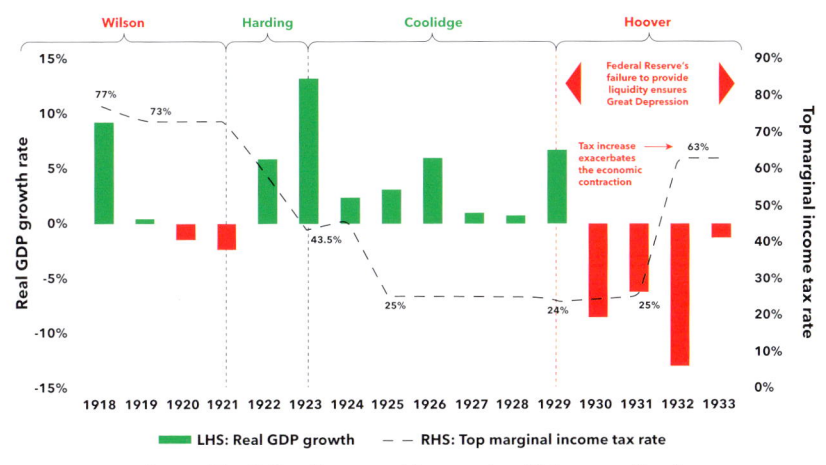

Source: Tax Policy Center and International Monetary Fund[24]

Before Hoover and the Fed's disastrous policies arrived, the economy, fuelled by the massively lowered tax rates, had boomed for a decade. As Chart 4.8 showed, the nation had seen a fiscal surplus for a full eleven years, even into 1930, reducing the national debt to that astoundingly low 16 per cent of GDP. Yet the debt rocketed back up when Hoover raised taxes, while at the same time, any bank in trouble, being unsupported by the Fed, knocked its problems on to the next bank, leading to a calamitous cascade of bank failures right across the country. Before that, in the 1920s, as shown in Chart 4.9, real GDP growth, fuelled by low taxes, had been strong for a full eight years, at an average of over 3 per cent a year, without precipitating inflation or over-heating.[*] It took the combined misguided efforts of Hoover and the Fed, and later Roosevelt, to bring that strong economic performance to a halt.

In summary, when it comes to tax, the message is to cut tax rates, especially on businesses; simplify the tax code; broaden the tax base. Implement tax cuts while simultaneously cutting expenditure. With support from institutions such as the Bank of England, pursuing policies that fully resonate with the government's own programme, then reduce taxes further, eventually so that tax revenues are some 30 per cent of GDP, as the economy grows.[†] The schedule on pp. 329–30 of Volume One shows the details and timing of the various needed cuts.

STEP SIX: STRENGTHEN FREE MARKETS AND FREE TRADE WHILE ENSURING SOUND MONEY

In Chapters 1 and 2 of this volume, I laid out the principles and practices of free markets and free trade. Not much more needs to be said, but to summarise for free markets:

- Privatise more! The more the economy is in the private sector, with competition and demanding management, the more productive and efficient it will be.

---

[*] The wonderful book *Once in Golconda* by John Brooks shows how the 1929 stock market boom and crash was a function of commercial and investment bank illegality rather than, as some have alleged, an over-heating economy.
[†] The government has other (non-tax) sources of revenue. They tend to be around 3–4 per cent of GDP. Tax revenues can therefore fall a few points below spending levels and we can still end up with a balanced budget, or even (as in 2000) a surplus.

- Create tighter licensing requirements on state-monopoly utilities. (This is one of a number of areas where *better*, not *more*, regulation is needed.)
- For the semi-nationalised utilities that are in financial trouble, force creditors and particularly bondholders to take a haircut and come into possession of the company. Those lenders will then, in future, be far more chary of allowing the utilities to lever up and will enforce discipline and compliance with the utilities' number one task – namely, to serve the country's citizens.
- Work harder to eliminate monopolies and oligopolies, and fight back against unionised public-sector employee cartels. Eliminate all public-sector defined-benefit pension schemes.
- Remove subsidies, particularly in the energy sector, and discourage rent seekers.
- Ban sock-puppet charities.
- Remove NIMBY powers from local councils.
- Reform the bankruptcy code to a US-style Chapter II structure, so that companies can fail more swiftly and be taken over more swiftly by their creditors, rather than putting them into the hands of receivers and thus subjecting them to an expensive, drawn-out, inefficient, growth-destroying limbo of months or years of economic inactivity and deconstruction into parts that are sold off individually.

And for free trade:

- Continue to make and improve trade deals everywhere around the world, especially with those countries where our common-law-based approach and our compatible service and product offerings are particularly welcomed.

- For imports, eschew both tariff and non-tariff barriers – even when that's not reciprocated.
- Support exporting companies to overcome the protectionist barriers of other countries with, for example, easy-to-navigate apps that take the company through how to deal with protectionist barriers or help them with calculation/collection/payment of charges. In general, encourage other countries not to be protectionist. Speak publicly and loudly about the benefits of free trade.

These activities, to support free markets and free trade, go hand-in-hand with the steps on expenditure, tax and regulation that were discussed in previous pages of this epilogue. The objective is to achieve, after ten years in office, an open, fast-growing economy, run on free-market principles, that gives its citizens not just wealth but the goods and services they want – cheaply and efficiently.

PULLING THIS TOGETHER INTO A SUCCESSFUL, LONG-TERM PLAN

The preceding pages have outlined not just a vast set of needed activities, but also the needed radical change of approach and belief across the UK. If both were achieved, despite the difficulties, we would reap enormous rewards for our country – and political reward for the government that implemented it successfully.

The objective is to bring together a combination of restraint on expenditure; lower taxes; and more effective regulation across the economy, so as to achieve over time a small-state, low-tax, minimally regulated economy – all within the context of financial sobriety and acceptable levels of state expenditure, with an open, predominantly private-sector, freely trading economy.

These multiple objectives make the creation and implementation

EPILOGUE

of a potentially successful plan complex – and, of course, any economic plan will always encounter unplanned-for obstacles, just as soon as it is introduced into the real world. However, this epilogue has offered a view on how and when to go about these issues:

- For government cuts, some can be done immediately by requiring a return to 2019 levels. Some, such as procurement, can be done in the medium term. Some can only be done in the long term, after busting state employee monopoly behaviour.
- For tax, again, some changes can be immediate, such as corporate tax reduction; some in the medium term, such as reductions in National Insurance contributions; some in the long term. The key is to get costs down so that tax cuts can be implemented without fiscal strain, while at the same time not being too shy about quickly getting rid of some of the most egregious, growth-reducing taxes.
- For regulatory reduction, the quicker the better; abolition of growth-restricting regulation can kick-start growth all across the economy. These will in turn potentiate a free-market private sector, while shrinking the state. Regulations that restrict product features or pricing should be the first to go.
- For trade, continue to seek opportunities to sign, extend and deepen free-trade deals, while being the global champion of free trade, explaining and promoting its benefits in international forums.

An overall sequencing might look something like that outlined in Chart 4.10, next.

The evidence outlined in both volumes in this book, and from the recent history of our country, is that we can achieve and benefit from a smaller government sized at around 33 per cent of the overall economy, with tax rates that take no more than 30 per cent of GDP and an overall lessening of regulation that would boost enterprise, providing more personal and economic freedom.

Chart 4.10: Getting the Economy Growing Again

There is an appropriate sequencing for introducing changes.

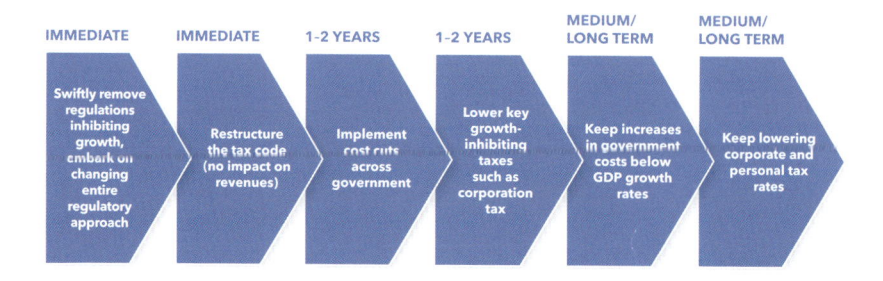

IMMEDIATE	IMMEDIATE	1-2 YEARS	1-2 YEARS	MEDIUM/ LONG TERM	MEDIUM/ LONG TERM
Swiftly remove regulations inhibiting growth, embark on changing entire regulatory approach	Restructure the tax code (no impact on revenues)	Implement cost cuts across government	Lower key growth-inhibiting taxes such as corporation tax	Keep increases in government costs below GDP growth rates	Keep lowering corporate and personal tax rates

Achieving such a set of changes for the country would be a great task. Of course, the proposed actions set out are extraordinarily ambitious. Many will argue that it would be impossible to get a government elected on that programme – but Milei was elected with a far more radical manifesto. Of course, we are not Argentina (yet); it may be that our crisis has to get worse before the electorate becomes convinced that such steps are the only option that can be taken. But the conversation has to start somewhere, and the programme laid out in this book is detailed, doable and defensible. Judging by our model and its conservative parameters, all the UK has to do is to return to the kind of structure we had at the end of the Major/beginning of the Blair years, and we can then expect our country's economy to turn around quickly.

I hope that this book has both shown how to do that, and given hope that it can be done.

APPENDIX A

METHODOLOGY FOR CHART 3.1

The classification of sectors used for Chart 3.1 is as follows: 'Government, health and education' incorporates the following:

- public administration and defence
- compulsory social security
- education
- human health and social work activities

'Outsourced government activities' incorporates:

- Electricity, gas, steam and air conditioning supply
- water supply, sewerage, waste management and remediation activities
- creative, arts and entertainment activities
- libraries, archives, museums and other cultural activities

'Quasi-governmental sectors' incorporates:

- agriculture
- mining and quarrying
- manufacture of food products, beverages and tobacco
- manufacture of refined petroleum products

- manufacture of chemicals and chemical products
- manufacture of basic pharmaceutical products and pharmaceutical preparations
- manufacture of basic metals and metal products
- manufacture of transport equipment
- construction
- land transport and transport via pipelines
- water transport
- air transport
- postal and courier activities
- accommodation and food service activities
- programming and broadcasting activities
- financial and insurance activities
- security and investigation activities
- gambling and betting activities

All other sectors are classified as 'mostly free market'.

APPENDIX B

THE GROWTH MODEL

In Appendix B of Volume One, we detailed the particulars of our growth model, referred to throughout both volumes of the book. The model is used to estimate the impact on economic growth of implementing our proposed policies over a fifteen-year period. It takes the most recent numbers, up to and including most of 2024, as its starting point (although the real-world commencement of the fifteen-year period is likely to be 2028 or 2029 at the earliest).

Here, we describe, in addition, how the model was extended to include the topics discussed in this second volume.

The model itself is a modified version of the World Bank's long-term growth model (LTGM),[1] which itself is based on the well-known neoclassical Solow–Swan growth model (specifically, the enhanced version that includes human capital).[2] In this appendix, we reiterate the specifications of this model, add in the new variables and outline the final growth scenario used in the summary section of this book. This scenario incorporates the free-trade, free-market and sound money approaches that were discussed in this volume, adding the (conservatively) estimated additional impact from these approaches on top of the impact from the proposed policy changes discussed in Volume One.

THE SOLOW–SWAN MODEL

This well-known model, from which we derive our own, is based on an aggregate Cobb–Douglas production function with human capital:

$$Y_t = A_t K_t^{1-\beta} (h_t L_t)^\beta$$

Where at any given time t:
Y_t = output (GDP)
A_t = total factor productivity (TFP)
K_t = capital stock
h_t = human capital per worker
L_t = number of workers in the economy[*]
β = labour share in output

The number of workers in the economy is $L_t = N_t \omega_t \rho_t$, where at any time t:

N_t = total population
ω_t = share of working-age population in total population
ρ_t = labour force participation rate (share of working-age population who are employed or actively seeking employment)

Capital stock evolves according to the following difference equation, which states that its current level is equal to its previous level, adjusted for depreciation δ and new investment I_t:

---

[*] A fair criticism of this model is that it assumes that any new member of the workforce has the same level of human capital and is as productive as the average current member. Thus, the model can significantly overestimate the positive impact of immigration on GDP growth, especially given the cost of the additional national infrastructure that is needed to support the additional numbers. Our own calculations assume much less immigration in the fifteen-year period than in the past few years, so reduce the size of any such overestimates.

APPENDIX B

$$K_{t+1}=(1-\delta)K_t+I_t.$$

The model is calibrated for the UK economy using the following parameters:

Variable	Value	Source
β	0.59	Penn World Table version 10.01[3]
δ	0.0397	Penn World Table version 10.01
K_o/Y_o	3.5	IMF Investment and Capital Stock dataset[4] and Penn World Table version 10.01, average value for 2019

A conventional version of the Solow–Swan model has one important drawback: it assumes that the path of the key variable, Total Factor Productivity (TFP), is exogenous. As a central new feature of this approach, we extend the Solow–Swan model using our findings on the impact on TFP from four variables: the three key drivers discussed in Volume One (government expenditures as a percentage of GDP, tax revenues as a percentage of GDP and level of business regulations) and a fourth variable, trade freedom, which is discussed in Volume Two. (In our calculations for Volume One, we fix that fourth variable at a constant level.)

These four factors are defined as follows:

I_t^{exp} – index of government expenditures, scaled from 0 to 10
I_t^{tax} – index of tax revenues, scaled from 0 to 10
I_t^{reg} – index of business regulations, scaled from 0 to 10
I_t^{trade} – freedom of trade index, scaled from 0 to 10

The index of government expenditures is constructed as follows:

$$I_t^{exp}=10\,(G_{max}-G_t)\,/\,(G_{max}-G_{min})$$

G_t is government expenditures as a percentage of GDP, G_{max} and G_{min} are set at 70 per cent of GDP (the largest observed number for G_t since 1975 in our sample of countries, rounded up to the nearest whole percentage) and 11 per cent of GDP (the smallest observed amount value for G_t in our sample of countries, rounded down to the nearest whole percentage) respectively. A lower value of I_t^{exp} reflects a higher level of government expenditures G_t.

The index of tax revenues is similarly constructed as follows:

$$I_t^{tax} = 10\ (T_{max} - T_t) / (T_{max} - T_{min})$$

Where T_t denotes tax receipts as a share of GDP, T_{max} and T_{min} are set at 51 per cent of GDP (the highest level of tax revenues rounded up to the nearest whole percentage) and 21 per cent of GDP (the lower level of tax revenues rounded down to the nearest whole percentage) respectively. A lower value of the index I_t^{tax} reflects a higher level of taxation T_t.

For the index of business regulations I_t^{reg} and the freedom of trade index I_t^{trade}, we use the business regulations component (5C) and tariffs component (4A) of the Fraser Institute's Economic Freedom of the World ranking. Both indices are originally scaled from 0 to 10. A lower value I_t^{reg} corresponds to a higher regulatory burden, whereas a lower value of I_t^{trade} corresponds to higher trade barriers.

We then construct a composite index I_t by averaging the data for each of the four variables and then rescaling from 1 to 100:

$$I_t = (I_t^{exp} + I_t^{tax} + I_t^{reg} + I_t^{trade})/4\ \ 99/10 + 1,$$

APPENDIX B

TOTAL FACTOR PRODUCTIVITY AND THE COMPOSITE INDEX

To obtain a quantitative relationship between TFP growth and our composite index of the aggregation of the four variables, we constructed a regression model in which the TFP growth rate is a function of a contemporaneous value of the composite index:

$$g_t^{TFP} = \xi_0 + \xi_1 \ln I_t + \varepsilon_t,$$

where:

g_t^{TFP} = TFP growth rate in year t
I_t = composite index at t, scaled from 1 to 100
ξ_0, ξ_1 = regression coefficients
ε_t = residuals

The alert reader will have noticed an implicit assumption in our approach, which is to give equal weight to each of the four measures. It would, of course, be better if we could have concluded on the relative degree of impact on growth of changes in each separately. However, the high correlation between the variables, particularly the first two, makes problematic any stab at estimating the differing effects of individual variables. Assuming a similar level of impact for each variable should lead to calculated outcomes that could be a degree – but most likely only to a degree – inaccurate.[*]

Our regression analysis was conducted using, as a sample, the

---

[*] We discover, to our pleasure, that the World Bank came to almost identical conclusions in its own use of this model. See p.77 of their long-term growth model paper, linked to in the text.

twenty-three developed countries that have been long-standing members of the OECD, 2000–2019.[*]

The TFP growth-time series is derived from the Penn World Tables (PWT) version 10.01 database. The time series for government expenditures and revenues come from the IMF's Public Finances in Modern History database. The table below summarises the regression results.

As previously noted, the model implies one-to-one correspondence between TFP growth and GDP-per-capita growth.

Chart A.1: TFP Growth against Changes in Our Composite Index, 2000–2019

Regressing TFP growth on our composite index confirms the positive relationship between those factors and TFP. The UK's position on the scatter plot shows how Britain's economic shape has deteriorated in the past two decades.

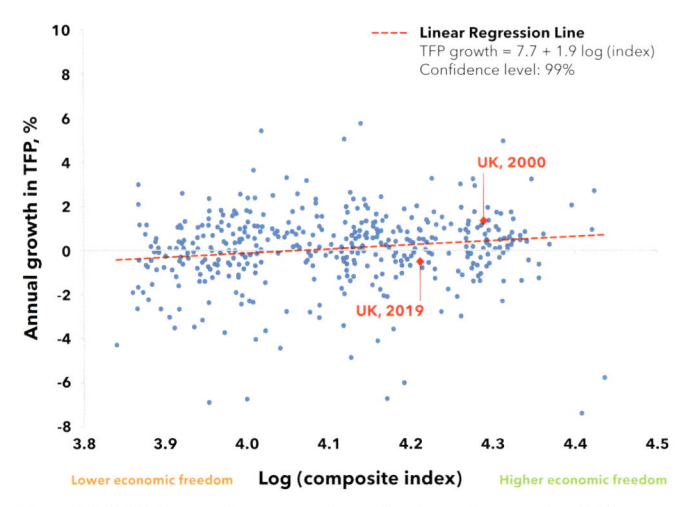

Source: Penn World Tables version 10.01, Fraser Institute, International Monetary Fund, OECD, moyniteam analysis[5]

---

[*] Australia, Austria, Belgium, Canada, Denmark, Finland, France, Germany, Greece, Iceland, Ireland, Italy, Japan, Luxembourg, Netherlands, New Zealand, Norway, Portugal, Spain, Sweden, Switzerland, United Kingdom and the United States.

APPENDIX B

If the UK could just return its overall TFP to the levels we had in 2000, growth would increase by some one third of 1 per cent per annum: almost 5 per cent over the fifteen-year forecast period. Adopting our proposed actions would take TFP beyond that and thus improve growth by significantly more.

Chart A.1 illustrates the validity of the relationship posited in our model. The two red data points evidence the deterioration of the UK's economy between 2000 and 2019.[*] Further detail of the UK's deterioration, for each of the four factors used in the model, is shown in Chart A.2.

Chart A.2: Four Composite Index Variables
The UK's Position, 2000 versus 2019

The UK was, even by 2019, in much worse shape than it was in 2000 on three of the four variables that make up our composite index. We can expect that by 2024, we are in even worse shape. Our position has improved (somewhat) only on the variable of trade freedoms.

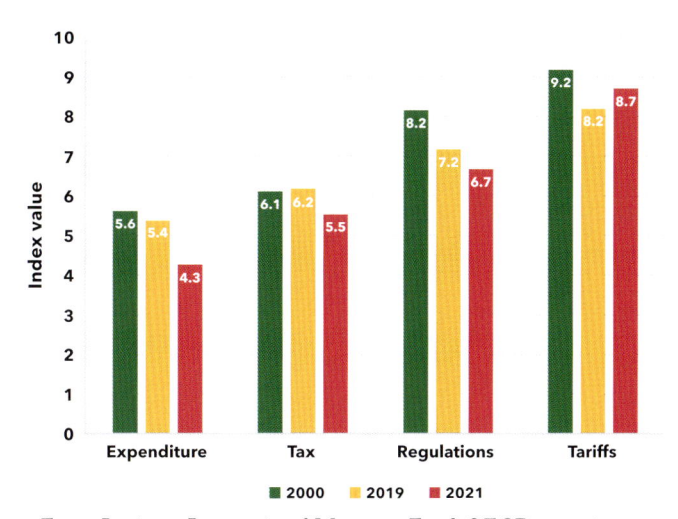

Variable	2000	2019	2021
Expenditure	5.6	5.4	4.3
Tax	6.1	6.2	5.5
Regulations	8.2	7.2	6.7
Tariffs	9.2	8.2	8.7

Source: Fraser Institute, International Monetary Fund, OECD, moyniteam analysis[6]

---

[*] The UK's 2019 TFP growth was negative.

THE ALL-POLICIES SCENARIO

In addition to the three scenarios for the UK that we discussed in Volume One, we created a further scenario, an all-policies scenario. This assumes, first, that we succeed with the proposed optimisations of the size of government, taxes and regulation – as reviewed in Volume One. The model then relaxes the freedom of trade index, which is assumed to be fully optimised after the first five years and is assumed to continue at that optimal ($I_t^{trade} = 10$) level thereafter. Assuming the free-market approach has been implemented, the labour force participation rate is assumed to gradually improve over fifteen years, achieving in year fifteen the participation level that Sweden enjoys today. We also assume that human capital growth recovers, reaching after the first five years the average level that we saw in the UK 1991–2000. To reflect economic improvement resulting from the free-market and sound money policies we advocate, the investment level ten years from now is hypothesised to reach the 2023 level of Sweden.

As with the previous three scenarios, the total population N_t and working population ω_t in the UK is supposed to evolve in line with the ONS principal projection of 30 January 2024.[7] Non-tax receipts are assumed to account for the constant 4.3 per cent of GDP based on the OBR Economic and Fiscal Outlook March 2024 figures.[8] Real GDP is expected to grow by 0.8 per cent in 2024/25, in line with the IMF's forecast at the time of writing.[9]

As discussed in the text, the addition of the three new policy approaches discussed in this volume leads, though we have been careful to stay at the conservative end of possible forecasts, to a significant amount of further economic growth, over and above the amount seen in the scenarios we laid out in Volume One.

NOTES

RECAP: THREE KEY DRIVERS OF ECONOMIC GROWTH

1 International Monetary Fund, 'Public Finances in Modern History', https://www.imf.org/external/datamapper/datasets/FPP
2 Victor Mallet and Paola Tamma, 'France's national auditor sounds alarm over national finances', *Financial Times*, 15 July 2024, https://www.ft.com/content/1d41857d-8d6d-4e0a-a44b-fc6fcce5650f

PROLOGUE: EVENTS SINCE PUBLICATION OF VOLUME ONE

1 Caroline Wheeler and Jill Treanor, 'Rachel Reeves hires City high flyers to unlock billions for Labour's economic plan', *The Times*, 10 March 2024, https://www.thetimes.com/uk/politics/article/rachel-reeves-unveils-big-business-squad-labour-wealth-fund-g6rjdq3j9
2 Nick Gutteridge, 'Reeves set to sign off above inflation rise in minimum wage', *Daily Telegraph*, 10 August 2024, https://www.telegraph.co.uk/politics/2024/08/10/reeves-set-to-sign-off-above-inflation-rise-in-minimum-wage/; Jo Faragher, 'Reeves confirms public sector pay rises of 5-6%', Personnel Today, 30 July 2024, https://www.personneltoday.com/hr/public-sector-pay-rises/
3 Dominic Penna, 'Civil Servants on over £100k rises by 40pc in a year', *Daily Telegraph*, 9 August 2024, https://www.telegraph.co.uk/politics/2024/08/09/civil-servants-earning-more-than-100000-rises-by-40pc/
4 Andrew Ellson, Steven Swinford and Oliver Wright, 'Train drivers to strike for three months despite £100m pay deal', *The Times*, 16 August 2024, https://www.thetimes.com/uk/transport/article/train-drivers-to-strike-for-three-months-in-wake-of-100m-pay-deal-rh5gp7q57
5 'Local government employers must improve pay offer to avoid strike threat', Unison, 4 September 2024, https://www.unison.org.uk/news/2024/09/local-government-employers-must-improve-pay-offer-to-avoid-strike-threat/
6 Jonathan Walker, '£40m private health bill for "public sector" staff', *Sunday Express*, 11 August 2024, https://www.pressreader.com/uk/sunday-express-1070/20240811/281934548246786
7 Szu Ping Chan and Tim Wallace, 'Record number of children on disability benefits after autism and ADHD surge', *Daily Telegraph*, 13 August 2024, https://www.telegraph.co.uk/business/2024/08/13/record-number-children-disability-benefits-autism-adhd/
8 HM Treasury and The Rt Hon Rachel Reeves MP, 'Chancellor statement on public spending and inheritance', Gov.uk, 29 July 2024, https://www.gov.uk/government/speeches/chancellor-statement-on-public-spending-inheritance
9 'Rachel Reeves' tax updates for non-doms: What you need to know', Gravita, https://www.gravita.com/rachel-reeves-tax-update-non-doms-2025/
10 Matthew Lesh, 'Shadow Expenses: uncosted regulatory burdens in election manifestos', Institute for Economic Affairs, 27 June 2024, https://iea.org.uk/publications/shadow-expenses-uncosted-regulatory-burdens-in-election-manifestos/
11 'Civil service expanding diversity teams across the board', Guido Fawkes, 14 August 2024, https://order-order.com/2024/08/14/civil-service-expanding-diversity-teams-across-the-board/
12 Sam Fleming, Valentina Romei and Delphine Strauss, 'UK government finances are on an "unsustainable" path, watchdog warns', *Financial Times*, 12 September 2024, https://www.ft.com/content/8d131ebf-d06a-478c-8c42-943abfac2449; 'Fiscal risks and sustainability – September 2024', Office for Budget Responsibility, 12 September 2024, https://obr.uk/frs/fiscal-risks-and-sustainability-september-2024/

INTRODUCTION: THREE FREE-MARKET APPROACHES THE UK SHOULD EMBRACE ANEW

1. Peter A. Hall, 'The evolution of economic policy', in Howard Machin et al. (eds), *Developments in French Politics II* (Palgrave, 2001), https://scholar.harvard.edu/files/hall/files/evolution_of_econ_pol_2001.pdf
2. École nationale d'administration', Wikipedia, https://en.wikipedia.org/wiki/%C3%89cole_nationale_d'administration
3. Tim Congdon, 'There is still no alternative to monetarism', CapX, 2 August 2024, https://capx.co/there-is-still-no-alternative-to-monetarism/
4. Ben Bernanke, 'Why can't your neighbour burn down his house?', The Decision Lab, https://thedecisionlab.com/thinkers/economics/ben-bernanke#
5. 'Classical Liberalism', Wikipedia, https://en.wikipedia.org/wiki/Classical_liberalism

CHAPTER 1: LET FREE MARKETS THRIVE

1. Matt Ridley, 'How to be PM: ten rules for the next Tory leader to live by', *The Spectator*, 6 August 2022, https://www.spectator.co.uk/article/how-to-be-pm-ten-rules-for-the-next-tory-leader-to-live-by/
2. Poppy Koronka, 'The struggling GPs battling to keep NHS afloat', *The Times*, 16 August 2024, https://www.thetimes.com/article/ce655610-514b-4dfe-9415-8d1cf2496024?shareToken=9ec6bee332d232cfa9129381b00263c6
3. Leonard E. Read, 'I, Pencil: my family tree as told to Leonard E. Read', via Econlib Books, 5 February 2018, https://www.econlib.org/library/Essays/rdPncl.html
4. Alexander Barmine and Max Eastman, *One who survived: the life story of a Russian under the Soviets* (Pickle Partners Publishing, 2010), https://www.amazon.com/One-Who-Survived-Russian-Soviets/dp/1163190993?dplnkId=8587bab8-2c52-4b42-a902-c923ba2f1947&nodl=1
5. F. A. Hayek, 'The use of knowledge in society', *The American Economic Review*, vol. 35, no. 4, September 1945, pp. 519–30, https://statisticaleconomics.org/wp-content/uploads/2013/03/the_use_of_knowledge_in_society_-_hayek.pdf
6. Johnny Fulfer, 'Milton Friedman: The Economist who shaped Neoliberalism in the Cold War era', The Economic Historian, 14 March 2024, https://economic-historian.com/2018/09/milton-friedman-free-market/
7. Christine S. Wilson, 'Milton Friedman is still right: marking the 35th anniversary of *Free Markets for Free Men*', United States of America Federal Trade Commission, 12 October 2019, https://www.ftc.gov/system/files/documents/public_statements/1553170/wilson_-_cpac_brazil_remarks_10-12-19.pdf
8. Milton Friedman, 'Free Markets for Free Men', Chicago Booth Review, 17 October 1974, https://www.chicagobooth.edu/review/free-markets-free-men
9. Anthony B. Kim, 'US slips to worst-ever score in 2023 Index of Economic Freedom', The Heritage Foundation, 1 March 2023, https://www.heritage.org/international-economies/commentary/us-slips-worst-ever-score-2023-index-economic-freedom; Heritage Foundation, 'Preface', The Index of Economic Freedom, October 2023, https://www.heritage.org/index/pages/report
10. Steven E. Landsburg, 'What aspiring economists aren't being taught', *Wall Street Journal*, 2 August 2024, https://www.wsj.com/articles/what-aspiring-economists-arent-being-taught-a3f73484
11. 'EU investigating Apple, Google and Meta's suspected violations of new Digital Markets Act', CBS News, 25 March 2024, https://www.cbsnews.com/news/eu-apple-google-meta-investigation-new-digital-markets-act-antitrust-law/
12. 'Commission fines JCB for unlawful distribution agreements and practices', European Commission press release, 21 December 2000, https://ec.europa.eu/commission/presscorner/detail/en/IP_00_1526; Foo Yun Chee, 'Dyson wins fight against EU energy labelling rules', Reuters, 8 November 2018, https://www.reuters.com/article/idUSKCN1ND1NL/
13. 'Volkswagen emissions scandal', Wikipedia, https://en.wikipedia.org/wiki/Volkswagen_emissions_scandal
14. 'Does the US suffer ten times the foodborne disease that the UK does?', Jorvik Food Safety Services, 12 May 2020, https://foodsafetyteam.org/does-the-us-suffer-ten-times-the-foodborne-disease-that-the-uk-does
15. 'Defunding Politically Motivated Campaigns', Conservative Way Forward, https://www.conservativewayforward.com/_files/ugd/acef4a_5b5ec1d9017f40b987a68110f70d276c.pdf
16. Gill Plimmer and Ella Hollowood, 'Water companies pay £2.5bn in dividends in two years as debt climbs by £8.2 bn', *Financial Times*, 15 April 2024, https://www.ft.com/content/c3cdfefb-c912-4699-bb7f-72c5c6515757
17. Tim Congdon, 'How have changes in regulation affected UK bank credit since the Great Recession?', Institute of Monetary Research and the University of Buckingham, September 2021, https://mv-pt.org/wp-content/uploads/2021/10/2021-10-06-Research-Paper-9-Congdon-Screen.pdf
18. Peter Cambell and Jim Pickard, 'Carmakers in UK to face EV sales targets despite delay to petrol vehicle ban', *Financial Times*, 21 September 2023, https://www.ft.com/content/1d3201e1-bfbf-4eb2-aca1-06c83d87b1e6

NOTES

19 Ben Southwood, Samuel Hughes and Sam Bowman, 'Foundations: Why Britian has stagnated', https://ukfoundations.co/
20 'Electricity Prices', Global Petrol Prices, December 2023, https://www.globalpetrolprices.com/electricity_prices/
21 Amanda Jasi, 'Fertiliser producer's plan to shut UK's largest ammonia plant triggers agriculture and food security concerns', The Chemical Engineer, 9 August 2023, https://www.thechemicalengineer.com/news/fertiliser-producer-s-plan-to-shut-uk-s-largest-ammonia-plant-triggers-agriculture-and-food-security-concerns/
22 HM Treasury, 'Public Expenditure Statistical Analyses 2023', Gov.uk, 19 July 2023, https://www.gov.uk/government/statistics/public-expenditure-statistical-analyses-2023
23 'GDP output approach, low level aggregates, UK quarter 1 (Jan to March 2024)', Office for National Statistics, https://www.ons.gov.uk/file?uri=/economy/grossdomesticproductgdp/datasets/ukgdpolowlevelaggregates/current/previous/v83/gdplowlevelaggregates2024q1.xlsx
24 'Are free markets history?', The Economist, 5 October 2023, https://www.economist.com/leaders/2023/10/05/are-free-markets-history
25 Prime Minister's Office, 10 Downing Street, The Rt Hon Greg Clark MP, and the Rt Hon Theresa May MP, 'PM Theresa May: we will end UK contribution to climate change by 2050', Gov.uk, 12 June 2019, https://www.gov.uk/government/news/pm-theresa-may-we-will-end-uk-contribution-to-climate-change-by-2050
26 Department for Business, Energy & Industrial Strategy, Prime Minister's Office, 10 Downing Street, Department for Environment, Food & Rural Affairs, Department for Transport, The Rt Hon Greg Hands MP, 'UK's path to net zero set out in landmark strategy', Gov.uk, 19 October 2021, https://www.gov.uk/government/news/uks-path-to-net-zero-set-out-in-landmark-strategy
27 David Turver, 'The Climate Change Committee releases 2024 progress report and rails at Government for failing to meet its emissions targets and failing to make electricity cheaper. Spot the problem, here?', Daily Sceptic, 5 August 2024, https://dailysceptic.org/2024/08/05/climate-change-committee-contradictions/
28 Mark J. Perry, 'What nation on earth has reduced its carbon emissions more than any other, Part II?', AEI, 8 November 2017, https://www.aei.org/carpe-diem/what-nation-on-earth-has-reduced-its-carbon-emissions-more-than-any-other-part-ii/
29 Jonathan Leake, 'Britain will need gas to avoid blackouts for decades', Daily Telegraph, 22 October 2023, https://www.telegraph.co.uk/business/2023/10/22/national-gas-jon-butterworth-britain-fossil-fuels-blackouts/
30 Vaclav Smil, *Power Density: A key to understanding energy sources and uses* (MIT Press, 2015), https://direct.mit.edu/books/monograph/4023/Power-DensityA-Key-to-Understanding-Energy-Sources
31 Simon Jack and Noor Nanji, 'Britishvolt: UK battery start-up collapses into administration', BBC News, 17 January 2023, https://www.bbc.co.uk/news/business-64303149
32 'Offshore wind subsidies per MWh generated continue to rise', Renewable Energy Foundation, 1 August 2021, https://www.ref.org.uk/ref-blog/370-offshore-wind-subsidies-per-mwh-generated-continue-to-rise#:~:text=On%20the%20basis%20of%20official%20RO%20and%20CfD,total%2C%20with%20Hornsea%20taking%2011%25%20or%20%C2%A3480%20million
33 Chris Morrison, 'Net Zero electricity fantasies to cost British consumers £100 billion over next six years', Daily Sceptic, 25 November 2023, https://dailysceptic.org/2023/11/25/net-zero-electricity-fantasies-to-cost-british-consumers-100-billion-over-next-six-years/
34 David Turver, 'Debunking the cheap renewables myth', Daily Sceptic, 16 May 2024, https://dailysceptic.org/2024/05/16/debunking-the-cheap-renewables-myth/
35 Max Colchester, Joe Wallace and Benoit Faucon, 'Global gas shortage stings UK, showing shortcomings in its energy transition', Wall Street Journal, 30 September 2021, https://www.wsj.com/articles/global-gas-shortage-stings-u-k-showing-shortcomings-in-its-energy-transition-11633005732?st=v768y0j29mkjbka&reflink=article_email_share
36 Wester van Gaal, 'Germany begins dismantling wind farm for coal', Euobserver, 29 August 2023, https://euobserver.com/green-economy/arf0893c11
37 Sam Tobin, 'UK's new coal mine sent "adverse international signal", campaigners say', Reuters, 16 July 2024, https://www.reuters.com/sustainability/climate-energy/uks-new-coal-mine-sent-adverse-international-signal-campaigners-say-2024-07-16/; Christina McSorley and Georgina Rannard, 'New coalmine in doubt after "error" in planning decision', BBC News, 11 July 2024, https://www.bbc.co.uk/news/articles/c99w1qjp8qk0
38 Department for Energy Security and Net Zero, 'Industrial energy price indices', Gov.uk, 27 June 2024, https://www.gov.uk/government/statistical-data-sets/industrial-energy-price-indices
39 'Electricity Prices', Global Petrol Prices, December 2023, https://www.globalpetrolprices.com/electricity_prices/

40. Florence Jones, 'China continues permitting the equivalent of two coal-fired power plants per week', Power Technology, 30 August 2023, https://www.power-technology.com/news/china-permitting-two-coal-fired-power-plants-per-week/#:~:text=China%20is%20continuing%20a%20coal-fired%20power%20plant%20permitting,equivalent%20of%20two%20coal-fired%20power%20plants%20per%20week
41. Michael Sheridan, 'Do treaties matter? Not to China', CEPA, 12 May 2023, https://cepa.org/article/do-treaties-matter-not-to-china/
42. Paul Bolton, 'Gas and electricity prices during the "energy crisis" and beyond', House of Commons Library Research Briefing, 2 September 2024, https://commonslibrary.parliament.uk/research-briefings/cbp-9714/
43. Rainer Zitelmann, 'Socialism: the failed idea that never dies', Forbes, 16 March 2020, https://www.forbes.com/sites/rainerzitelmann/2020/03/16/socialism-the-failed-idea-that-never-dies/?sh=6f4e9f1b23cc
44. Hannah Ritchie and Pablo Rosado, 'Nuclear Energy', Our World in Data, July 2020 (revised in April 2024), https://ourworldindata.org/nuclear-energy
45. 'Death rates per unit of electricity production', Our World in Data, https://ourworldindata.org/grapher/death-rates-from-energy-production-per-twh
46. Michael Shellenberger, 'It sounds crazy, but Fukushima, Chernobyl, and Three Mile Island show why nuclear is inherently safe', Forbes, 11 March 2019, https://www.forbes.com/sites/michaelshellenberger/2019/03/11/it-sounds-crazy-but-fukushima-chernobyl-and-three-mile-island-show-why-nuclear-is-inherently-safe/?sh=37ba36a11688
47. US Energy Information Administration (EIA), 'First new US nuclear reactor since 2016 is now in operation', Today in Energy, 1 August 2023, https://www.eia.gov/todayinenergy/detail.php?id=57280#:~:text=Georgia%20Power%20expects%20another%20similar,Palo%20Verde%20plant%20in%20Arizona
48. Office of the Premier, 'Ontario breaks ground on world-leading small modular reactor', Ontario Newsroom, 2 December 2022, https://news.ontario.ca/en/release/1002543/ontario-breaks-ground-on-world-leading-small-modular-reactor
49. 'The global fusion industry in 2023', Fusion Industry Association, https://www.fusionindustryassociation.org/wp-content/uploads/2023/07/FIA%E2%80%932023-FINAL.pdf
50. 'The global fusion industry in 2023', Fusion Industry Association, https://www.fusionindustryassociation.org/wp-content/uploads/2023/07/FIA%E2%80%932023-FINAL.pdf
51. Uri Gat, H. L. Dodds, 'Molten Salt Reactors – safety options galore', OSTI.gov, 1 June 1997, https://www.osti.gov/biblio/469120#:~:text=There%20are%20safety%20concerns%20associated,the%20MSBR%2C%20the%20expansion%20of
52. Carley Willis and Joanne Liou, 'Safety in Fusion: An inherently safe process', International Atomic Energy Agency, May 2021, https://www.iaea.org/bulletin/safety-in-fusion
53. Jack Devanney, 'The trouble with fusion', Gordian Knot News, 18 February 2024, https://jackdevanney.substack.com/p/the-trouble-with-fusion; Emily Hayes, 'Nuclear power in the UK', House of Lords Library, 1 December 2021, https://lordslibrary.parliament.uk/nuclear-power-in-the-uk/
54. Sam Dumitriu, 'Why Britain is building the world's most expensive nuclear plant', The Spectator, 2 May 2024, https://www.spectator.co.uk/article/why-britain-is-building-the-worlds-most-expensive-nuclear-plant/
55. Mark A. Zupan, 'The Virtues of Free Markets', Cato Journal, vol. 31, no. 2, spring/summer 2011, https://ciaotest.cc.columbia.edu/journals/cato/v31i2/f_0022693_18678.pdf
56. Daniel Heil, 'Capitalism vs Socialism', Hoover Institution, 21 April 2021, https://www.hoover.org/research/capitalism-vs-socialism-2
57. Nick Beams, 'Social inequality and the fight against capitalism', World Socialist Website, 25 October 2016, https://www.wsws.org/en/articles/2016/10/25/pers-025.html
58. David Brooks, 'I was once a socialist. Then I saw how it worked', New York Times, 5 December 2019, https://www.nytimes.com/2019/12/05/opinion/socialism-capitalism.html?smid=nytcore-ios-share&referringSource=articleShare&ugrp=c&pvid=499840E8-3CAE-4F3F-BC43-0671F8DB7FE5; John M. Echols III, 'Does socialism mean greater equality? A comparison of East and West along several major dimensions', American Journal of Political Science, vol. 25, no. 1, February 1981, pp. 1–31, https://www.jstor.org/stable/2110910; Ayaan Hirsi Ali, 'The false appeal of socialism', Hoover Institute, 21 September 2020, https://www.hoover.org/research/false-appeal-socialism
59. 'Gini Coefficient by Country 2024', World Population Review, https://worldpopulationreview.com/country-rankings/gini-coefficient-by-country
60. Matt Ridley, The Origins of Virtue (Penguin, 1996), https://en.wikipedia.org/wiki/The_Origins_of_Virtue
61. World Income Inequality Database, https://view.officeapps.live.com/op/view.aspx?src=https%3A%2F%2Fwww.wider.unu.edu%2Fsites%2Fdefault%2Ffiles%2FData%2FWIID_28NOV2023.xlsx&wdOrigin=BROWSELINK

NOTES

62 'Gini Coefficient by Country 2024', World Population Review, https://worldpopulationreview.com/country-rankings/gini-coefficient-by-country

CHAPTER 2: LET FREE TRADE FLOURISH

1 Andreas Bergh and Therese Nilsson 'Globalization and Absolute Poverty – A Panel Data Study', IFN Working Paper No. 862, 6 December 2013, https://papers.ssrn.com/sol3/papers.cfm?abstract_id=2363784

2 OECD, ILO, World Bank, WTO, 'Seizing the benefits of trade for employment and growth', final report, 11 November 2010, www.wto.org/english/news_e/news10_e/oecd_ilo_wb_wto_report_e.pdf

3 Office for National Statistics, 'UK trade: January 2024', 13 March 2024, https://www.ons.gov.uk/economy/nationalaccounts/balanceofpayments/bulletins/uktrade/January2024#monthly-trade-in-services

4 Office for National Statistics, 'UK trade: May 2024', 11 July 2024, https://www.ons.gov.uk/economy/nationalaccounts/balanceofpayments/bulletins/uktrade/may2024#uk-trade-data

5 Sophie Hale and Emily Fry, 'Open for Business? UK Trade Performance since leaving the EU', Resolution Foundation, 28 February 2023, https://economy2030.resolutionfoundation.org/reports/open-for-business/

6 'Britain's services exports are booming despite Brexit. Why?', *The Economist*, 9 May 2023, https://www.economist.com/britain/2023/05/09/britains-services-exports-are-booming-despite-brexit-why

7 'Quarterly GDP and components – expenditure approach, national currency', OECD, Release of 15 August 2024, https://data-explorer.oecd.org/vis?df[ds]=DisseminateFinalDMZ&df[id]=DSD_NAMAIN1%40DF_QNA_EXPENDITURE_NATIO_CURR&df[ag]=OECD.SDD.NAD&df[vs]=1.1&dq=Q.Y.ITA%2BUSA%2BJPN%2BDEU%2BFRA%2BCAN…P62%2BP61……L..&to[TIME_PERIOD]=false&vw=tb&pd=2013-Q4%2C2024-Q2 ; ONS, https://www.ons.gov.uk/file?uri=/economy/nationalaccounts/balanceofpayments/datasets/tradeingoodsmretsallbopeu2013timeseriesspreadsheet/current/mret.xlsx

8 'Quarterly GDP and components – expenditure approach, national currency', OECD, https://data-explorer.oecd.org/vis?df[ds]=DisseminateFinalDMZ&df[id]=DSD_NAMAIN1%40DF_QNA_EXPENDITURE_NATIO_CURR&df[ag]=OECD.SDD.NAD&df[vs]=1.1&dq=Q.Y.ITA%2BUSA%2BJPN%2BDEU%2BFRA%2BCAN…P62%2BP61……L..&to[TIME_PERIOD]=false&vw=tb&pd=2013-Q4%2C2024-Q2; ONS data file, https://www.ons.gov.uk/file?uri=/economy/nationalaccounts/balanceofpayments/datasets/tradeingoodsmretsallbopeu2013timeseriesspreadsheet/current/mret.xlsx

9 ONS data file, https://www.ons.gov.uk/file?uri=/economy/grossdomesticproductgdp/datasets/ukgdpolowlevelaggregates/current/gdpolowlevelaggregates2024q2.xlsx

10 James Cook and Megan Bonar, 'Grangemouth oil refinery could cease operations by 2025', BBC News, 22 November 2023, https://www.bbc.co.uk/news/uk-scotland-tayside-central-67497023; 'UK announces proposal to permanently close ammonia plant at Billingham complex', CF Industries, 25 July 2023, https://www.cfindustries.com/newsroom/2023/billingham-ammonia-plant

11 ONS data file, https://www.ons.gov.uk/file?uri=/economy/nationalaccounts/balanceofpayments/datasets/tradeingoodsmretsallbopeu2013timeseriesspreadsheet/current/mret.xlsx

12 ONS, 'UK total trade by all countries', seasonally adjusted, Q1 2024, https://www.ons.gov.uk/file?uri=/economy/nationalaccounts/balanceofpayments/datasets/uktotaltradeallcountriesseasonallyadjusted/januarytomarch2024/tradequarterlyq124seasonallyadjusted.xlsx

13 International Monetary Fund, 'World Economic Outlook (April 2024)', https://www.imf.org/en/%20Publications/WEO/weo-database/2024/April/

14 Paul Wiseman, 'Trump or Biden? Either way, US seems poised to preserve heavy tariffs on imports', Associated Press, 21 May 2024, https://apnews.com/article/trump-biden-trade-tariffs-china-inflation-1c17b1d22308ob7a594326905380845a#

15 'Brand Finance's Global Soft Power Index 2024: USA and UK ranked top nations brands, China takes third place, overtaking Japan and Germany', Brand Finance, 29 February 2024, https://brandfinance.com/press-releases/brand-finances-global-soft-power-index-2024-usa-and-uk-ranked-top-nation-brands-china-takes-third-place-overtaking-japan-and-germany

16 'What next? A special report on the world economy', *The Economist*, 8 October 2022, https://www.economist.com/weeklyedition/2022-10-08

17 'Comparative advantage', Wikipedia, https://en.wikipedia.org/wiki/Comparative_advantage

18 Williams Johnson, 'Motorsport Valley: The biggest hub of motor racing in the world', Medium, 26 July 2019, https://medium.com/inside-the-motorsport-valley-the-biggest-hub-of/the-motorsport-valley-the-biggest-hub-of-motor-racing-in-the-world-ab13e16e4d36

19 Kirstie McDermott, 'A guide to the Silicon Fen tech sector', Growth Business, 20 July 2022, https://growthbusiness.co.uk/a-guide-to-the-silicon-fen-tech-sector-20192/

20. 'UK Tech Ecosystem Evolution: The Global Talent Visa's Impact', Tech Nomads, https://www.technomads.io/blog/uk-tech-ecosystem-evolution-the-global-talent-visas-impact
21. Radomir Tylecote, 'The New trade route: The story of the IEA, Brexit and the UK's new approach to global trade', IEA, 23 June 2021, https://iea.org.uk/publications/the-new-trade-route-the-story-of-the-iea-brexit-and-the-uks-new-approach-to-global-trade/
22. Jeffrey A. Frankel and David H. Romer, 'Does Trade Cause Growth?', *American Economic Review*, vol, 89, no. 3, June 1999, pp. 379–99, https://www.aeaweb.org/articles?id=10.1257/aer.89.3.379
23. Jon Moynihan, 'Gravity models, free trade and game theory: How the *bien pensant* "experts" of the Remain camp allowed their prejudices to distort their thinking', Brexit Central, 16 June 2017, https://brexitcentral.com/gravity-models-remain-prejudices-distort/
24. Douglas A. Irwin, 'Does Trade Reform Promote Economic Growth? A Review of Recent Evidence', NBER Working Paper 25927, June 2019, https://www.nber.org/system/files/working_papers/w25927/w25927.pdf
25. Robert J. Barro, 'Determinants of Economic Growth: A Cross-Country Empirical Study', NBER Working Paper 5698, August 1996, https://www.nber.org/papers/w5698
26. Dong-Hyeon Kim and Shu-Chin Lin, 'Trade and Growth at Different Stages of Economic Development', *Journal of Development Studies*, vol. 45, no. 8, 2009, pp. 1211–24, https://econpapers.repec.org/article/tafjdevst/v_3a45_3ay_3a2009_3ai_3a8_3ap_3a1211-1224.htm
27. Tarlok Singh, 'Does International Trade Cause Economic Growth? A Survey', *The World Economy*, vol. 33, no. 11, November 2010, pp. 1517–64, https://onlinelibrary.wiley.com/doi/abs/10.1111/j.1467-9701.2010.01243.x
28. Andrew Berg and Anne O. Krueger, 'Trade, Growth, and Poverty: A Selective Survey', IMF Working Paper No 03/30, 28 February 2003, https://papers.ssrn.com/sol3/papers.cfm?abstract_id=879105
29. Jean-Jacques Hallaert, 'A History of Empirical Literature on the Relationship between Trade and Growth', *Mondes en Développement*, vol. 34, no. 135, 2006, https://papers.ssrn.com/sol3/papers.cfm?abstract_id=1671544
30. William R. Cline, 'Trade Policy and Global Poverty', Peterson Institute for International Economics number 379, April 2004, https://ideas.repec.org/b/iie/ppress/379.html
31. Robert E. Baldwin, 'Openness and Growth: What's the Empirical Relationship?', NBER Working Paper 9578, March 2003, https://www.nber.org/papers/w9578
32. L. Alan Winters, 'Trade Liberalisation and Economic Performance: An Overview', *The Economic Journal*, vo. 114, no. 493, February 2004, https://onlinelibrary.wiley.com/doi/abs/10.1111/j.0013-0133.2004.00185.x
33. Francisco Rodriguez and Dani Rodrik, 'Trade Policy and Economic Growth: A Sceptic's Guide to Cross-National Evidence', NBER Working Paper 7081, April 1999, https://www.nber.org/papers/w7081
34. T. N. Srinivasan and Jagdish Bhagwati, 'Outward-Orientation and Development: Are Revisionists right?', Economic Growth Center discussion paper 806, Yale University, September 1999, http://www.econ.yale.edu/growth_pdf/cdp806.pdf
35. Corey Iacono & Matt Palumbo, *In Defense of Classical Liberalism: An Economic Analysis*, ISBN: 1500963933 https://www.amazon.co.uk/Defense-Classical-Liberalism-Economic-Analysis/dp/1500963933
36. 'Economic Freedom Ranking', Fraser Institute, https://www.fraserinstitute.org/economic-freedom/map?geozone=world&page=map&year=2021
37. Groningen Growth and Development Centre, 'Penn World Table version 10.01', University of Groningen, https://www.rug.nl/ggdc/productivity/pwt/?lang=en
38. Michael Burrage, 'Myth & Paradox of the Single Market: How the trade benefits of the EU membership have been mis-sold', Civitas, January 2016, https://www.civitas.org.uk/email-resources/myth-and-paradox.pdf
39. Thomas Brown, 'Renewing the UK's trading relationship with Commonwealth countries', House of Lords Library, 2 July 2021, https://lordslibrary.parliament.uk/renewing-the-uks-trading-relationship-with-commonwealth-countries/
40. International Monetary Fund, 'Direction of Trade Statistics (DOTS)', https://data.imf.org/?sk=9d6028d4f14a464ca2f259b2cd424b85&sid=1409151240976
41. Taxation and Customs Union, 'TARIC, the integrated Tariff of the European Union', European Commission, https://taxation-customs.ec.europa.eu/customs-4/calculation-customs-duties/customs-tariff/eu-customs-tariff-taric_en
42. Paul Seddon and Kate Whannel, 'UK halts trade negotiation with Canada over hormones in beef ban', BBC News, 26 January 2024, https://www.bbc.co.uk/news/uk-politics-68098177
43. Catherine McBride, 'Hear, hear for suspended food tariffs', Briefings for Britain, 19 April 2024, https://www.briefingsforbritain.co.uk/hear-hear-for-suspended-food-tariffs/

NOTES

44 Dominic Pino, 'Brits should not be taxed extra for buying Moroccan Tomatoes', NR Capital Matters, 27 September 2024, https://www.nationalreview.com/corner/brits-should-not-be-taxed-extra-for-buying-moroccan-tomatoes/
45 Dominic Webb, 'Progress on UK free trade agreement negotiations', House of Commons Library, 8 April 2024, https://commonslibrary.parliament.uk/research-briefings/cbp-9314/
46 Office for Budget Responsibility, 'Brexit analysis', 17 April 2023, https://obr.uk/forecasts-in-depth/the-economy-forecast/brexit-analysis/
47 James Forder, 'The benefits of joining the CPTPP go far beyond the headline figures', Institute for Economic Affairs, 31 March 2023, https://iea.org.uk/the-benefits-of-joining-the-cptpp-go-far-beyond-the-headline-figures/
48 Patrick Minford with David Meenagh, *After Brexit, What Next? Trade, Regulation and Economic Growth* (Edward Elgar, 2020), https://www.amazon.com/After-Brexit-What-Next-Regulation/dp/1839103086; House of Commons Exiting the European Union Committee, 'EU Exit Analysis Cross Whitehall Briefing', Scribd, January 2018, https://www.scribd.com/document/373310656/EU-Exit-Analysis-Cross-Whitehall-Briefing
49 Joe Barnes, 'French Fisherman blockade Channel Tunnel and Calais port over licence row', *Daily Telegraph*, 26 November 2021, https://www.telegraph.co.uk/world-news/2021/11/26/french-fishermen-blockade-channel-tunnel/
50 Melanie Gower, Stefano Fella and Ilze Jozepa, 'After Brexit: Visiting, working and living in the EU', House of Commons Library, 28 November 2023, https://commonslibrary.parliament.uk/research-briefings/cbp-9157/
51 Ruby Hinchliffe and Henry Samuel, 'Punished enough by Brexit: France could relax 90-day rule for British second home owners', *Daily Telegraph*, 13 November 2023, https://www.telegraph.co.uk/money/property/second-homes/france-brexit-visa-rule-relax-british-second-homes/
52 Lottie Goss, 'Dog-friendly holidays in Europe: how post-Brexit rules affect your trip', *Daily Telegraph*, 3 August 2023, https://www.telegraph.co.uk/travel/advice/does-brexit-mean-pet-passports-travelling-dog-cat/
53 Ben Chapman, 'Brexit: One in four small export businesses have stopped selling to the EU, poll finds', *The Independent*, 29 March 2021, https://www.independent.co.uk/news/business/brexit-small-businesses-exports-sales-b1824008.html
54 David Trimble, 'Ditch the Protocol: the EU Threat to Northern Ireland', Briefings for Britain, 5 February 2022, https://www.briefingsforbritain.co.uk/ditch-the-protocol-the-eu-threat-to-northern-ireland/
55 Philip Brien, 'Service Industries: key economic indicators', House of Commons Library, 5 August 2024, https://commonslibrary.parliament.uk/research-briefings/sn02786/#:~:text=The%20service%20industries%20include%20the,employment%20in%20January%E2%80%93March%202024
56 Michael Burrage, 'Myth and Paradox of the Single Market: How the trade benefits of the EU membership have been mis-sold', Civitas, January 2016, https://www.civitas.org.uk/email-resources/myth-and-paradox.pdf
57 Department for Business and Trade and the Rt Hon Kemi Badenoch MP, 'UK and Florida sign pact to boost trade', Gov.uk, 14 November 2023, https://www.gov.uk/government/news/uk-and-florida-sign-pact-to-boost-trade
58 Matthew Ward, 'Statistics on UK Trade with the Commonwealth', House of Commons Library, 6 November 2023, https://commonslibrary.parliament.uk/research-briefings/cbp-8282; Department for Business & Trade, 'Trade and Investment Factsheets', https://assets.publishing.service.gov.uk/media/65f95aeed977c2001f9b807b/brazil-trade-and-investment-factsheet-2024-03-21.pdf
59 'Kenya wants to pioneer a new African approach to global warming', *The Economist*, 14 September 2023, https://www.economist.com/middle-east-and-africa/2023/09/14/kenya-wants-to-pioneer-a-new-african-approach-to-global-warming
60 Thomas Lambie, 'Miracle Down Under: How New Zealand Farmers Prosper without Subsidies or Protection', CATO Institute, 7 February 2005, https://www.cato.org/free-trade-bulletin/miracle-down-under-how-new-zealand-farmers-prosper-without-subsidies-or; Michael Farren, 'Subsidies prevent farmers from reaching their full potential', The Hill, 15 October 2018, https://thehill.com/opinion/finance/411379-subsidies-prevent-farmers-from-reaching-their-full-potential/
61 Louis Ashworth, 'Britain, consultation nation', *Financial Times*, 23 January 2024, https://www.ft.com/content/8d3ed4d7-6ab3-487d-81ee-3fd337b68538
62 'Academic year 2022/23, Level 2 and 3 attainment age 16-25', Gov.uk, 25 April 2024, https://explore-education-statistics.service.gov.uk/find-statistics/level-2-and-3-attainment-by-young-people-aged-19

CHAPTER 3: LET SOUND MONEY PREVAIL

1. Bank of England, 'Quantitative easing', https://www.bankofengland.co.uk/monetary-policy/quantitative-easing
2. ADB Institute, 'History of Bank of Japan's more than two decades of unconventional monetary easing with special emphasis on the frameworks pursued in the last 10 years', May 2023, https://www.adb.org/publications/history-of-bank-of-japan-s-more-than-two-decades-of-unconventional-monetary-easing-with-special-emphasis-on-the-frameworks-pursued-in-the-last-10-years
3. John Mullin, 'The Fed, the stock market, and the "Greenspan Put"', Federal Reserve Bank of Richmond, Econ Focus First Quarter 2023, https://www.richmondfed.org/publications/research/econ_focus/2023/q1_federal_reserve
4. Bank of England Database, Data Viewer, 2014-2024, https://www.bankofengland.co.uk/boeapps/database/fromshowcolumns.asp?Travel=NIxSTxTDxSUx&FromSeries=1&ToSeries=50&DAT=RNG&FD=1&FM=Jan&FY=2014&TD=24&TM=Jan&TY=2024&FNY=&CSVF=TT&html.x=52&html.y=27&C=JPZ&Filter=N; United Kingdom Debt Management Office, Gilts in Issue, https://www.dmo.gov.uk/data/pdfdatareport?reportCode=D1A
5. FRED, 'Interest Rates: Long-Term Government bond yields', https://fred.stlouisfed.org/series/IRLTLT01GBM156N
6. Tim Congdon (ed.), *Money in the Great Recession* (Edward Elgar, 2017), https://sites.krieger.jhu.edu/iae/files/2019/05/Money_in_the_Great_Recession_Hanke_Ch7.pdf
7. Isolde Walters, 'I earn £105k but rely on cash-in-hand jobs to make ends meet', *Daily Telegraph*, 13 April 2024, https://www.telegraph.co.uk/money/jobs/earn-salary-over-100k-but-still-feel-broke/
8. 'True swing voters are extraordinarily rare in America', *The Economist*, 11 April 2024, https://www.economist.com/leaders/2024/04/11/true-swing-voters-are-extraordinarily-rare-in-america; Tony Driver, 'Swing states trust Trump more on the economy than Harris', *Daily Telegraph*, 19 August 2024, https://www.telegraph.co.uk/us/politics/2024/08/19/swing-states-trust-trump-more-on-the-economy-than-harris/
9. L. Randall Wray, 'From the State theory of modern money to modern money theory', Levy Economics Institute, working paper no. 792, March 2014, https://www.levyinstitute.org/publications/from-the-state-theory-of-money-to-modern-money-theory
10. John H. Cochrane, '"The deficit myth" review: years of magical thinking', *Wall Street Journal*, 5 June 2020, https://www.wsj.com/articles/the-deficit-myth-review-years-of-magical-thinking-11591396579?st=9tpivy7moduclr8&reflink=article_email_share
11. FRED, 'Currency conversions: US dollar exchange rate: average of daily rates: national currency: USD for Turkey', July 2024, https://fred.stlouisfed.org/series/CCUSMA02TRM618N
12. 'Currency manipulation: how competitive devaluation impacts global trade', Faster Capital, 4 June 2024, https://fastercapital.com/content/Currency-manipulation--How-Competitive-Devaluation-Impacts-Global-Trade.html
13. International Monetary Fund, 'Monetary policy and Central Banking', https://www.imf.org/en/About/Factsheets/Sheets/2023/monetary-policy-and-central-banking
14. Mark Horton and Asmaa El-Ganainy, 'Fiscal policy: taking and giving away', International Monetary Fund, https://www.imf.org/en/Publications/fandd/issues/Series/Back-to-Basics/Fiscal-Policy
15. Carmen M. Reinhart and Kenneth S. Rogoff, 'Growth in a Time of Debt', NBER Working Paper 15639, January 2010, https://www.nber.org/papers/w15639
16. Ruth Alexander, 'Reinhart, Rogoff… and Herndon: the student who caught out the profs', BBC News, 20 April 2013, https://www.bbc.co.uk/news/magazine-22223190
17. International Monetary Fund, 'General Government Debt, Percent of GDP', https://www.imf.org/external/datamapper/GG_DEBT_GDP@GDD/AUS/BEL/DEU/FRA/ISR/ITA/NLD/PRT/ESP/SWE/GBR/USA/CZE/JPN/CAN/GRC?year=2021
18. Charlotte Edwards and Faisal Islam, 'National debt forecast to treble over next 50 years', BBC News, 12 September 2024, https://www.bbc.co.uk/news/articles/cewlwkg82gg0
19. HM Treasury, 'Public Expenditure Statistical Analyses 2023', Gov.uk, 19 July 2023, https://www.gov.uk/government/statistics/public-expenditure-statistical-analyses-2023
20. International Monetary Fund, 'World Economic Outlook Database', https://www.imf.org/en/%20Publications/WEO/weo-database/2024/April/; FRED, 'Interest Rates: Long-term government bond yields: 10-year: main (including benchmark) for United Kingdom', https://fred.stlouisfed.org/series/IRLTLT01GBM156N
21. United Kingdom Debt Management Office, 'Gilt Market, Index Linked Gilts', https://www.dmo.gov.uk/data/gilt-market/index-linked-gilts/#keyevents

NOTES

22 United Kingdom Debt Management Office, 'Gilts in Issue', https://www.dmo.gov.uk/data/pdfdatareport?reportCode=D1A
23 Jon Moynihan, 'Rishi Sunak's tax hikes have a fundamental flaw', *Daily Telegraph*, 11 February 2023, https://www.telegraph.co.uk/news/2023/02/11/rishi-sunaks-tax-hikes-have-fundamental-flaw/
24 Bank for International Settlements, 'Debt securities statistics, Central government debt securities', BIS data portal, https://data.bis.org/topics/DSS/tables-and-dashboards/BIS,SEC_C2,1.0
25 National Treasury Management Agency, '2023: Annual Report and Financial Statements', https://www.designethos.co/ntma/documents/NTMA-2023-Master-WEB.pdf
26 United Kingdom Debt Management Office, 'Gilts in Issue', https://www.dmo.gov.uk/data/pdfdatareport?reportCode=D1A
27 Gunther Schnabl, 'Inflation is always and everywhere a monetary phenomenon, even in pandemic and war', Austrian Institute, 30 May 2022, https://austrian-institute.org/en/blog/inflation-is-always-and-everywhere-a-monetary-phenomenon-even-in-pandemic-and-war/
28 Professor Tim Congdon, 'The quantity theory of money: a new restatement', Institute of Economic Affairs, 19 June 2024, https://iea.org.uk/publications/the-quantity-theory-of-money-a-new-restatement/
29 John Greenwood, 'How to prevent future inflation: Lessons from the Covid inflation', Politeia, 2023, https://www.politeia.co.uk/wp-content/uploads/2023/12/PDF-J-Greenwood-29-December-2023-How-to-Prevent-Future-Inflation.pdf
30 Office for National Statistics, 'CPIH annual rate', 14 August 2024, https://www.ons.gov.uk/economy/inflationandpriceindices/timeseries/l550/mm23
31 Bank of England, 'Further details about M4 data', https://www.bankofengland.co.uk/statistics/details/further-details-about-m4-data
32 Tim Congdon, Institute of International Monetary Research, May 2024, https://mailchi.mp/8e0ccfbb8371/which-economic-thoughtcomes-out-best-from-the-last-decade-8256123?e=94eb42f62d
33 Bank of England, 'Yield Curves', https://www.bankofengland.co.uk/statistics/yield-curves
34 BDO United Kingdom, 'A steady increase of "zombie" companies in the UK mid-market – the latest update', March 2024, https://www.bdo.co.uk/en-gb/insights/advisory/mergers-and-acquisitions/a-steady-increase-of-zombie-companies-in-the-uk-mid-market-the-latest-update
35 Tim Congdon, 'The debate over "quantitative easing" in the UK's great recession and afterwards', in Tim Congdon (ed.), *Money in the Great Recession* (Edward Elgar, 2017), pp. 57–77, https://mv-pt.org/wp-content/uploads/2020/05/mgr.02-Chapter-2-Congdon.pdf
36 Mervyn King, *The End of Alchemy: Money, Banking and the Future of the Global Economy* (W. W. Norton & Company, 2016), https://www.amazon.co.uk/End-Alchemy-Banking-Future-Economy/dp/0393247023
37 Bank of England, 'Bank rate increased to 2.25% – September 2022', 22 September 2022, https://www.bankofengland.co.uk/monetary-policy-summary-and-minutes/2022/september-2022
38 Jon Moynihan, 'How the Bank broke the Government', The Critic, December/January 2023, https://thecritic.co.uk/issues/december-january-2023/how-the-bank-broke-the-government/; Jon Moynihan, 'Did Liz Truss really cause the bond market rout?', CapX, 6 February 2023, https://capx.co/did-liz-truss-really-cause-the-bond-market-rout/; Alexandra Scaggs and Louis Ashworth, 'LDI: the better mousetrap that almost broke the UK', *Financial Times*, 29 September 2022, https://www.ft.com/content/f4a728a5-0179-48bd-b292-f48e30f8603c; Caitlin Ostroff, Jean Eaglesham and Chelsey Dulaney, 'UK Regulator pushed pensions to load up on LDIs', *Wall Street Journal*, 4 October 2022, https://www.wsj.com/articles/u-k-regulator-pushed-pensions-to-load-up-on-ldis-11664908870
39 Graham Hand, 'Tim Congdon warned us and we ignored him on inflation', First Links, 1 February 2023, https://www.firstlinks.com.au/congdon-warned-us-ignored-him
40 International Monetary Fund, 'Inflation rate, average consumer prices', https://www.imf.org/external/datamapper/PCPIPCH@WEO/OEMDC/ADVEC/WEOWORLD
41 Office for National Statistics data, https://www.ons.gov.uk/generator?uri=/economy/inflationandpriceindices/bulletins/consumerpriceinflation/july2024/9d4ce6f5&format=xls
42 Ben King, 'Bank makes history as it reverses quantitative easing', BBC News, 1 November 2022, https://www.bbc.co.uk/news/business-63474176
43 Professor Tim Congdon, 'Institute of International Monetary Research', May 2024, https://mailchi.mp/8e0ccfbb8371/which-economic-thoughtcomes-out-best-from-the-last-decade-8256123?e=94eb42f62d
44 Monetary Policy Committee, 'Monetary Policy Report', Bank of England, May 2024, https://www.bankofengland.co.uk/monetary-policy-report/2024/may-2024
45 Professor Tim Congdon, CBE, 'Institute of International Monetary Research, May 2024, https://mailchi.mp/8e0ccfbb8371/which-economic-thoughtcomes-out-best-from-the-last-decade-8256123?e=94eb42f62d

46 Bank of England, 'Inflation Calculator', https://www.bankofengland.co.uk/monetary-policy/inflation/inflation-calculator
47 Thomas Weston, 'Making an independent Bank of England work better', Economic Affairs Committee, House of Lords Library, 15 April 2024, https://lordslibrary.parliament.uk/economic-affairs-committee-report-making-an-independent-bank-of-england-work-better/
48 Nicholas Macpherson, 'Treasury Orthodoxy: Fact or Fiction?', Strand Group, Edinburgh, 1 November 2022, https://thestrandgroup.kcl.ac.uk/wp-content/uploads/Lord-Macpherson-Speech-HMT-Orthodoxy-1-November-2022.pdf
49 Tim Congdon, 'There is still no alternative to monetarism', CapX, 2 August 2024, https://capx.co/there-is-still-no-alternative-to-monetarism/
50 Ken Clarke, *Kind of Blue: A Political Memoir* (Macmillan, 2016), https://www.amazon.co.uk/Kind-Blue-Political-Ken-Clarke/dp/1509837191
51 Dr Matthew Partridge, 'Great frauds in history: BCCI – Agha Hasan Abedi's dodgy bank', Money Week, 27 January 2020, https://moneyweek.com/investments/investment-strategy/600706/great-frauds-in-history-bcci-agha-hasan-abedis-dodgy-bank
52 'Why Britain's Treasury must change its ways', *The Economist*, 16 November 2023, https://www.economist.com/britain/2023/11/16/why-britains-treasury-must-change-its-ways
53 Will Dunn, 'How the Treasury quietly runs Britain', *New Statesman*, 26 October 2022, https://www.newstatesman.com/culture/books/book-of-the-day/2022/10/how-the-treasury-quietly-runs-britain
54 Tim Wallace, 'Why Javier Milei's chainsaw economics won IMF's approval when Trussonomics didn't', *Daily Telegraph*, 13 December 2023, https://www.telegraph.co.uk/business/2023/12/13/javier-milei-argentina-shock-therapy-devaluing-peso/
55 David Smith, 'Forecasters are floored by inflation yet again', *The Times*, 19 February 2023, https://www.thetimes.co.uk/article/6985ce96-aeef-11ed-b94f-fc4969750d6e?shareToken=8838ccb30917d21926f47996d0ec669a
56 Jessica Elgot & Peter Walker, 'Labour crackdown on non-doms may raise no money, officials fear', *The Guardian*, 25 September 2024, https://www.theguardian.com/uk-news/2024/sep/25/labour-crackdown-on-non-doms-may-raise-no-money-officials-fear
57 'Torsten Bell's pals running OBR', Guido Fawkes, 3 October 2022, https://order-order.com/2022/10/03/office-for-budget-responsibilitys-not-so-independent-leadership/; 'Another tax-loving Torsten Transfer', Guido Fawkes, 6 October 2022, https://order-order.com/2022/10/06/another-obr-analyst-transferred-from-torstens-resolution-foundation-supports-massive-tax-rises/; 'Another leftist hire for the OBR', Guido Fawkes, 4 July 2023, https://order-order.com/2023/07/04/another-leftist-hire-for-the-obr/
58 'About us', Resolution Trust, https://resolutiontrust.org/about-us
59 Will Hazell, 'OBR economist said Corbyn debt plan would boost GDP', *Daily Telegraph*, 16 December 2023, https:// www.telegraph.co.uk/politics/2023/12/16/corbyn-debt-plans-could-boost-gdp-said-obr-economist/
60 Catherine McBride, 'Repeatedly disproven OBR forecasts? It's time to adopt "when the facts change"', Global Britain, https://globalbritain.co.uk/repeatedly-disproven-obr-forecasts-why-not-adopt-when-the-facts-change/
61 Phillip Inman and Larry Elliott, 'Head of OBR says lack of budget details led to "work of fiction" forecasts last year', *The Guardian*, 23 January 2024, https://www.theguardian.com/politics/2024/jan/23/head-of-obr-says-lack-of-budget-details-led-to-work-of-fiction-forecasts-last-year
62 Jon Moynihan, 'How the Bank broke the Government', The Critic, December/January 2023, https://thecritic.co.uk/issues/december-january-2023/how-the-bank-broke-the-government/; Jon Moynihan, 'Did Liz Truss really cause the bond market rout?', CapX, 6 February 2023, https://capx.co/did-liz-truss-really-cause-the-bond-market-rout/
63 Will Dunn, 'The QE theory of everything', *New Stateman*, https://www.newstatesman.com/business/economics/2024/02/the-qe-theory-of-everything
64 Faisal Islam, 'The inside story of the mini-budget disaster', BBC News, 25 September 2023, https://www.bbc.co.uk/news/business-66897881
65 Economic Affairs Committee, 'Making an independent Bank of England work better', House of Lords, 27 November 2023, https://publications.parliament.uk/pa/ld5804/ldselect/ldeconaf/10/10.pdf

CONCLUSION: RETURNING THE UK'S ECONOMY TO GROWTH

1 Moyniteam analysis; International Monetary Fund, 'World Economic Outlook Database', April 2024, https://www.imf.org/en/%20Publications/WEO/weo-database/2024/April/

EPILOGUE: AND HERE'S HOW WE DO IT

1 'An ideological shift? Gen Z teens identify as more conservative than their parents at higher rates than

NOTES

millennials did', The Up and Up, 28 March 2024, https://www.theupandup.us/p/gen-z-teens-conservative-shift-gallup-data

2   International Monetary Fund, 'World Economic Outlook Database', April 2024 edition, https://www.imf.org/en/%20Publications/WEO/weo-database/2024/April/

3   'Revealed: Liz Truss's unpublished growth agenda', *The Spectator*, 9 February 2023, https://www.spectator.co.uk/article/revealed-liz-trusss-unpublished-growth-agenda/

4   Robert Marstrand, 'Argentina's 10-point freedom plan (the Milei pact)', Of Wealth by Rob Marstrand, 11 March 2024, https://ofwealth.substack.com/p/argentinas-10-point-reform-plan-the

5   John Curtice and Alex Scholes, 'Roles and responsibilities of government: have public expectations changed?', National Centre for Social Research, September 2023, https://natcen.ac.uk/sites/default/files/2023-09/BSA per cent2040 per cent20Role per cent20and per cent20responsibilities per cent20of per cent20government.pdf

6   Faisal Islam, 'The inside story of the mini-budget disaster', BBC News, 25 September 2023, https://www.bbc.co.uk/news/business-66897881; 'OBR Forecasts: £60-70bn hole post Kwarteng's mini-budget', PKPI Growth & Tax Advisors, updated 25 December 2023, https://www.pkpi.uk/post/obr-forecasts-likely-to-show-60bn-70bn-hole-after-kwarteng-s-mini-budget

7   Simon Kemp, 'Digital 2023 deep-dive: Twitter use jumps after Elon Musk's acquisition', Datareportal, 28 January 2023, https://datareportal.com/reports/digital-2023-deep-dive-the-potential-outlook-for-twitter

8   Ben Wright and Matthew Field, 'How Elon Musk got away with firing 6,000 people', *Daily Telegraph*, 12 June 2024, https://www.telegraph.co.uk/news/2024/06/12/elon-musk-fire-x-staff-6000-jobs/

9   Tevye Markson, 'Hunt confirms timeline for 66,000 service job cuts in Autumn Statement', Civil Service World, 22 November 2023, https://www.civilserviceworld.com/professions/article/hunt-confirms-timeline-for-66000-job-cuts-in-autumn-statement

10 Jim Pickard, 'Boris Johnson sets out plans to cut up to 90,000 civil servants', *Financial Times*, 13 May 2022, https://www.ft.com/content/4d1ba055-167a-4ddd-ba9c-1505535dd890?shareType=nongift

11 'Sniffly civil servants shirking work', Guido Fawkes, 5 February 2024, https://order-order.com/2024/02/05/skiving-civil-servants-blasted-for-taking-1-8-million-sick-days/

12 '£100 million of taxpayers' cash wasted on trade union pilgrims', Guido Fawkes, 4 June 2018, https://order-order.com/tag/pilgrims/

13 'MPs respond to further £101 million in trade union subsidies', TaxPayers' Alliance, 26 June 2022, https://www.taxpayersalliance.com/mps_respond_to_further_101_million_in_trade_union_subsidies

14 Tim Knox, 'Civil service needs chief executives to drive real change', *The Times*, 12 April 2023, https://www.thetimes.com/uk/politics/article/civil-service-needs-chief-executives-to-drive-real-change-vgcb5g862

15 Ryan Dubé and Silvina Frydlewsky, 'Argentina scrapped its rent controls. Now the market is thriving', *Wall Street Journal*, 25 September 2024, https://www.msn.com/en-us/money/realestate/argentina-scrapped-its-rent-controls-now-the-market-is-thriving/ar-AA1r5n7B

16 Mary Pilon, 'How Bill Clinton's welfare reform changed America', History, 29 August 2018, https://www.history.com/news/clinton-1990s-welfare-reform-facts

17 'Retained EU Law – public dashboard', https://app.powerbi.com/view?r=eyJrIjoiMDY2MjAwZDMtMzcwOC00Zjc4LTk3NDQtMzNkNDIyMTlhYTcwIiwidCI6ImNiYWM3MDA1LTAyYzEtNDNlYi11NDk3LWU2NDkyZDFiMmRkOCJ9&disablecdnExpiration=1715290751

18 Alan Halsall, *Last Man Standing: Memoirs from the front line of the Brexit Referendum* (Finito Publishing, 2024), https://www.amazon.co.uk/Last-Man-Standing-Memoirs-Referendum-ebook/dp/B0DBV4553N?dplnkId=edb4e64a-f2b0-41ca-8384-1fb4a145a052&nodl=1

19 UK Public Spending, 'Multiyear Download of UK Government Spending', March 2024, https://www.ukpublicspending.co.uk/download_multi_year#copypaste

20 International Monetary Fund, 'World Economic Outlook Database', April 2024, https://www.imf.org/en/Publications/WEO/weo-database/2024/April/

21 Ciara Nugent and Claire Jones, 'IMF chief confident in "pragmatic" Milei despite setbacks', *Financial Times*, 1 February 2024, https://www.ft.com/content/79b4e7e2-9b1a-4b1b-8ff6-efc6f1bd960c

22 Tax Policy Center, 'Historical Highest Marginal Income Tax Rates', 11 May 2023, https://www.taxpolicycenter.org/statistics/historical-highest-marginal-income-tax-rates; International Monetary Fund, 'Gross public debt, percent of GDP', https://www.imf.org/external/datamapper/d@FPP/USA; The White House, 'Historical Tables', https://www.whitehouse.gov/omb/budget/historical-tables/

23 Ivan Pongracic Jr, 'The Great Depression according to Milton Friedman', Foundation for Economic Education, 1 September 2007, https://fee.org/articles/the-great-depression-according-to-milton-friedman/

24 Tax Policy Center, 'Historical Highest Marginal Income Tax Rates', 11 May 2023, https://www.taxpolicycenter.org/statistics/historical-highest-marginal-income-tax-rates; International

Monetary Fund, 'Real GDP growth rate, percent', https://www.imf.org/external/datamapper/rgc@FPP/USA

APPENDIX B: THE GROWTH MODEL

1. Norman V. Loayza and Steven Pennings, 'The Long Term Growth Model', World Bank, 2022, https://documents1.worldbank.org/curated/en/099627211072228496/pdf/IDU052ad90a40e67f040f80ab3b0cfbec815be8d.pdf
2. Robert M. Solow, 'A contribution to the theory of economic growth', *Quarterly Journal of Economics*, vol. 70, no. 1, February 1956, pp. 65–94, https://www.jstor.org/stable/1884513
3. Groningen Growth and Development Centre, 'Penn World Table version 10.01', University of Groningen, https://dataverse.nl/api/access/datafile/354095
4. 'Investment and Capital Stock Dataset', International Monetary Fund, https://data.imf.org/?sk=1ce8a55f-cfa7-4bc0-bce2-256ee65ac0e4
5. Groningen Growth and Development Centre, 'Penn World Table version 10.01', University of Groningen, https://www.rug.nl/ggdc/productivity/pwt/?lang=en; 'Economic Freedom', The Fraser Institute, https://www.fraserinstitute.org/economic-freedom/map?geozone=world&page=map&year=2021; International Monetary Fund, 'World Economic Outlook April 2024', https://www.imf.org/en/Publications/WEO/weo-database/2024/April; OECD, https://data-explorer.oecd.org/
6. 'Economic Freedom', The Fraser Institute, https://www.fraserinstitute.org/economic-freedom/map?geozone=world&page=map&year=2021; International Monetary Fund, 'World Economic Outlook April 2024', https://www.fraserinstitute.org/economic-freedom/map?geozone=world&page=map&year=2021; 'OECD Data Explorer', OECD, https://data-explorer.oecd.org/
7. Office for National Statistics, 'Principal Projections – UK Population in age groups', 30 January 2024, www.ons.gov.uk/peoplepopulationandcommunity/populationandmigration/populationprojections/datasets/tablea21principalprojectionukpopulationinagegroups
8. Office for Budget Responsibility, 'Economic and fiscal outlook', March 2024, https://obr.uk/efo/economic-and-fiscal-outlook-march-2024/
9. International Monetary Fund, 'World Economic Outlook Database', https://www.imf.org/en/Publications/WEO/weo-database/2024/April/

ACKNOWLEDGEMENTS

I would like to thank in particular the members of the moyniteam, that helped me create the two volumes of this book: Michelle McGhie, Mikhail Traykovskiy and Mathew Thurley. All have spent over a year helping to pull everything together, page by page, with Michelle keeping the overall shape and structure of the book from spinning out of control and Mikhail providing not just a vast amount of research and data but also a good portion of what original thought leadership and analysis can be found in these pages.

Great thanks also are due to Norman Blackwell, Roger Bootle, Terry Burns, Tom Clougherty, Robert Colville, Tim Congdon, Paul Cox, Iain Duncan Smith, Matthew Elliott, James Forder, Lance Forman, Fred de Fossard, Regan Hall, Dan Hannan, Tim Healey, Chris Howarth, Martin Howe, Corey Iacono, Julian Jessop, Mervyn King, Norman Lamont, the late Nigel Lawson, Don Lessard, Nic Lewis, John Longworth, Charlotte Lynch, Gerard Lyons, Catherine McBride, Chris McGhie, Douglas McWilliams, Dan Masterton of the Mighty Pie, Sam Miley, Patrick Minford, Kristian Niemietz, Christopher Nieper, John O'Connell, Matt Palumbo, Barney Reynolds, Abdel Karim Saddedine, Matthew Sinclair, Liam Strong, James and Margaret Thompson and Toby Young for their various and extensive help and direction on the project. Thanks are also due, of course, to the many economic and political thinkers and writers whose works are referenced in this book, and listed on the website that can be accessed from the QR code provided on the contents page. Economic models and data were validated by the economic consultancy CEBR.

I would also like to thank the wonderful team at Biteback, who have nurtured the birth of this book over the last year, helping in so many different ways: James Stephens, Olivia Beattie and my editor, Catriona Allon. I also heartily thank the PR team of Suzanne Sangster, Katrina Power, Suzanne Evans and Nell Whitaker.

I apologise to any of the numerous people who have given me invaluable advice over the years, whose assistance I have now, due to my failing wits, omitted to mention here. Any mistakes, errors, misunderstandings, misrepresentations or outright falsehoods are of course, and regardless of any attempted or even achieved help to my understanding that I may have received from others, entirely my own fault.

A particularly heartfelt thank you to my boon and greatly loved friend of many years, the much-admired artist John Springs. His superbly executed covers on both volumes are in most cases, I am sure, the only reason anyone has purchased a copy.

Lastly, and above all, I thank my dear helpmate and wife Patricia for her selfless and buoyant support throughout the long and torturous process that led to publication of these two volumes; and indeed throughout our forty-four years of married life together.

INDEX

Page references in *italics* refer to charts.

4 factors impacting TFP 261, *265*

all-policies scenario *193*, 266

balance of payments 177, 179, 180
Bank of England 135, 148, 184, 185, 252
    global financial crisis 174
    independent 180, 181, 213
    inflation 135, 148, 149, 154, 155, 162, 213
    quantitative easing/tightening 97–9, 144, 145, 147, 154, 180–81, 212
    Treasury orthodoxy and 163, 168, 169, 174
    Truss government 173
    under democratic control 222
Barber boom (1972) 177–8
Barro, Robert J. 72, 73
Bastiat, Frédéric 51, 60, 68, 80
Bell, Torsten 172
Biden administration 88, 89
Black Wednesday 160, 161, 162, 174, 178
Brexit 14, 16, 28
    free trade confusion 53, 69
    goods exports after 58, 89
    Northern Ireland 85
    post-Brexit 51, 53, 58
    predicted economic effects 82, 83, 172
    referendum 174, 231
Brown, Gordon 3, 162, 173, 181, 186
budget deficit 1918–33 (US) *250*
Burns, Terry 159, 161
business ecosystems 66, 68
Butler boom (1955) 177, 179

CBAM (Carbon Border Adjustment Mechanism) 35, 90, 91
CFD (Contract for Difference) strike price *29*
China 4, 34, 36, 42, 46–7, 61, 62, 76, 89
City of London 226
civil service 29, 213–22, 246
Clarke, Ken 161
Cobden, Richard 69, 80
commercial competitors in nuclear technology *40*, *41*
comparative advantage 55, 60, 63–8, 86, 87, 92–4, 111–16
competition 2, 8, 10, 13–15, 17–19, 27, 190, 226
competitive advantage 38, 55, 60, 64–8, 86, 87, 92–4, 110, 112–16
Congdon, Tim 4, 5, 19, 20, 142, 144, 151, 154, 156, 158
containerisation 71
Corn Laws 52, 60, 68, 69, 91
cost of living 81, 82, 148, 153, 156
Covid-19 130, 131, 140
    exporting performance since 54
    Omicron variant 244
    private insurance since 19
    quantitative easing during 99, 100, 145, 148, 150, 151, 153, 173
    Sunak, Rishi 178
CPI (Consumer Price Index) *153*
CPTPP (Comprehensive and Progressive Agreement for Trans-Pacific Partnership) 82, 83, 87
currency management 110, *116*

debt ratio 1918–33 (US) *250*
democratic mandate 197, 198–211
deregulation 27, 223–39, 246
    economic impact of 164
    ensuring 236–9
    government approach 225, 227, 238
    nuclear 223–4
    opportunities 225–8

digital trade 71
dirigism 1–3, 42
economic
    activity 21, 35, 120, 123, 126, 165, 182, 248
    collapse 107, 147, 150
    development 34, 243
    forecast 163, 170, 172, 214
    ignorance 1, 4, 171
    institutions 186, 212
    management 165, 206
    officials 176, *176*, 185
    policy 6, 109, 125, 146, 159, 165, 169, 173, 175–85, 186
    progress 15, 73
    strategy 172, 185, 202
    theory 51, 60, 63, 147
    tools 175, 179, 183
economics 61, 127
    demand-side 125, 177, 179
    Hayekian 142, 147, 149, 163, 181
    Keynesian 100, 140
    liberal 14, 213
    supply-side 125, 164, 165, 178
    trickle-down 164
Economist, The 26, 53, 63, 90, 166
economy
    capitalist 164
    Commonwealth 87
    communication of a plan to reform *248*
    communist 5
    evolution of (UK) *56*
    free market 1, 6, 7, 9, 48, 202
    goods 55
    government management *176*
    high-growth 1, 195
    no-growth xiii
    sequence for growth *256*
    services 55
    'status quo' forecasted UK development *xxiii*, 192
    UK 13, 17, 36, 54–6, 86, 189
    US 76, 99
    zombie 100, 150, 167
electricity prices 22, 32, *33*, 34, 56
energy policy 35
Energy Price Guarantee 34
energy sector 28–36, 37, 44
entrepreneurial creativity 11
equalitarian/equalitarianism 49
equality of opportunity 47
EU tariffs 62, 76, 78, 79, 81

European Central Bank 146, 168
European Common Market 76–8, 87
European Exchange Rate Mechanism (ERM) 160, 161, 174
exchange rate 5, 108–9, 113, 116–17, 158, 160–61, 179–80, 182

Forder, James 83
forecasts/forecasting 83, 151, 154, 156–7, 265, 266
    OBR and 129, 130, 163, 170–72, 174, 185, 213, 214
fracking 30, 31, 32, 35, 57, 234–6
Frankel, Jeffrey 69, 70
Fraser Institute 73, 74, 75, 262
free agent 8
free exchange 8, 9, 10, 13
free market
    activities 17, 28
    approaches 1–6, 31, 42, 44, 49, 211, 213, 236, 242, 266
    conditions 24, 25
    definition 7
    economies 1, 6, 7, 9, 26, 45, 48, 63, 202, 203, 213
    energy sector (UK) 28–36
    foundations 7
    government interference with 5, 7, 9, 13, 14, 19–22, 26, 27, 28, 67
    nuclear energy 39
    policies 2, 169, 214
    principles 10, 19, 44, 254
    sectors 24, *25*, 26, 37
    suppression 14, 15, 16
free market versus captive sectors (UK) *25*, 257–8
free trade 51–95, 158, 191, 195, 253–4, 255
    Adam Smith 63, 64
    benefits 60
    Brexit and 53, 69
    economic growth 51, 189, 259
    importance of 51, 52
    policy 81, 190
Friedman, Milton 12, 139, 140, 142, 153, 250
fuel price indices (UK) *33*

gas 30–35, 234–6
GATT (General Agreement on Tariffs and Trade) 61, 62, 69
GDP (Gross Domestic Product)
    annual growth rate *xix*
    debt as a percentage of 129, *129*
    debt-to-GDP ratio 128, 136, 137, 189, 192, 251

INDEX

growth 75, 83, 91, 109, 113, 130, 191–2, 252
   growth in the 1920s (US) *251*
   growth rate 75, 191, 206, 239, 240
   per capita xiv
   reaching 33 per cent *204*
   real xiv, 204, 252, 266
gilts 99, 134, 135, 145, 147, 181, 227
Gini coefficient 46, *46*, 47, 49, 50
global financial crisis 2008 97, 100, 104, 144, 146, 174, 182, 190
goods exports (UK) 54, *55*, 56–8, *59*, 77
government
   activities 17, *25*, 257
   bonds 97–9, *131*, 132, *134*
   central 11
   civil service, relationship with 214–221, 222
   Conservative 177, 186, 187, 200, 223, 228, 248
   currency management *116*
   debt 124, 127, *129*, *134*, 241
   energy sector interference 28–36
   expenditure 124, 152, 180, 197, 204, 205, 239–47, 261–2
   free market, interference with 5, 7, 9, 13, 14, 19–22, 26–36, 67
   Johnson government 28, 147
   Labour 130, 170, 171, 174, 189
   large 4*5*, 8, 190, 210
   local 221, 245
   management of institutions *212*
   management of the economy *176*
   May government 28, 228
   nuclear sector interference 36–44
   public perceptions of *210*
   quasi- 17, 24, *25*, 257
   size 14, 189, 194, 210, 211, 240, 242, 246, 255, 266
   size versus growth rate xix
   small/smaller 1, 6, 44, 50, 72, 116, 190, 191, 195, 222, 242, 255
   spending 24, 67, 110, 166, 173, 204, 206, 209
   subsidy 38, 40
   Sunak government 34
   Thatcher 160
   Truss government 34, 173, 183, 207, 242
   workers 17
'gravity theory' 69, 70, 71, 83
Great Depression, the 5, 61, 100, 104, 159, *251*
Greenspan Put, the 98, 143, *143*
growth
   creating an economic policy for 175–85
   EU versus Commonwealth 58, *59*

EU versus Rest of the World 58, *59*
   GDP (Gross Domestic Product) 75, 83, 91, 109, 113, 130, 191–2, 206, 252
   model 259–65
   money supply and inflation *141*
   rate 58, 74–5, 128, 154, 191, 202, 206, 239, 240, 247, 263
   Solow–Swan model 259, 260–62
   Total Factor Productivity (TFP) *264*
   trade openness and 60–66, 71–6, *74*, 75
   US GDP in the 1920s *251*

Hall, Peter 2
Halsall, Alan, *Last Man Standing* 231
Hayek, Friedrich von 10–12, 27, 36, 142, 147, 149, 163, 181
healthcare 19, 227, 243, 245
Heathcoat-Amory boom (1959) 177
Heritage Foundation index 14
Heseltine, Michael 161
household electricity prices *33*
Hurd, Douglas 161
hydrocarbons 22, 23, 30, 32, 43, 57, 68, 152

Iacono, Corey 73, 74
IMF (International Monetary Fund) 123, 166, 168–9, 173, 247, 264, 266
immigration 92, 163, 171, 188, 213
IMRP (Intermittent Market Reference Price) *29*
income
   developed economies (by quintile) *48*
   disposable 243
   distribution by country *46*
   national 127
   per capita 70
   stream 101, 102
   tax 124, 125, 177, 248, 249
   trends 44
income tax rate 1918–33 (US) *250*
Index of Economic Freedom 14, 44
index-linked bonds 132, 133, 134, *134*, 136
inequality 45, 46, 48, 49, 50
inflation
   asset 145, 182
   average rate 2022–3 *152*
   causes 133, 135, 139, 148, 149, 154, 159, 213, 222
   control 148, 153, 154, 157, 174
   effect on economy 139, 148
   expected 119
   high 133, 140, 143, 148, 150, 159, 196

inflation *cont.*
  hyperinflation 110, 130
  influence on national debt 131, *131*, 132
  low 121, 151, 153
  premium 119, 120
  price 148, 150
  UK CPI 2019–24 *153*
interest rates 97–100, 113–18, 142–7
  1975–2024 (UK) *143*
  managing 109, 118–23
Irwin, Douglas 71, 72, 73, 74

Jay, Peter 159
Johnson, Boris 28, 67, 85, 147, 173, 200, 217

Keynesian economics 4, 100, 142, 157, 165–6, 171, 173–4, 178–9, 202, 206, 213
  neo-Keynesian economics 106, 107, 125, 140, 147
Keynesianism 1, 5, 158–9, 160, 162

Laffer, Art 164
Laffer curve 163, 164, 165, 170
Lawson boom (1988–91) 178
Lawson, Nigel 140, 142, 161, 167, 180
Lazear, Edward 44–5
'levelling up' 67
liberal markets 63
liquidity 97–8, 100, 104, 114–21, 138, 142, 159, 181
living within one's means *203*
long-term growth model (LTGM) 259

McBride, Catherine 172
Macpherson, Lord Nicholas 158, 159, 162, 173
manufacturing industries 34, 54, 55, 112
market collusion 9, 13
market information 8
Maudling dash for growth (1963–4) 177
mercantilist/mercantilism 1, 3–4, 52, 63, 76, 80, 89
Milei, Javier 169, 196, 198, 207, 224, 247, 256
Minford, Patrick, *After Brexit, What Next?* 83
mini-budget (2022) 178
Mises, Ludwig von 10, 147
monetarism 5, 142, 154, 158, 159, 161, 162, 167
monopoly/monopolies 9, 13–15, 17–20, 25, 63, 67, 216, 253, 255
'Motorsport Valley' 66

national debt 108–9, 127–38, *129*, *131*, 162, 178, 192, 249, 251

net zero 28, 29, 34, 41, 54, 56, 200
New Statesman 166, 167, 168
NHS 10, 19, 202
nuclear 30, 31
  deregulation 223–4
  energy 22, 36, 37, 39, 223
  energy approaches *39*
  fission *40*, 42, 43
  fusion 39, *40*, 41, *41*, 42, 43
  list of commercial competitors *40*
  sector 22, 36–44
  small modular reactors (SMR) 37, 223, 224
  tokamak machine *39*, *40*, 41

OBR (Office for Budget Responsibility) 82–3, 129, 150, 155, 163, 167, 169–74, 181, 184–5, 213, 222
OECD (Organisation for Economic Cooperation and Development) 51, 53, 73, 74, 86, 264
oil exports (UK) *57*

Palumbo, Matt 73, 74
pensions 17, 146, 156, 178, 217, 227, 243, 246, 253
Pensions Act (2004) 227
Piketty, Thomas 45, 49
Pill, Huw 147, 148
'politically exposed persons' (PEP) 22
price mechanism 7, 8, 9, 11, 13
price theory 14
privatised sector 17, 18
product standards 13, 15, 16, 20, 62, 82
protectionism 60–63, 68–9, 81, 90, 116, 191
protectionist 4, 16, 35, 53, 75–6, 79–80, 86, 90, 91, 202
  barriers 58, 77, 82, 254
public debt reduction (EU) *240*

QE (quantitative easing) 97–107, 120–22, 140, 142–7, 149, 151, 173, 175, 182
QT (quantitative tightening) 98, 121–2, 154, 181, 184, 212

Reaganomics 164
Reeves, Rachel xxv–xxvii, 172
Reform UK 198, 201
regulation *see also* deregulation 20, 21, 26, 37, 43, 164, *265*, 189–91, 194
  business 126, 261, 262
  eliminating 13
  excessive 58, 190, 236

low 65, 72, 191
minimal 1, 6, 44
over- 22
planning 21, 223
reducing 229–30
regulators 7, 225, 228–34, 237–9
Reinhart, Carmen and Rogoff, Kenneth 127, 128, 130
renewables *29*, 30–33, 35, 37–9, 41–4
Resolution Foundation 53, 171, 172
Ricardo, David 51, 60, 63–5, 68, 80, 91
Ridley, Matt, *The Origins of Virtue* 9, 48, 49
Romer, David 69, 70
rule of law 7, 9, 13, 14, 26, 50
Russia 10, 32, 36, 76, 153, 165, 235

Samuelson, Paul 5
sanctity of contract 7, 9, 13, 26
services exports (UK) 52, 53, 54, *54*, 58, *59*, 89
Silicon Fen 66
Singapore 14, 48, 49, 138, 227
small modular reactors (SMR) 223
Smith, Adam 10, 51, 60, 63, 64, 80
Smoot–Hawley Tariff Act (US) 61
social democracy 44, 49, 137
socialism 45, 49
Solow–Swan growth model 259, 260, 261
sound money 5, 6, 97, 185, 189–91, 195, 198, 239, 249, 255, 266
Spectator, The 43, 207
'status quo' development (UK) xxiii, xx, 130, 192, 225
Stein, Herbert 146
Sunak Covid chancellorship (2020–22) 178
Sunak, Rishi 88, 155, 173, 180
Switzerland 14, 23, 93, 111–12, 152

tariffs 4, 61–3, 68, *75*, 76, 78, 80, 81, 91, 191, 262, *265*
tax
    cuts 137, 170, 177, 206, 211, 223, 246, 249, 252, 255
    high 50, 54, 58, 107, 123, 126, 195, 207
    income 124, 125, 177, 248, 249, *250*
    low 1, 6, 44, 67, 116, 171, 222, 242, 249, 254
    rates in the 1920s (US) *251*, 252
    reduction 239, 248–52, 255
    revenues 35, 75, 124, 170–71, 195, 205, 208, 244, 252, 261–2
    Solow–Swan model 260–62
ten-year gilt bond yield (UK) *99*

TFP (Total Factor Productivity) 260–5, *264*
Times, The 159, 168, 170
tokamak machine 41
trade
    barriers 61, 73, 81, 82, 82, 91, 262
    Common Market membership and 76, 77, 78, 83, 85
    Commonwealth countries 76, 77, 78, 87, 88
    free *see* free trade
    freedom 63, 73, *75*, 76, 80, 89, 261
    goods trading partners 1960 versus 1980 (UK) *78*
    gravity theory 69, 70, 71, 83
    international 51, 90
    liberalisation 62, 70, 72, 73, 93
    Northern Ireland 85, 91
    openness 51, 60, 73, 74, 89
    policy 53, 60, 62, 71, 72, 80, 81, 82, 202
    UK/US 77, 88
Treasury orthodoxy 125, 157–75, 183
Trump, Donald 4, 62, 76, 105, 224
Turkish lira versus US dollar *111*

US dollar versus Turkish lira *111*

Wall Street Journal 14
wealth creators 208, 209
Windsor Framework 85, 91
WTO (World Trade Organization) 62, 63, 76